SOCIAL DEVELOPMENT

SOCIAL DEVELOPMENT

THE DEVELOPMENTAL PERSPECTIVE IN SOCIAL WELFARE

James Midgley

SAGE Publications
London • Thousand Oaks • New Delhi

First published 1995
Reprinted 1998, 1999

SAGE Publications Ltd
6 Bonhill Street
London EC2A 4PU

SAGE Publications Inc
2455 Teller Road
Thousand Oaks, California 91320

SAGE Publications India Pvt Ltd
32, M-Block Market
Greater Kailash – I
New Delhi 110 048

British Library Cataloguing in Publication Data

A catalogue record for this book is
available from the British Library

ISBN 0–8039–7772 7
ISBN 0–8039–7773 5 (pbk)

Library of Congress catalog card number 95–69626

Typeset by M Rules

IN MEMORY OF

Kiruba Moodley
and Betty J. Stewart

Contents

Acknowledgements

Many people have supported and facilitated my efforts to write this book. As usual, Dija encouraged my work. Harvill Eaton and Ed Zganjar backed this project from the beginning and helped me find time to write. Thanks also to Michelle Livermore, Jenny Poulter and Jim Albins who assisted in various ways. I am grateful to Jim Billups and Stewart MacPherson who reviewed the proposal and advised Sage to publish this book. Special thanks go to David Hill, Karen Phillips and Gillian Stern for having confidence in my ideas. Margaret Hardiman and Michael Sherradan gave helpful advice on the final manuscript. Margaret's fine eye for detail helped me avoid many errors while Michael's comments, particularly on theoretical issues, were incisive. Colin Hutchens was a supportive copy-editor and Nicola Harris managed the project through production. Julie Hodgkinson worked hard to ensure that the book was properly marketed. To them and many others who helped this book evolve and see completion, I am grateful.

I have dedicated this book to the memory of two dear friends with whom I shared my ideas on many happy occasions. Both are sadly missed.

James Midgley
Baton Rouge, Louisiana

Introduction

This book discusses an approach for promoting human welfare known as *social development*. Social development's most distinctive feature is its attempt to harmonize social policies with measures designed to promote economic development. While other institutionalized approaches for promoting social welfare such as philanthropy, social work and social administration have tangential links with economic development, none dynamically or purposefully harmonize economic and social objectives within a wider, development process. It is the emphasis on *development*, together with its universality and macro-focus, that differentiates social development from the other approaches for promoting social welfare.

Social development transcends the residual and institutional approaches which have dominated social welfare thinking in the past. While the residualist approach recommends that limited public resources be targeted on the most needy sections of the population, the institutional approach urges the extensive involvement of the state in all aspects of social welfare. Although these two approaches differ in the way they formulate policy proposals for allocating resources for social welfare, both create social interventions that are subsidiary to the economy and both are passively dependent on the economy for funding. Neither is concerned with the way resources for social welfare are generated or with the fiscal problems that occur in times of economic adversity. As recent events have revealed, subsidiarity and dependence have created an uncertain, erratic and unsatisfactory relationship between social policy and the economy.

The social developmental approach transcends the residualist–institutionalist debate by linking social welfare directly to economic development policies and programmes. It draws extensively on the experience of the developing countries of the so-called Third World where the need for social policies that are compatible with economic development is paramount. However, the social development approach is relevant to all societies where efforts are under way to promote economic development. It stresses the need for a wider commitment to economic development and emphasizes the importance of social interventions that are compatible with economic development objectives. As will be shown in the final chapter of this book, this compatibility is fostered in different ways.

As the twentieth century draws to a close, new approaches to promoting social welfare such as social development are urgently needed. The comprehensive 'welfare statism' which typified social policy thinking in the past has been widely criticized for failing to deal realistically with economic adversities and for neglecting to take the problems of recession, structural unemployment and other changing economic realities into account. Similarly, the minimalist welfare policies of the Radical Right which resulted in severe reductions in collective provision during the 1980s have not only exacerbated social needs but disquieted many concerned citizens. Recent electoral trends and public opinion surveys suggest that many voters are not opposed to state intervention as such but that they desire social programmes that are reasonable, equitable and pragmatic. As economic difficulties persist in many parts of the world, social programmes that are compatible with economic development are likely to attract widespread support. Social development offers an approach which not only is cognizant of wider economic realities but actively promotes development. It is primarily about development and the ways social interventions can be harmonized with development objectives.

DEVELOPMENT AND DISTORTED DEVELOPMENT

The term 'development' is widely used today. For most people, it connotes a process of economic change brought about by industrialization. The term also implies a process of social change resulting in urbanization, the adoption of a modern lifestyle, and new attitudes. Further, it has a welfare connotation which suggests that development enhances people's incomes and improves their educational levels, housing conditions and health status. However, of these different meanings, the concept of development is most frequently associated with economic change. For most people, development means economic progress.

The adoption of economic development prescriptions during the last century has produced impressive results. This is true of both the Western industrial countries and the developing countries of the Third World. While there are significant differences in the extent to which development goals have been attained, the pursuit of development has generated unprecedented growth rates in most countries. It is probable that the economic achievements of the last hundred years far exceed those of the last millennium. In addition, economic development has been ubiquitous and there are today relatively few countries that are characterized by an absence of at least some degree of economic development.

Levels of social welfare have also improved significantly. Compared to the situation at the end of the nineteenth century, ordinary people today have higher incomes and standards of living, live longer and healthier lives, are better educated than ever before and have access to health and social services to a degree that few would have predicted a hundred years ago. Official reports published by the United Nations and the World Bank reveal that significant social improvements have taken place not only in the Western industrial nations but in the Third World. Despite the images of poverty and deprivation the Third World invokes, life expectancy in many developing countries has increased significantly, levels of education have risen, access to health care, sanitation and clean drinking water has improved, and social programmes have expanded.

Critics of a pessimistic persuasion will, with justification, question the significance of these gains. They will note that grinding poverty still characterizes the lives of many millions of ordinary people in Africa, Asia and Latin America. Housing conditions in many Third World cities are atrocious, the spectre of starvation haunts millions of rural dwellers, homeless children roam the streets, too many young people still die premature deaths, and labour exploitation of both adults and children is widespread. Many will point out that even in the prosperous industrial nations, homelessness, inner city decay, need and neglect remain endemic. Those who believe that there has been little social progress over the last century will note that cataclysmic wars have caused the deaths of many millions of human beings, and observe that brutal dictatorships have subjugated whole nations for extended periods of time. They will point to the Holocaust and other genocidal campaigns, and to the ongoing racial and ethnic hatreds which perpetuate violence and brutality, and to the widespread subjugation of women.

The social achievements of recent decades are, therefore, decidedly mixed. While there has been real social progress during this century, the goal of achieving social welfare for all has certainly not been realized. In addition, there is evidence to show that the gains recorded in the decades following the Second World War have slowed, and in some cases have even been reversed. Official reports reveal that the incidence of poverty increased in many parts of the Third World, particularly in Africa and Latin America during the 1980s. In industrial countries such as Britain and the United States, studies reveal that the proportion of people living below official poverty lines has risen significantly during the last decade.

The phenomenon of persistent poverty in the midst of economic affluence is one of the most problematic issues in development today. In many parts of the world, economic development has not been accompanied by an attendant degree of social progress. This phenomenon is often referred to as *distorted development*. Distorted development exists in societies where economic development has not been accompanied by a concomitant level of social development. In these countries, the problem is not an absence of economic development but rather a failure to harmonize economic and social development objectives, and to ensure that the benefits of economic progress reach the population as a whole.

Despite a high degree of economic development, conditions of distorted development persist on an unacceptable scale in industrial countries such as Britain and the United States. In these countries, economic development has failed to eradicate poverty and raise levels of welfare for all. This is not to suggest that there has been no social progress in these two countries. Indeed, it is clear that both enjoy high standards of living. The problem is rather that significant sections of the population have failed to benefit from economic growth. In these countries, the problem of distorted development is most blatant in decayed inner city areas and in deprived rural communities. Inner cities are increasingly devastated not only in physical but in social terms as well. It is here that poverty, unemployment, crime, family disintegration, violence, drug use and social deprivation are most marked.

The problem of distorted development in the industrial countries is also manifested on a regional basis. One example is the Mississippi Delta region of the United States where levels of poverty are the highest in the country, and where infant mortality rates are higher than in several Third World nations. And yet, the region is not characterized by an absence of economic development. One of the world's most heavily concentrated petro-chemical complexes runs along the Mississippi river from Baton Rouge to New Orleans. In addition to having several major oil refineries, multinational firms along the river produce huge amounts of fertilizers, industrial chemicals and similar products. The region also contains several large cities which serve as centres for transportation, trade, commerce, tourism and government services. It is also a major agricultural centre where advanced farming technologies are employed to produce rice, cotton, soya, sugar, vegetables and many other crops, often for export. Its coastal areas are rich in fishing resources and afford excellent opportunities for modern aquaculture. However, the region is characterized by poverty and social neglect. The coexistence of economic development and social deprivation in the region is a classic example of distorted development.

Conditions of distorted development persist in many Third World countries as well. As was noted earlier, relatively few developing countries have experienced little or no economic development since the Second World War. However, in many of these countries, the development process is highly distorted. Perhaps the most dramatic examples of the disjunction between social and economic goals are to be found in Latin America where rates of economic growth have been impressive but where poverty and deprivation are perpetuated. While many Latin American countries have experienced rapid economic growth and a significant degree of industrial development, social conditions among large sections of the population have improved only marginally. In these societies, economic development has not been accompanied by a concomitant degree of social development. Typically, the distribution of income and wealth in these societies is highly skewed, ostentatious wealth and abject poverty coexist, investments in education and the social services are low, and the rate of unemployment and underemployment is often high.

Similar examples of distorted development are to be found in Africa and Asia and particularly in those countries where economic prosperity has been achieved through exploiting natural resources. In pre-independence Namibia, for example, the development of the country's extensive mineral wealth ensured high standards of living for the white minority but left the African majority in conditions of abject poverty. A similar situation exists today in Gabon. Popularly known as 'Africa's Emirate' because of its oil wealth, Gabon has the highest per capita income of any African country. However, 70 per cent of homes in the capital city have no drinking water or sanitation, and the proportion of children attending primary school is lower than in many other poorer African nations.

Distorted development is manifested not only in poverty, deprivation, low health status and inadequate housing but in the exclusion of sections of the population from full participation in development. In many societies, ethnic and racial minorities are discriminated against and barred from utilizing opportunities that can improve their standards of living. Small groups of indigenous people are particularly disadvantaged. Often isolated in remote regions, or relegated to dismal reservations with few opportunities for advancement, these groups live in conditions of poverty and deprivation which can be directly attributed to racism, discrimination and their low social position in society.

Another example of distorted development is the oppression of women, and the perpetuation of conditions of deprivation for hundreds of millions of women around the world. Although women are major contributors to economic development, they do not share adequately in its benefits. While their labour is critical to the rural economy, the urban informal sector and increasingly the industrial and service sectors, their incomes are lower than those of men, their status is inferior and many live in conditions of deprivation and dependency. A related manifestation of distorted development in many Third

World countries is the position of children where millions of children work under exploitative conditions to support the precarious income of their families. Their exclusion from educational opportunities, adequate health care and a sense of security and well-being ensures that poverty and deprivation are perpetuated for future generations.

Distorted development is also manifested in the environmental degradation which particularizes many societies where the exploitation of natural resources characterizes development efforts. The wealth which is derived from these resources is very considerable but too often it brings few benefits to local people or the wider society. Worse, the ravaging of these resources results in permanent environmental damage which jeopardizes the well-being of future generations.

A similar problem arises from profligate military expenditures. Despite heavy indebtedness, many countries continue to arm their military establishments with the latest and most destructive weapons. These expenditures not only mortgage future generations but divert scarce resources from projects that can foster both economic and social development. While the military expands, investments in productive enterprise, education and other forms of human capital formation stagnate, perpetuating conditions of poverty and deprivation.

Societies with distorted development may be contrasted with societies where a better balance between economic and social development has been found. European countries such as Austria, Sweden and Switzerland have the highest levels of living in the world today not only because of their economic achievements, but because of their systematic efforts to promote social development. They have invested extensively in human and social capital, and have high levels of educational attainment, extensive health and social services and effective forms of social protection. Consequently, they have a low incidence of poverty and deprivation, and are characterized by relatively low levels of crime and violence. The problem of distorted development has also been minimized in some developing countries such as Costa Rica, Singapore and Taiwan where systematic efforts have been made to foster economic development while simultaneously ensuring that social development objectives are promoted. Although these countries are not utopias, free of social problems and tensions, they have ensured that economic development has been accompanied by a real commitment to social development.

However, these countries are a minority and, today, the problem of distorted development remains widespread, particularly in the Third World. Distorted development also poses a serious problem in the newly liberated Eastern European countries and in the former states of the Soviet Union. To address the problem of distorted development in these and other societies, measures are needed that promote economic development and, at the same time, ensure that social development is given high priority. Fortunately, it seems that the need to address the disjunction between economic and social objectives through a dynamic process of social development is again being recognized.

THE NEED FOR SOCIAL DEVELOPMENT

The pressing social problems arising from distorted development are now attracting more attention. The harsh political attitudes of the 1980s which attributed social deprivation to idleness, irresponsibility, excessive government intervention and other simplistic interpretations have softened. While many believed just a decade ago that the resurgence of free market forces would resolve social problems, faith in the simple solutions offered by the proponents of unfettered capitalism has weakened. Today, many recognize that the challenges facing society require concerted action on the part of government, communities and individuals, and that global social needs can only be addressed in a meaningful way through pragmatic policies and programmes that directly address welfare issues.

The acceptance of the notion of sustainable development and the publication in the early 1990s of a series of reports on 'human development' by the United Nations are indicative of a renewed international concern for people's welfare. In the United States, efforts to address the problems of deprived regions such as the Mississippi Delta through a combination of economic development and social programmes are a further indication of recognition of the need for purposeful action. Most promising has been the decision of the United Nations to convene the World Summit on Social Development in 1995. This event reveals that, after a period of neglect, social welfare is again an important issue for international discussion. With the support of the world's leaders, the prospect of revitalizing the social development approach seems better than ever before.

As was noted earlier, social development is an approach to promoting people's welfare that is well suited not only to enhancing the quality of life for all citizens but to responding to the problems of distorted development. The conditions of concomitant prosperity and deprivation that characterize so many countries today can best be remedied through an approach that integrates economic and social objectives. The concentrations of poverty which persist on an unacceptable scale in the industrial countries can be dealt with most effectively through a combination of economic and social measures. Similarly, the widespread poverty which coexists with affluence in the Third World cannot be remedied by social measures that operate independently of economic solutions.

Social development offers a comprehensive macro-perspective that focuses on communities and societies, emphasizes planned intervention, promotes a dynamic change-oriented approach which is inclusive and universalistic, and above all seeks to harmonize social interventions with economic development efforts. The social development approach uniquely integrates economic and social objectives. It not only recognizes the critical importance of economic development in raising standards of living, but actively seeks to harness economic development for social goals. It is for this reason that social development will be defined in this book as a process of promoting people's welfare in conjunction with a dynamic process of economic development.

The emergence of social development as an approach for promoting social welfare, and its direct linkage with economic development, may be traced to the efforts of British colonial social administrators in Africa in the 1940s and 1950s to identify forms of social welfare which would be compatible with the emphasis being placed on economic development at the time. After the United Nations embraced the social development approach in the 1960s, these ideas were widely disseminated throughout the developing world. Through the efforts of a small group of social workers in the the United States, the social development approach was introduced into the industrial countries as well.

However, the social development perspective is not widely known in the industrial countries today. Nor is it generally accepted in academic circles. In addition, the field is still theoretically underdeveloped and there is much confusion about what social development entails in programmatic terms. Even the term is still poorly defined. While a substantial number of articles, reports and other documents on social development have been written, the literature is highly fragmented. Apart from two edited books which appeared in the early 1980s (Jones and Pandey, 1981; Sanders, 1982), no comprehensive textbook on the subject has previously been published.

This problem is compounded by the existence of widely different approaches to social development. While several conceptual approaches to social development have been formulated, none have gained universal acceptance. Because no attempt has yet been made to analyse and systematize these different approaches, social development not only is conceptually fragmented but is conducive to hortatory exhortation rather than the articulation of specific interventions. Consequently, there is much confusion about what social development entails.

THE PURPOSE AND SCOPE OF THIS BOOK

This book attempts to fill a gap in the literature by offering an overview of social development. It is designed primarily for those working in the fields of social policy, social work, applied sociology and development studies who have a familiarity with current world events, contemporary social issues and social science theories. The book uses both factual information and theoretical formulations to frame the discussion. It attempts to provide a summary of competing ideological and theoretical approaches to social development while, at the same time, explicating the author's own normative perspective. Hopefully, this will not only permit readers to understand the different conceptual and policy approaches which have emerged in the field, but will help them to reach their own conclusions and to challenge those approaches with which they disagree.

Chapter 1 offers an introductory definition of the concept of social development. It contrasts the social development approach with other established approaches for promoting social welfare. These approaches are philanthropy, social work and social policy. It examines the different ways the term 'social development' has been used in different disciplinary fields in the past, and it identifies key elements in the social development perspective. Using the insights of contemporary political economy, it suggests that social development is the broadest and most inclusive of various approaches to enhancing people's well-being today.

Chapter 2 continues the process of articulating the social development perspective by tracing its historical evolution. Ideas in the history of social thought which have influenced social development are examined and the impact of more recent events such as the adoption of planning and the emergence of the welfare state on social development are discussed. The term's colonial origins are traced, and its adoption and popularization by the United Nations are reviewed. Efforts to promote the social development approach in the industrial countries are also examined. The chapter ends by discussing the impact of Radical Right-wing political movements on social development in the 1980s. It notes that despite serious setbacks for social development, there is currently a resurgence of interest in the field.

Chapter 3 discusses various theoretical debates in social development. The chapter begins by discussing the relevance of different types of social science theory to social development. Drawing on these different types of theory, an attempt is made to summarize and analyse key controversies in social development. These controversies are examined with reference to a conception of social development as a process. The discussion examines various debates attending the nature of underdevelopment as a pre-existing state, the nature of the social development process and the prospect of attaining social development goals.

Chapter 4 draws on the theoretical ideas discussed in the previous chapter and attempts to identify major strategic approaches for realizing social development goals. All are characterized by an attempt to link social interventions to economic development efforts. As will be seen, some of these strategies are more successful at integrating social and economic elements than others. Various strategic approaches to social development are examined with reference to prevailing ideological beliefs about the best way of attaining social development objectives. Their prescriptions for social development as well as their strengths and weaknesses are discussed.

Chapter 5 seeks to formulate a synthesis of the major strategies within the framework of what is called the *institutional perspective*. The institutional perspective draws on the work of social scientists who believe that the major institutions of society (including the state, market and community) need to be mobilized to promote economic and social change. These social scientists have attempted to forge an accommodation between different ideological positions to foster the adoption of strategies based not on one approach but on a synthesis of individualist, communitarian and statist ideologies.

Drawing on their ideas, it will be argued that the promotion of social development depends on the integration of the economic and social domains, and on combining diverse strategies for the promotion of social welfare. However, it will be argued that the successful promotion of social development requires that the state plays a leading role in integrating economic and welfare institutions and in utilizing the market, community and the public sector. This activist role for the state is described as *managed pluralism*. It is argued that social development's strategic approach of managed pluralism currently offers the most realistic prospect for promoting human well-being. Examples are given of countries where the state has adopted managed pluralism in an attempt to achieve a synthesis between economic and social welfare goals.

The idea of social development and the approach articulated in this book is inherently controversial and there are many who will criticize it. Indeed, many have already done so. In addition to the objections that have been made to the different social development strategies described later on, criticisms of the social development approach have been levied on ideological, conceptual and technical grounds. However, most critics focus on the overall assumptions and values of social development. Social development has been accused of being utopian, too wide-ranging to be meaningful, technically unsustainable and even of being conducive to totalitarianism. These and other criticisms have come from both the radical political right and Marxist left, and from new conceptions of social change such as those embodied in postmodernist theory. These and other criticisms are considered in more depth in chapter 3.

While criticisms of social development must be taken seriously, they can be countered. In addition to its topical emphasis on linking economic and social policies to promote development, social development's strength is its flexible, undogmatic and pragmatic approach. It seeks to combine the insights of many different scholars who have sought to analyse contemporary world conditions and to offer meliorative prescriptions for current social problems. Its very methodology is conducive to consensus building and applying wide-ranging solutions to the ongoing social crises facing humankind. As such, it offers an effective basis for social action. Hopefully, the remainder of this book will explicate the social development approach in interesting and useful ways.

1
A Definition of Social Development

There is an urgent need to respond to the problem of distorted development described in the introduction to this book. By seeking to harmonize social policies with measures designed to promote economic development, social development offers a unique response to this problem. It also offers a broad macro-perspective on social welfare, and applies a variety of strategies which seek to enhance the levels of living of the whole population. As such, social development offers a comprehensive and dynamic approach to promoting social well-being today.

This chapter provides an overview of the concept of social development. It also offers a formal definition of social development and a description of its key characteristics. The account provided in this chapter will be augmented subsequently, and many of the features of social development discussed here in a preliminary form will be developed later.

The chapter begins by linking social development with the concept of social welfare. It defines the concept of social welfare and examines different approaches for promoting social welfare. These include social philanthropy, social work and social administration. Social development is defined as an approach to social welfare which offers an effective response to current social problems. By describing the differences between social development and these other approaches, it is hoped that the unique features of the social development approach will be clarified.

The chapter then formulates a formal definition of social development which frames the discussion in the rest of the book. This definition is inspired by the insights of modern-day political economy which offers an interdisciplinary perspective on current social and economic problems, and deals explicitly with ideological issues.

Finally, the chapter examines other definitions of social development which have been formulated in different academic fields in the past. These are discussed so that the definition provided in this book can be put into perspective. As will be shown, the term 'social development' has been defined in different ways in fields as diverse as psychology, sociology, social work and development studies. Although each field views social development differently, these various disciplines have all contributed to the formulation of the social development perspective.

THE CONCEPT OF SOCIAL WELFARE

Social development may be viewed as an approach for promoting people's welfare (or social well-being). Social development may be contrasted with other approaches such as social philanthropy, social work and social administration. All have been institutionalized as approaches for promoting social welfare. Before reviewing these different approaches, the meaning of the term 'social welfare' needs to be discussed. The notion of social welfare is central to the concept of social development, and the way the term is used in this book.

The term 'social welfare' is today widely misused. Although its original meaning was a noble one, referring broadly to a state of social well-being, contentment and prosperity, most people today equate the term with charity or, in the United States, with public assistance for poor families and their children. In the United States, social welfare has almost become a term of abuse. Women who obtain welfare are known as 'welfare mothers' and they are often accused of being lazy, of not wanting to work and of exploiting government services. This is paradoxical because the founders of the United States used the term 'welfare' in a broad sense to connote the economic, social and political well-being of the nation.

The meaning adopted in this book reflects the wider connotation of the concept of social welfare. As used here the term 'social welfare' refers to a social condition, and not to the charity given by philanthropic individuals, charities or public assistance provided by governments. The book will argue that a condition of social welfare exists when families, communities and societies experience a high degree of social well-being.

It is difficult to define social welfare or social well-being precisely. The concept has both subjective and objective aspects and it can be defined either in descriptive, qualitative terms or by using empirical measures. Although there is no consensus about the characteristics of the condition of social welfare, perhaps the most significant contribution has been made by social scientists who have attempted to quantify its components.

Social scientists who have sought to develop quantifiable measures of social welfare have used various techniques to come to grips with the concept. One technique compares key statistics or indicators which measure social conditions. These statistics are known as indicators because they give some 'indication' of social conditions in different communities and societies. Examples of commonly used indicators are the unemployment rate, the infant mortality rate, the crime rate, the literacy rate and statistics relating to life expectancy, school enrolment, poverty and other social conditions. High rates of crime, unemployment, poverty and similar problems are indicative of a low level of social welfare. Conversely, communities that have low unemployment, poverty and crime rates, and high rates of life expectancy and literacy, are said to have a higher degree of social welfare.

Another technique is to combine these indicators into a single index of social welfare. As Nancy Baster (1972) reported, this idea was first developed at the United Nations Research Institute for Social Development in Geneva in the 1960s where social scientists defined social welfare in terms of the 'level of living' of societies. Subsequent composite indicators of social welfare such as the PQLI (Physical Quality of Life Index) of D. M. Morris (1979), the Index of Social Progress invented by Richard Estes (1985), and the more recent Human Development Indicator developed by the United Nations Development Programme (1990) are based on a few key components.

In addition, some social scientists have conducted surveys to ask citizens about their social concerns and anxieties, and their perception of social well-being. The findings of these surveys have then been compared with similar surveys undertaken in different communities, regions and countries to provide some insights into people's subjective feelings of well-being. In this way, it is possible to discover what social situations are associated with a positive perception of social welfare and those that are not.

A Definition of Social Welfare

It is also possible to define social welfare in conceptual terms and many definitions of this kind have been formulated in the past. In this book, a condition of social welfare (or social well-being) is conceived of as comprising three elements. They are, first, the degree to which *social problems are managed*, second, the extent to which *needs are met* and, finally, the degree to which *opportunities for advancement are provided*. These three elements apply to individuals, families, groups, communities and even whole societies. The three elements thus operate at different social levels and need to apply at each level if a society as a whole is to enjoy a reasonable state of social well-being.

All families, communities and societies have *social problems* but they differ in the extent to which they manage them. For example, conflicts are managed quite well by some families but in others they seriously damage relationships, and sometimes result in the disintegration of the family. Crime and violence are more effectively prevented and controlled in some communities than others. Similarly, while some societies have implemented policies for keeping the rate of unemployment down, others have not been able to deal with this problem effectively. Generally, societies which are able to manage these and other problems have a higher degree of social welfare than others. An inability to manage social problems results in a condition that Richard Titmuss (1974) called 'social illfare'.

All human beings, families, communities and societies have *social needs* which must be met if people are to experience social contentment. Needs refer to basic biological survival requirements such as nutrition, safe drinking water, shelter and personal safety but needs also exist at the level of communities and societies. Today, it is widely agreed that there is a necessity for communities and societies to have adequate levels of education and health care, harmonious social interaction, safe drinking water and social security. Communities and societies which meet these social needs experience a collective sense of well-being.

Finally, social welfare exists in communities which create *social opportunities* for people to advance and realize their potential. Societies with rigid social barriers that impede advancement are often characterized by a high degree of discontentment. Similarly, societies which fail to provide education, job opportunities and other means by which people can realize their potential often have high rates of crime and violence as people seek alternative, illegitimate means for improving their social position. The absence of opportunities is a major cause of social illfare in society.

These three dimensions – the management of social problems, the meeting of needs and the enhancement of opportunities – combine in a complex way to comprise the basic requirements for attaining a condition of social well-being. When all three requirements are met in any particular community or society, it may be argued that the community or society enjoys a satisfactory level of welfare. When these requirements are not met, it may be claimed that the community or society has failed to attain a satisfactory level of welfare.

Of course, this approach to defining social welfare is not intended to offer a precise set of standards for judging whether communities or societies enjoy an adequate level of social welfare. The use of quantitative measures such as official social statistics or indicators provides a more effective basis for making judgments of this kind. However, the definition which has been offered here provides some insights into the meaning of the concept.

APPROACHES FOR PROMOTING SOCIAL WELFARE

Today, most people associate the term 'social welfare' with the provision of government social services. However, it is only in relatively recent times that governments in Europe and North America expanded the public social services and assumed a major responsibility for promoting social welfare. For most of human history, individuals, with the support of their families, have been responsible for their own welfare. They attempted to solve their problems through their own efforts, and through hard work sought to earn the income they needed to meet their social needs.

While individual and family responsibility has traditionally been the primary means of promoting social welfare, other forms of support have also evolved. In most societies, culturally prescribed obligations require relatives, kin and even neighbours to assist those in need. Similarly, the world's great religions have long prescribed that alms be given as a religious duty, and, in some cases, this duty evolved into complex systems of charitable provision. Religious charity fostered the emergence of a highly organized approach for promoting people's welfare which, by the nineteenth century, catered for the needs of many needy people. Organized charity also promoted the emergence of professional social work. Similarly, it stimulated government involvement in social welfare.

Today, it is possible to identify three institutionalized approaches for promoting social welfare. The first is *social philanthropy* which relies on private donations, voluntary effort and non-profit organizations to meet needs, solve problems and create opportunities. The second is *social work* which relies on professional personnel to foster welfare goals by working with individuals, groups and communities. The final approach relies on government intervention through a variety of statutory social services. This latter approach may be called the *social administration* approach. This approach is also known as the social service or social policy approach.

All three approaches for promoting people's welfare have been widely adopted throughout the world. They may be contrasted with the social development approach which has not been widely adopted. As will be shown, the key difference between the social development approach and the other approaches is the attempt to link social policies and programmes directly to a comprehensive process of economic development.

Social Philanthropy and Charitable Giving

Social philanthropy seeks to promote social welfare through encouraging the provision of private goods and services to needy people. While the systematic promotion of social philanthropy is a relatively recent development, philanthropy has ancient roots. For most of human history, social welfare has been provided by private citizens in the form of charity and, as was noted earlier, acts of charity were often prescribed and motivated by religious beliefs. In ancient Judaism, for example, farmers were expected to leave a portion of the harvest for the needy. In early Christianity, churchgoers were required to give tithes to help the poor. In Islam, the principles of *zakat* governed the giving of charity. Of course, these practices are still required today, and religious charity remains a major means of helping those in need.

Social philanthropy was implemented not only through individual acts of charity, but through organizations which provided specialized services to those in need. In Christianity, the first organizations to provide services of this kind were the monasteries which catered for the sick, the homeless and abandoned children. In time, specialized institutions that provided residential care for different groups of needy people such as the elderly, the mentally ill and orphans evolved. The provision of residential services to care for the needy became a major means of implementing the social philanthropy approach.

Although residential institutions were the most common form of social philanthropy, non-residential services were also provided. These services expanded very rapidly in the nineteenth century. By the middle of the century, a great variety of philanthropic organizations had been established in the cities of Europe and North America. Most provided poor relief in the form of food, clothing and other forms of material support. Others offered counselling and advice with social problems. Some were concerned with moral reform, seeking to rescue children and young women from alcohol abuse, vagrancy and prostitution. In time, the need to coordinate the activities of the different charities became a major concern of philanthropic leaders. As a result of their efforts, several coordinating agencies emerged. One of the first was the Charity Organization Society which not only sought to improve the coordination of philanthropic effort but formulated new techniques that resulted in the creation of professional social work.

At about this time, social philanthropy became increasingly secular. Although religious organizations had traditionally dominated charitable activity, many new charities without specific religious affiliations began to emerge. Much social philanthropy is now secular in character although, of course, religiously affiliated charities still operate on a large scale.

Today, a plethora of charitable organizations provide income, goods or services to needy people. Social philanthropy focuses primarily on those who cannot care for themselves, and it does not provide goods or services to the population as a whole. Historically, the providers of charity have drawn a sharp distinction between those who are 'deserving' and 'undeserving'. The deserving include the elderly, the disabled, children and others who cannot take care of themselves. The undeserving are the able-bodied unemployed, and those who have fallen into need because of some behavioural problem such as drug abuse or crime. Generally, those who receive social philanthropy are passive recipients of goods and services. Philanthropy is dependent on the good will of donors and on the willingness of governments to use tax-payers' money to supplement charitable activities.

Not all philanthropy is concerned with the provision of charitable relief to the needy. During the nineteenth century, when charitable activities were expanding rapidly in Europe and North America, some philanthropic leaders sought to bring about social reforms and improve social conditions. These leaders, who were often well-connected members of the upper middle class, sought to use their influence to solicit the support of political and business leaders. They used their connections to persuade governments to introduce new social services, to enact laws that prevented exploitation and discrimination, or to introduce measures that protected the vulnerable.

Many commentators have been sceptical of the achievements of philanthropic reformers, claiming that those with power and influence always protect their own interests, and only offer minor concessions that fail to bring about significant social changes. However, the successes of the reformers cannot be denied. Indeed, there are many historical examples of successful social reforms even though these reforms were not always introduced for altruistic reasons. Sometimes, reforms have come about because of a fear of social unrest and sometimes because political groups embracing reform proposals have done so in order to win elections. In other cases, the status and connections of social reformers have been critical factors resulting in the adoption of proposals primarily because of their ability to exercise influence.

Whatever the reason, philanthropic reform has produced significant results at different times. In the United States, the end of the nineteenth century is known as the Progressive Era because a large number of major reforms were introduced. An important social reformer at the time was Jane Addams who was well connected and able to exert influence on those in political office. She had a good relationship with President Teddy Roosevelt and was able to influence his policies. In Britain, leading members of the Fabian Society such as Beatrice and Sidney Webb actively promoted social reform. They adopted a strategy of 'permeation' by which they sought to gain the support of political leaders and to influence their policies.

The social philanthropy approach has been most successful in the industrial nations but similar developments have taken place in many developing countries as well. In addition, there has been a rapid growth in the number of international philanthropic agencies that specialize in finding resources for economic, social and community projects. Some of these agencies such as Oxfam have become large, multinational organizations with large budgets and extensive programmes. While most philanthropic endeavour promotes a conception of social welfare based on the provision of goods and services to needy people, many of these international philanthropies have also promoted the social development approach.

Social Work and Professional Intervention
Social work is an organized approach for promoting social welfare which uses professionally qualified personnel to deal with social problems. Social work emerged in the industrial countries during the latter half of the nineteenth century. It originated out of the efforts of the Charity Organization Society, which was founded in London in the 1860s, to systematize charitable activity. The organization's leaders were highly critical of the widespread practice of giving indiscriminate charity to the needy. They argued that help should only be given after a careful investigation of the circumstances of clients had been made, and it had been determined that they were deserving and had no other means of support. In addition, they believed that assistance should be given for a limited time. Those who received aid should be helped to find work or some other means of becoming independent. Employment would engender self-respect and contribute to the well-being of society.

To implement its ideas, the Charity Organization Society recruited educated women volunteers who made home visits to investigate the circumstances of applicants for aid. The volunteers also developed treatment plans designed to rehabilitate recipients. They also provided counselling, believing that many people who were in poverty had behavioural problems that contributed to their situation. These early charity visitors laid the foundation for the emergence of modern-day social work which is still primarily concerned with treating the social problems of needy people.

Since the nineteenth century, social work has undergone considerable professional and academic development and it has spread around the world. Information provided by the International Association of Schools of Social Work shows that social work has gained widespread recognition (Rao, 1983). When the association was founded in 1929, it had only a few member schools, chiefly in the industrial countries. In 1973, its membership had grown to 459 schools in 66 countries. By 1983, it had 476 member schools. In more recent times, many more schools have been created in Eastern Europe and the former states of the Soviet Union (Hokenstad et al., 1992).

Social work's most distinctive feature is its reliance on professionally educated personnel to treat social problems and enhance the well-being of individuals, families, groups and communities. Although many lay people regard social work as a form of charitable endeavour practised by altruistic citizens, this image is incorrect. Social workers are required to obtain a professional qualification usually at university institutions. They take a variety of academic courses which enhance their understanding of human behaviour, psychopathology and social problems. They also learn how groups and communities function. They are taught different techniques of intervention and different approaches to helping their clients. Because of their professional interests, they combine theoretical study with supervised practical placements in social agencies which provide an adequate preparation for working directly with clients. Social work is characterized by its focus on direct intervention and by its use of professionally trained workers who can deal effectively with social problems.

Today, social workers serve in a great variety of settings in both the public and the voluntary sectors. However, in most countries, the great majority of social workers are employed in local and central government social service organizations where they work in fields as diverse as child welfare, school social work, social assistance, medical social work, corrections, housing, gerontology and psychiatric social work. Others are employed in non-profit social agencies and more are today finding work in for-profit agencies such as drug rehabilitation, employment assistance and psychiatric facilities. In some countries, such as the United States, many are in private practice counselling clients for a fee (Hopps and Pinderhughes, 1992).

Traditionally, social workers have provided remedial services which seek to treat the social problems of individuals and families. This emphasis on social treatment reflects the profession's historical commitments. In the nineteenth century, when social work first emerged, it was generally accepted that most social problems including poverty, homelessness, ill health, illiteracy and crime were caused by individual malfunctioning. Many believed that social ills could be remedied by counselling, and by helping people to improve their social functioning. While these social workers recognized that some needy people can never function independently, they believed that most needy people can be treated and helped to become self-reliant again.

Today, social work relies heavily on counselling and other forms of remedial intervention to deal with people's social problems. It must be stressed, however, that there are other forms of social work which do not provide remedial services. Non-remedial forms of social work include social policy, social work research, non-therapeutic group work, the planning of local social services and community action. In addition, there is a small but highly activist group of social workers which has sought to infuse a social development perspective into the profession. However, these activities are peripheral to the profession's primary concern with individual pathology and the treatment of social problems. While some social workers are involved in non-remedial activities, the social work approach to promoting social well-being depends heavily on a remedial approach to social welfare. As will be shown later in this chapter, some social workers are encouraging the adoption of the social development perspective in social work. However, much more needs to be done before a development thrust will be accepted by the profession.

Social Administration and the Provision of Welfare Services

The social administration approach seeks to promote people's welfare by creating governmental social programmes that enhance the well-being of citizens through providing a variety of social services. This approach is also known as the social policy or social service approach. Unlike social philanthropy, which directs private charity to those in need, the social administration approach directs public resources towards larger groups of citizens and, often, all citizens are included. The social administration approach is based on the idea that governments are responsible for the welfare of their citizens, and that they should provide a range of services to promote social welfare.

The Poor Laws, which were enacted during the reign of Queen Elizabeth I in England, are often regarded as the beginning of government involvement in social welfare. However, there are earlier examples of state-sponsored social provision such as Hammurabi's Code in ancient Babylon which protected widows and orphans (Chambliss, 1954). Nevertheless, the Elizabethan Poor Laws were the most comprehensive of early forms of government social intervention. Unlike previous statutory provisions which were localized, inadequately managed and limited in coverage, poor relief under the Elizabethan laws was centralized, governed by clear rules and regulations and implemented throughout the country. The Poor Laws also laid the foundation for modern-day social assistance programmes which provide income support and other benefits to people who cannot work and who have little or no other source of income (de Schweinitz, 1943).

While the Poor Laws focused only on the neediest sections of society, they legitimated the involvement of the state in social welfare. Despite opposition, governments had by the nineteenth century become increasingly responsible for public health and education, for regulating working conditions in the mines and factories, and for preventing the exploitation of women and children. Under the influence of middle-class reformers, the growing strength of the trade unions and the spread of socialist ideas, governments began to introduce public education, social security and health care for the working class. During the twentieth century, government social service provisions in the industrial countries expanded further and by the 1950s became quite extensive, covering large sections of the population. In many countries, coverage by some social services has become universal. For example, in Britain social security and health care were introduced after the end of the Second World War to cover the whole population.

Examples of modern-day social services include public education, social security, health care, housing, family allowances and similar services. The governments of many Western industrial countries have established extensive social service programmes and these countries are accordingly known as *welfare states*. The social administration approach is, therefore, inextricably linked to the contemporary welfare state.

There have been parallel developments in Third World countries (Hardiman and Midgley, 1982, 1989; MacPherson, 1982). Although the social services in these countries are not as extensive or well funded, most have also increased governmental involvement in social welfare. This process was begun by colonial administrators who first introduced limited public social services in the colonies in the 1930s and 1940s. After independence, many Third World governments extended these provisions. Although the social services have not always been appropriate to local needs, and have frequently catered primarily for urban populations, there is no doubt that state intervention has contributed significantly to the social improvements which have been recorded in the Third World. These improvements have been most marked in education and health care. While the situation in many developing countries is far from satisfactory, significant improvements in school attendance, literacy rates, access to medical care, and the control of communicable diseases have taken place because of the provision of social services by Third World governments.

During the 1980s, many governments cut social expenditures, reduced the social services and privatized or contracted out programmes to commercial providers. In the developing countries, massive debts and the imposition of structural adjustment policies severely curtailed government social expenditures. Governments in many industrial countries have also curtailed their social service expenditures. These reductions reflect a wider ideological antipathy to the statist interventionism which has characterized most of the twentieth century. With the ascendancy of Radical Right-wing governments, the social services have been significantly curtailed (Glennerster and Midgley, 1991).

However, there is widespread disenchantment with the Radical Right's approach today. As is now widely recognized, the retrenchment of the welfare state has not brought greater prosperity and social well-being as the Radical Right had promised but has instead been accompanied by increased levels of poverty, deprivation, inner city decay, crime and violence. On the other hand, the weaknesses of the conventional social administration approach has been recognized and new approaches are being examined. One such approach is social development which offers the prospect of transcending the limitations of the social administration approach, and linking social welfare more effectively with economic development.

THE SOCIAL DEVELOPMENT APPROACH

Social development differs from social philanthropy, social work and social administration in several ways. Unlike philanthropy and social work, social development does not deal with individuals either by providing them with goods or services, or by treating or rehabilitating them. Instead, social development focuses on the community or society, and on wider social processes and structures.

The social development approach is also comprehensive and universalistic. Unlike social philanthropy and social work, social development does not cater only to needy individuals but seeks to enhance the well-being of the whole population. Social development is also dynamic, involving a process of growth and change. Unlike the other approaches which are primarily concerned with maintaining adequate levels of welfare, social development transcends this static posture by actively promoting a developmental process.

However, social development's most distinctive feature is its attempt to link social and economic development efforts. Social development explicitly seeks to integrate social and economic processes, viewing both elements as integral facets of a dynamic process of development. It is this emphasis on *development* that characterizes the social development approach. Within the process of development, social and economic development form two sides of the same coin. Social development cannot take place without economic development and economic development is meaningless unless it is accompanied by improvements in social welfare for the population as whole.

The attempt to integrate social and economic policies and programmes in order to promote people's welfare distinguishes social development from the other approaches. Generally, social philanthropy and social work do not address economic issues. There are, of course, some exceptions such as the efforts of philanthropic organizations, particularly in developing countries, to establish local economic development projects. These were mentioned earlier. Also, as was shown earlier in this chapter, some social workers have attempted to promote a developmental approach in social work. More recently, there have been proposals to infuse community social work with economic development projects (Midgley and Simbi, 1993; Galaway and Hudson, 1994). However, these efforts are peripheral to social work's mainstream activities which continue to be primarily concerned with remedial intervention.

The social administration approach would appear to have a direct association with economic activities. The social services depend on government revenues derived from taxes generated by the economy, and it is in the interest of the providers of social programmes to ensure that social and economic policies are harmonized. In addition, founders of the social administration approach such as William Beveridge insisted that economic growth and full employment were a necessary condition for social prosperity. Nevertheless, the social administration approach continues to compartmentalize the social services from the economy and few efforts have been made to harmonize social and economic policies. Instead, in most industrial countries, the relationship between the social services and the economy has been one of dependence and subsidiarity. The social administration approach is primarily concerned with the provision of services, with meeting minimum standards of welfare, and with supporting the elderly, the disabled, the unemployed and other dependent groups. The social services are subsidiary to the economy in terms of their importance, and they are dependent on the economy for funding. This involves a reliance on the taxes generated by the economy and particularly on incomes earned through employment.

However, this is a shaky dependence. For example, if the economy experiences recession, the revenues needed to fund the social services decline and the fiscal pressures on governments increase. Similarly, the need for social services is likely to be higher during times of economic adversity when more people need assistance and when government revenues are generally lower. It was the growing demand for services in a context of economic stagnation that was exploited by the Radical Right in its appeals to voters in the 1970s and 1980s. The social services were defined by the Radical Right as a primary cause of economic decline which could only be remedied by curtailing the expansion of the welfare state. In addition, the social services have come under increasing pressure as populations have aged and as larger numbers of people now depend on government provisions. The problem has been exacerbated by tax resistance and continued economic difficulties.

Unlike the social administration approach, social development seeks to harmonize social interventions with economic development effort. It has been extensively informed by the efforts of developing countries to integrate economic and social policies within a concerted thrust for development. As was noted earlier, social development first emerged within the context of Third World development.

While the social development approach differs significantly from the other approaches, it also shares common features with them. Like these approaches, social development is committed to promoting the welfare of the population. Like them, it also stresses the need for intervention. It does not accept that social welfare occurs automatically as the result of 'natural' processes. Nor does the social development approach negate the other approaches, or minimize their efforts to enhance people's well-being. Social development does not, for example, invalidate the social administration approach but, within the context of economic development, seeks to link the social services to economic development in a dynamic way.

Social development may also be viewed as an extension of the residual–institutional dichotomy which has been widely cited in the literature on social welfare (Wilensky and Lebeaux, 1965; Titmuss, 1974). These 'welfare models' have been extensively used to classify social programmes, different social welfare approaches and even whole societies in terms of whether social welfare caters only for needy people who meet specified income criteria or whether it promotes the well-being of the population as a whole. Those who use this taxonomy point out that residual social welfare is limited, remedial and stigmatizing, while institutional welfare is universalistic and a 'normal', front-line and integral part of society.

These models may also be linked to the social welfare approaches described earlier. Philanthropy and social work are sometimes regarded as residualist forms of social welfare while the social administration approach is often seen as representing the institutional view. However, neither model explicitly addresses development issues. Indeed, both assume that the costs of social welfare will be met from the revenues generated by the economy. The social development approach is, therefore, a third model of social welfare which promotes a developmental perspective in social welfare.

Characteristics of Social Development
Social development will be defined in this book as *a process of planned social change designed to promote the well-being of the population as a whole in conjunction with a dynamic process of economic development.* Like most other formal definitions, it suffers from weaknesses. However, it attempts to capture the essence of the social development perspective. The elements of this perspective will be discussed in more detail in the subsequent chapters of this book but, at this stage, key aspects of the definition will be highlighted.

First, as has been emphasized already, the process of social development is inextricably *linked to economic development*. It is this aspect which gives social development a unique character when compared to other institutionalized approaches for enhancing people's welfare. Although social development is similar to the other approaches because it focuses on social problems and implements social policies and programmes that enhance welfare, it does so within the context of the development process. The other major approaches for promoting social welfare do not seek to relate social interventions directly to development. This issue will be discussed further in this chapter.

Second, social development has an *interdisciplinary focus* which draws on the insights of the various social sciences. As has been noted already, social development is particularly inspired by modern-day political economy. Drawing on the insights of political economy, social development offers an interdisciplinary basis for analysing and dealing with current social problems and for promoting social welfare. Social development also fosters an ability to deal with these concerns at the national and international levels. It also addresses values, beliefs and ideologies explicitly. By dealing directly with ideological issues, social development is better able to formulate interventions which can be debated and critically evaluated. The influence of political economy on social development will be examined in more detail later in this chapter.

Third, the concept of social development invokes a sense of *process*. Social development is a dynamic concept in which the notion of growth and change is explicit. The very term 'development' explicitly connotes a sense of positive change. Standard dictionary definitions indicate that development is a process of growth, change, evolution or movement. As will be seen in chapter 3, the social development process is defined in conceptual terms as having three aspects: first, a pre-existing social condition that social development seeks to change; second, the process of change itself; and, finally, the end state in which social development goals are accomplished.

Fourth, the process of change, as conceived by the advocates of social development, is *progressive in nature*. At a time when the ideal of progress can be easily ridiculed, the proponents of social development proclaim a faith in the prospect of human betterment. Many believe that there is no alternative. As social conditions in many parts of the world have deteriorated over the last decade, nihilism, cynicism and despair make no contribution whatsoever to reversing the trend. Advocates of social development argue that a return to notions of social improvement is urgently needed.

Fifth, the process of social development is *interventionist*. The proponents of social development reject the idea that social improvements occur naturally as a result of the workings of the economic market or of inevitable historical forces. Instead, they believe that organized efforts are needed to bring about improvements in social welfare. They believe that human beings are not swept along by tides of events, but that they are able to influence their own future in the context of wider social, economic and political forces. The process of social development is, therefore, directed by human beings who implement specific plans and strategies to foster social development goals.

Sixth, social development goals are fostered through various *strategies*. These strategies seek, either directly or indirectly, to link social interventions with economic development efforts. They are supported by different *beliefs or ideologies* about how social development goals can best be attained. These 'ideologies' have historically been opposed to one another, and the theories and strategies they have inspired are also in conflict with each other. However, current social development thinkers have adopted a less doctrinaire position and many now argue for a pragmatic viewpoint which fosters a synthesis of different strategies. While they recognize the difficulty of achieving a synthesis of this kind, they believe that disparate ideological approaches to social development can be harmonized. Indeed, it is likely that the current ideological climate which characterizes the post-Cold War era, will sustain a synthesis of this kind.

Seventh, social development is concerned with the population as a whole and it is, therefore, *inclusive* or *universalistic* in scope. As was noted earlier, social development differs from philanthropy and the social treatment approaches in that it does not focus primarily on needy individuals. Instead, the proponents of social development advocate the adoption of a macro-focus which directs attention to communities, regions and societies. While social development is particularly concerned with those who are neglected by economic growth or excluded from development (such as the inner city poor, impoverished rural dwellers, ethnic minorities and women), its concern for these groups takes place within a wider universalistic context of interventions that promote the welfare of all. Another aspect of social development's universalism is its *spatial focus*. Within the context of its universalism, social development seeks to promote social welfare within specific spatial settings such as inner city areas, rural communities, cities, regions or countries.

Finally, the goal of social development is the *promotion of social welfare*. As shown earlier, the term 'welfare' is used in this book in its broadest meaning to connote a condition of social well-being which occurs when social problems are satisfactorily managed, social needs are met and social opportunities are created. The condition of social welfare is fostered through various mechanisms or institutions. With its interventionism, commitment to progress, macro-focus, universalism, integration of social policy with economic growth, socio-spatial focus and eclectic, pragmatic approach, social development is the most inclusive of all approaches for promoting social welfare today.

OTHER CONCEPTIONS OF SOCIAL DEVELOPMENT

The definition of social development offered in this chapter is only one of several in current use. Other definitions of the term have been formulated in academic subjects such as psychology, sociology, social work and development studies. An understanding of these different usages will help not only to clarify the field, but to put the definition used in this book into perspective.

Academic research in these different disciplines has also contributed to the definition of social development which is used in this work. As was suggested earlier, the political economy approach inspires thinking about social development. It offers a convivial intellectual framework for exploring ways of linking economic and social processes that enhance human welfare. Also, because of its interdisciplinary character, it has successfully incorporated the insights of these different subjects.

Social Development and Psychological Development
In psychology, the term 'social development' is widely used to refer to childhood development and particularly to the acquisition of social skills by children. Psychologists who specialize in this field are known as developmental psychologists. As will be readily apparent, psychologists use the term 'social development' in a very specific sense, and their definition has little bearing on the way the term is used in this book.

Although psychologists define social development very differently from the way the term is used here, ideas associated with its psychological meaning have influenced some social workers who have written about social development. Drawing on psychological ideas, these social workers believe that social development is a process of positive personal growth which contributes cumulatively to the well-being of society as well. They believe that societies can be improved if individuals experience personal development and learn to relate to each other in more positive ways. One exponent of this approach is Henry Maas (1984) whose writings draw extensively on psychological ideas. Maas's conception of social development will be examined later in this chapter.

Sociology, Social Development and Social Change
The term 'social development' is not widely used in sociology today except by sociologists involved in Third World development but it was

quite popular in the early decades of this century. The term was first used in the context of sociological studies of social change which was a important field of sociological inquiry at the turn of this century. Most leading sociologists of the time defined social change (or social evolution as it was also known) as a process which transforms small, simple and homogeneous communities into large, complex and heterogeneous societies and promotes modernity.

A major issue among sociologists concerned with the study of social change was whether human beings could or should seek to influence the process of change. Many sociologists at the time rejected any attempt to direct society's evolution. The famous British sociologist, Herbert Spencer, was particularly opposed to government intervention in social affairs and he even opposed the giving of charity. He argued that efforts by human beings to interfere with the natural process of change will disrupt the evolutionary development of society, and impede its progress towards higher levels of civilization.

Other sociologists disagreed with Spencer and argued that attempts should be made to influence social evolution. In the United States, a major critic of Spencer's ideas was Lester Ward who coined the term 'applied sociology'. Ward defined applied sociology as a branch of sociology concerned with the improvement of social conditions. Another writer who disagreed with Spencer was the British sociologist, Leonard Hobhouse, who published a book entitled *Social Development* in 1924. Hobhouse believed that rational human action can steer the process of social change in desirable directions. This required government involvement and the adoption of planning. Hobhouse did not believe that government intervention was inevitably beneficial but he disagreed with Spencer's view that government action will inevitably retard the process of social evolution.

Hobhouse's ideas were not new. Indeed, the belief that social science should be applied to improve society had previously been advocated by the French social philosophers Count Henri Saint-Simon and his colleague, Auguste Comte, a mathematician who invented the term 'sociology'. Hobhouse was, however, one of the first social scientists to use the term 'social development' in a systematic way. He was also one of the first to define social development as a process by which governments can adopt rational planning to foster social integration and well-being. His concept of social development subsequently influenced government officials who believed in the value of economic and social planning.

However, Hobhouse and the interventionists were in a minority and, during this century, most sociologists opposed any involvement in policy making and in social welfare. A few did, nevertheless, advocate the application of sociological knowledge for purposes of social planning.

Among the first to popularize the term 'social planning' was Charles North (1932), and it was subsequently adopted by other sociologists and social workers as well. Later proponents of social planning include Warren Bennis and his colleagues who published an edited collection of articles on the subject of 'planned change' in 1961, and Szymon Chodak whose book on 'societal development' appeared in 1973.

While these sociologists all define social development as a process of 'planned' or 'guided' change, they discuss the topic in highly abstract ways. Bennis et al., for example, defines planned change as 'the application of social technology derived from systematic and appropriate knowledge' for the purpose of 'creating intelligent action and change.' (1961: 3). Although this definition is uncontentious, the book fails to provide a set of specific prescriptions for applying social technology to create intelligent action. Other sociological accounts of 'planned' or 'guided' social development have been equally vague about how social development can be translated into specific policies and programmes. Many authors have urged that guided change should promote desirable values such as democracy, freedom, opportunity and similar ideals without specifying how this is to be achieved. In addition, few of these sociologists have focused specifically on social welfare issues and have viewed 'guided' social change as a means for promoting modernity.

The absence of clearly defined policies and programmes in the sociological literature has hampered the popularization of social development in sociological circles. Although sociologists working in the field of Third World development are familiar with the term, it has not been extensively informed by sociological ideas. Indeed, as Hall and Midgley (1988) suggested, much more work needs to be done before sociology has articulated a specific approach to development policy. Nevertheless, while sociologists have not defined social development in specific programmatic terms, the emphasis on change, intervention and progress in sociological accounts of social development has extensively informed the social development perspective.

Social Work and Social Development

The term 'social development' gained popularity in social work circles in the early 1980s, largely through the efforts of a small group of social workers in the United States who had been involved with the international agencies or who had worked in developing countries. Early publications in the field by Frank Paiva (1977), John Jones and Rama Pandey (1981) and Daniel Sanders (1982) all reflect this influence, and were important in fostering the social development approach in social work.

Although social workers have attempted to promote the social development perspective, many have defined social development in a highly abstract and idealized way which offers few specific proposals for action. Many definitions of social development formulated by social workers are so broad as to be meaningless. Consequently, it is not clear what social workers mean when they define social development.

One example of this problem is Salima Omer's (1979) definition which describes social development as a process concerned with 'achieving an integrated, balanced and unified social and economic development of society' and as one that 'gives expression to the values of human dignity, equality and social justice' (1979: 15). Social development, she points out, is holistic, international in scope, interdisciplinary, intersectoral and interregional. The goal of social development, she notes, is to 'create humanistic societies devoted to achieving peace in the world and progress for all people' (1979: 16). While these are noble ideals, Omer's definition does not say what social development entails as a professional activity, who will be responsible for social development, how social development goals will be realized, or what roles social workers will play in social development.

Many other definitions of social development by social workers are equally broad, idealistic and unclear about practical matters. Some commentators such as Gary Lloyd (1982) have been quite exasperated with the abstract and nebulous definitions offered by many social workers. Lloyd points out that most social work definitions fail to offer either a coherent theory of social development or guidance of any practical value as to how desired social development ideals are to be attained. Instead, Lloyd contends, the social work literature comprises a 'set of values, aspirations and heuristic notions' that are 'hortatory rather than prescriptive' (1982: 44–5). While he notes that the term 'social developer' had emerged in the social work literature to connote the professional deployment of professional personnel in the field, most definitions fail to articulate the role of social developer in tangible terms.

Although Lloyd's criticism is valid, it should be recognized that some social workers have attempted to define social development in more specific, practical terms. Among these are, first, a group who define social development from a psycho-social perspective as a process of personal growth and self-actualization. These writers claim that processes which enhance the functioning of individuals and result in their self-improvement also result in the improvement of society. Social development thus operates primarily at the individual level but, if successful, it creates a more harmonious and responsible society. As was noted earlier, a major exponent of this approach is Henry Maas (1984: 3) who has defined social development as a process in which 'people become increasingly able to interact competently and responsibly'. Maas goes on to point out that 'the more often they engage in socially responsive interaction, the more likely they are to help create a caring and sharing society'.

A second group of social workers who have defined social development in practical terms have attempted to equate social development with what is known in American social work as 'indirect' or macro-practice. Macro-practice includes community organization, social policy making, social planning and social work administration. The most systematic exposition of this approach is offered by Irving Spergel (1978) who defines social development as macro-structural practice concerned with promoting community and societal well-being. In a subsequent publication, Spergel (1982) provides a detailed account of the activities of an agency director named Ed who planned, implemented and managed a new project for young offenders. Using the project as a case study, Spergel argues that Ed's activities embody the social developer's role.

Although both the individualistic and the indirect practice approaches to social development attempt to identify actual practice roles for social workers, neither differs significantly from social work's current, conventional forms of intervention. In Maas's approach, social development is hardly different from the conventional activities of case-workers or group workers who help individuals experience personal growth and self-actualization through counselling or organized group experiences. Similarly, Spergel's approach hardly differs from social work's long-standing responsibility for community organization, neighbourhood activism and public sector social welfare administration. Despite the claim that social development is a new modality in social work, these activities have been a part of social work for many years. To define them as social development does little more than relabel them and use the term 'social development' as a synonym for well-established social work endeavours.

A third group of social workers who have attempted to formulate a workable definition of social development have relied on the approach developed in the interdisciplinary field of development studies. Many have previous experience of Third World development, and this has informed the way they use the term. Examples include the publications of Frank Paiva (1977, 1982), John Jones and Rama Pandey (1981), Daniel Sanders (1982), Doreen Elliott (1993), James Billups (1994) and Roland Meinert and the late Ezra Kohn (Meinert and Kohn, 1987; Meinert, Kohn and Strickler, 1984). Although these attempts offer promising directions for future research, they have not yet resulted in the adoption of a generally accepted social development perspective in social work.

It is clear that much more needs to be done if a coherent and unique social work perspective on social development is to emerge. It is also necessary that social work transcend the idealized and hortatory approach which has been used so extensively in the past. Although social workers are interested in social development and have been involved in social development endeavours in the past, renewed efforts must be made to define a unique social work approach to social development. On the other hand, the contribution of social work to social development needs to be acknowledged. Social workers popularized social development in the industrial countries and they have been enthusiastic proponents of the social development approach. In addition, their focus on practical issues has reinforced social development's essential programmatic commitments. In the future, they may well foster the emergence of a coherent approach to professional intervention in the field.

Social Development and Development Studies

The term 'social development' has been used most extensively in the interdisciplinary field of development studies, primarily to refer to the provision of social services in developing countries. Specifically concerned with Third World development, this meaning has informed many definitions which are used today. It also informs the definition which is used in this book.

As will be shown in chapter 3, this use of the term was promoted by British colonial welfare administrators who wished to link social welfare services more closely to economic development efforts. At the time, economic development was a primary goal for colonial governments and nationalist independence movements alike. The colonial welfare officers were anxious to introduce programmes that transcended the remedial social welfare services which had been introduced into the colonies and they wanted to make a positive contribution to economic development. Traditional social work services which catered for the destitute, beggars, young offenders, the disabled and other conspicuously needy groups were augmented by mass literacy and community development programmes which, it was believed, would foster a developmental approach in social welfare. The term 'social development' emerged from these efforts. Collectively, it referred to two aspects of colonial welfare policy: namely, remedial social work services and community development programmes.

It was largely through the United Nations that the term spread around the world in the 1950s and 1960s. The term was widely adopted by the governments of Third World countries as well as non-governmental organizations. Although the United Nations initially used the term in the same way as the British to refer to a combination of remedial social work and community development, by the 1960s, when the First Development Decade was launched, United Nations officials questioned this definition. They urged that the concept of social development be broadened to transcend its limited focus on social work and community development, and deal with wider issues such as raising the levels of living of the population, promoting popular participation and integrating economic and social planning.

Today, the term 'social development' is used in the context of Third World development to mean different things. Some experts use the term narrowly to refer to the services provided by government ministries or departments of social welfare in developing countries. As was noted earlier, this was the original meaning of the term. Often, this usage reflects an attempt on the part of government agencies to make their programmes more relevant to the needs and circumstances of their countries. It is for this reason that ministries or departments of social welfare in many countries have changed their names and are now known as ministries of social development. In this context, the term 'social development' therefore covers both traditional social work services such as residential care, probation and social casework as well as community development programmes, women's activities, youth services, nutrition and day care for children.

Other experts use the term 'social development' more broadly to cover all the social services. In addition to the social work or social welfare services, the term includes health, education, housing and related fields. In this approach, social development refers to the major social service sectors, and is often used in the context of national planning to connote the planning and coordination of the social services. Social development is, therefore, a synonym for social sectoral planning and for the government ministries and departments that provide these services. An example of this approach is provided in Hardiman and Midgley's (1982, 1989) work on social policy in developing countries which discusses policy issues affecting the major social services in the Third World.

Other authorities have extended the scope of the term even further to cover the social services as well as a wider range of social policies and programmes that directly affect the social well-being of the populations of developing countries. In these definitions, social development is an umbrella term which covers the major social services, land reform, rural development, people's participation, population planning and national strategies to ameliorate poverty and raise levels of living. This wider definition comes closest to the political economy approach which is used in this book to provide a theoretical perspective for social development endeavour.

Political Economy and Social Development
Political economy is an approach which seeks to apply the combined insights of economics, political science and social theory to societal

concerns, at both national and international levels. The term was first used in the seventeenth century to refer to the management of the economic affairs of the state but by the end of the last century, it had been replaced by the modern-day term 'economics'. By the early twentieth century, the term 'political economy' was reserved to describe the work of eighteenth- and nineteenth-century thinkers such as Adam Smith, David Ricardo and Karl Marx. With the revival of Marxist social science in the 1960s, the term again came into vogue and while at first regarded as an approach favoured by the left, it is now used by social scientists of all political persuasions (Coleman, 1972).

Political economy is not a distinctive discipline, and few universities today have separate departments of political economy. Although political economy is usually associated with the discipline of economics, it is really an interdisciplinary approach in the social sciences which seeks to integrate the insights of the major social science disciplines. It is more of a perspective or style in social science thinking rather than a formal discipline or sub-discipline. It focuses directly on topical social and economic questions, deals explicitly with values and ideologies, fosters a macro-perspective and readily addresses both national and international issues.

The political economy approach to social development was pioneered by the international agencies and particularly the United Nations as an integral part of an effort to foster social and economic progress among the newly independent developing countries. As will be shown in the next chapter, the United Nations originally adopted the British definition of social development to connote a combination of remedial social work and community development programmes. However, by the 1960s, officials at the United Nations began to advocate a broader approach which defined social development in terms of policies and programmes that were intimately linked with economic development and enhanced standards of living among the population as a whole. This approach drew extensively on the insights of political economy.

Social development also addresses issues which have traditionally been the purview of political economy. Political economy is concerned with human societies as they are grounded in economic activities, and it addresses questions of welfare, poverty, wealth and opportunities for advancement. Social development is concerned with similar issues. It combines the insights of different social sciences to analyse pressing human problems, and it proposes various strategies to deal with them. It is concerned with the role of the state and other major institutions in responding to social need. It involves values and deeply held beliefs. Discussions about these values and beliefs are often very controversial.

The insights of modern-day political economy have extensively informed thinking in social development. The language, ideas, approaches and issues which advocates of social development have employed have been significantly influenced by political economy. Although political economy has not developed its own definition of social development, the contribution of political economy to social development has been considerable.

2
The Historical Context

Although the last chapter offered a formal definition of social development, the term is still defined in different ways. Some of these different usages were described at the end of the previous chapter. To better understand the definition used in this book, it is useful to trace social development's historical evolution. As will be shown in this chapter, social development has been promoted by different groups of people, and influenced by different ideas and events. An understanding of how these people, ideas and events contributed to the evolution of social development gives further insights into social development's meaning.

The chapter begins by examining the role of ideas about societal change and social intervention in social development. It reviews the contribution of those who believe that it is possible and desirable to direct the process of change. The way the emergence of the welfare state and the adoption of planning in the industrial nations affected the idea of social development is also discussed. The chapter traces the evolution of social development as a practical approach for promoting social welfare. It describes the role of colonial welfare administrators who first applied the term to social welfare in the years following the Second World War. Its popularization by the United Nations is then examined. Reference is made to the adoption of the term in the industrial countries largely through the efforts of American social workers. The chapter notes that events in the 1980s have had a negative affect on social development. Although Radical Right-wing political groups effectively opposed social development and retarded its spread, there are indications that social development is again being accepted as a viable approach for enhancing social welfare.

As will be seen, these ideas and events have exerted considerable influence on the evolution of the present-day social development approach. Ideas about the nature of social change and ways of directing social change are central to social development thinking today. Similarly, social development has been affected by the expansion of government social services and the adoption of economic planning during this century. Although the influence of these ideas and events was not explicitly recognized, they played a critical role in shaping the social development approach which emerged in the 1950s and 1960s.

THEORIES OF SOCIAL CHANGE AND INTERVENTION

As was shown in the last chapter, social development involves a *process of change* which is fostered through *deliberate human action*. Social development is not, therefore, a natural, spontaneous process but requires organized intervention. The notions of change and intervention are central to social development and they exert an important influence on social development theory today. Therefore, to properly understand the nature of social development, an appreciation of the theory of social change and the concept of social intervention is needed.

Explanations of social change are very old. Social historians such as Rollin Chambliss (1954) have shown that the Greek philosophers wrote extensively about social change and that, before them, ideas about social change had emerged within the myths, legends and religions of the ancient civilizations. For example, the ancient Chinese had well-developed beliefs about social change. In Chinese culture, change was viewed as a never-ending process of cycles. The ancient Chinese believed that society first grows and becomes more organized and prosperous, but then declines into disorganization and decay. Eventually, the cycle is reversed, and society once again moves towards greater order and prosperity. The ancient Chinese also believed that planetary forces are responsible for the process. Ancient Indian civilization held a similar cyclical view of change but, unlike the Chinese, the Indians believed that the cycle of progress and decline began with an original 'Golden Age' from which society declined into a never-ending process of cycles.

The idea of a decline from a 'Golden Age' occurs in many other cultures as well. Judaism, Christianity and Islam all teach that Adam and Eve, the original human beings, lived happily in paradise until they were tempted and sinned. This resulted in their expulsion from paradise and a decline into a state of suffering which will only be alleviated when the Messiah comes to redeem humanity. These religions believe that God is the prime mover of change and change follows the destiny he prescribes for it.

These ancient ideas reveal that there are different beliefs about the direction and causes of social change. Although it has been widely accepted during this century that social change is a progressive process which produces significant improvements in society, not everyone shares this optimistic opinion. Like the ancients who viewed social change as a decline from a 'Golden Age', many people today believe that social conditions have deteriorated. Those who believe that conditions have deteriorated hold a *retrogressive or pessimistic conception* of change while those who believe conditions have improved have a *progressive or optimistic view*. In addition to these two dominant conceptions, there are explanations that view social change as a *cyclical process* consisting of alternating periods of progress and decline. As will be shown later, the modern idea of social development has been heavily influenced by the idea that social change is a progressive process.

To complicate matters further, it is possible to combine some of these approaches. Progressive theories may, for example, be combined with cyclical theories in the sense that change is viewed as a progressive process characterized by a cyclical rather than linear pattern of progress. Progressive theories may be divided into those that view social change as a linear process of steady improvement and those that regard social change as a process that passes through clearly identified stages or steps. In addition, there are some who view historical time as a static process in which no change occurs. H. W. Arndt (1978) notes that the 'stationary' conception of history dominated social thought in medieval Europe and that it was only challenged during the Renaissance and the Enlightenment. The Enlightenment in Europe was the period during the eighteenth century when social thinkers extolled the values of the new, modern society which was emerging to replace the old feudal system. Writers of the Enlightenment championed the idea of modernity which was characterized by individualism, rationality and progress. These themes pervaded the theories of social change which emerged at the time. As Robert Nisbet (1980) suggests, it was at this time that the idea of progress was popularized not only in social thought but in economics and other fields as well. For example, Adam Smith, one of the founders of modern economics, wrote that the progressive society experiencing positive social change brings benefits to all its members. On the other hand, he argued, 'the stationary state is dull; the declining one [is] melancholy' (Arndt, 1978: 7).

There are different explanations about the *causes of social change*. As was noted earlier, the ancient Chinese believed that the planets governed the process of change. For most of human history, it has been accepted that change is directed by a supreme being. It is only relatively recently that social thinkers have sought to attribute the causes of social change to social and economic factors within society itself. The idea that human beings can deliberately plan to foster and direct the process of change is even more recent.

The ancient Greeks made a major contribution to the understanding of social change. Many social science theories of social change are derived from their beliefs. The Greeks thought that their society had declined from an original 'Golden Age' and this belief found expression in the myths and legends which were written up by Hesiod. Later, this belief was challenged by the philosopher Heraclitus whose theory of social change combined cyclical and progressive elements. Heraclitus believed that societies are born, evolve, mature and decline, but he also suggested that the overall tendency is towards steady progress. Heraclitus believed that change is ever-present and that nothing in either the physical or social world remains static. He offered a sophisticated account of the cause of change, suggesting that it occurs when opposite elements fuse and create a new phenomenon. In time, the new phenomenon is opposed by another phenomenon and when these two fuse, yet another new phenomenon is created. The process of fusing opposites is known as the *dialectic*. Heraclitus argued that the dialectic propels change. His writings had an important affect on European social thinkers in the eighteenth and nineteenth centuries. Most accepted his view of social change as a progressive and inevitable process, and some thinkers such as Georg Hegel and Karl Marx adopted the dialectic to explain the causes of social change.

Plato was also influenced by Heraclitus but he tended to accept the retrogressive view of change, believing that the society in which he lived had declined from a higher state of civilization. However, he agreed with Heraclitus that societies, like human beings, grow and mature and then decline and die. Like the ancient Hebrews, Plato believed that social change is directed by a supreme being. He also believed that this being exerts more control over society in some periods of history than others. During the 'Golden Age', he was close to human beings and directed their affairs. However, when he loosened his hold over society, it began to decline. While Plato accepted the inevitability of change, he disliked change, preferring instead to live in a condition of stability and order.

Another important influence on the emergence of modern theories of social change was St Augustine, a leading scholar of the early Christian era. Indeed, Nisbet (1980) has argued that St Augustine's writings have exerted even more influence on modern theories of social change than those of the Greeks. He points out that many of the theories of social change that emerged after the Renaissance were inspired by Augustine's writings.

Augustine's view that social change is a progressive process which results in the steady improvement of society has been widely adopted. This idea has also influenced the concept of social development. Augustine also invented the technique of dividing the process of historical time into a series of discreet stages or epochs. Instead of viewing social change as a steady, ongoing flow of time, he categorized history into six distinct stages beginning with Adam and Eve and proceeding through various biblical stages up to his own time. Later, many writers adopted this technique, viewing social change as a process that proceeds episodically, in steps.

Augustine also argued that the process of change culminates in a final state of perfection. In addition to the six stages, he identified a seventh stage which would be a millennial 'Golden Age' in which human beings would live in peace and harmony on earth. This stage would be followed by the eighth and final stage when the earth passes away and believers go to heaven to live in everlasting happiness. For Augustine, the ultimate goal of social change is, therefore, social perfectibility. This idea was later developed by the utopians, and it has also exerted considerable influence on social development thinkers.

Finally, Augustine contributed to modern theories of social change by identifying the causes of change. While Augustine believed that God created time and directs the process of change, he was inspired by the Greek idea of the dialectic and believed that social change is propelled by conflicting forces. For Augustine, the basis of all social reality is the ongoing conflict between the 'City of Man' and the 'City of God', in other words between material and spiritual forces. When this conflict is finally resolved, time comes to an end.

Although very few studies of social change were published between the time of Augustine and the sixteenth century, one important theory was formulated by Ibn Khaldun, the fourteenth-century North African Islamic scholar. Ibn Khaldun's theory is significant because it was one of the first to attribute the cause of social change to human activities. Khaldun differentiated between two types of societies, the warlike nomadic tribes and the sedentary farmers and city dwellers. He pointed out that the nomads constantly attack sedentary people. Because of their superior strength and warlike habits, they eventually conquer them. The nomads settle down and rule the subjugated sedentary dwellers, but by doing so, they become sedentary themselves and lose their ability to wage war. In time, another nomadic group arrives to attack and conquer them. They too settle down and are, in turn, overthrown by other nomads. Ibn Khaldun believed that this cyclical process continues indefinitely. Although Ibn Khaldun's cyclical theory differs from most subsequent theories which view social change as a linear, progressive process, his emphasis on human conflict as the primary cause of change is historically important.

Many theories of social change were formulated by European philosophers during and after the Enlightenment. Most of these theories are optimistic, believing that societies evolve in a progressive, linear fashion. Another common element was the identification of different stages in the process of social change. Many theories of the time claimed that the final stage will be one of social perfection. However, the Enlightenment theories attributed the causes of social change to many different factors. These explanations can be divided into those that emphasize the role of human ideas and those that stress the role of economic or social forces in generating social change. The former explanations are known as *idealist* theories, while the latter are known as *materialist* theories.

Adam Smith was one of the first to suggest that social change occurs because of altered economic activities. He identified five stages in human history. The lowest stage, which is dominated by hunters, gradually gives way to the pastoral stage, which is dominated by herders. The herders are eventually replaced by primitive agriculturalists who are in turn replaced by advanced agriculturalists. The final stage is dominated by 'civilized men' who were, Smith believed, characterized by their 'improved manufacturers' and engagement in 'foreign commerce'. Changing economic activities thus propels human societies into higher stages of development. Smith's theory is an example of the materialist explanation of change.

On the other hand, Georg Hegel's explanation of social change emphasizes the role of human ideas as the primary cause of change. In addition to identifying different stages through which societies pass, he believed that different human ideas come into conflict at different stages of history. These conflicting ideas, which are expressed as a *thesis* and an *antithesis*, are eventually resolved through a process of *synthesis*. When a synthesis takes place, society is propelled into the next historical stage. The *synthesis* now becomes a new idea or *thesis*, which is eventually challenged by another new idea or *antithesis*. However, these two ideas are eventually resolved, moving society once again into a higher stage. Although Plato and other writers had previously emphasized the importance of human ideas in social change, Hegel's theory is probably the best known and most sophisticated example of the *idealist* explanation.

Karl Marx, and his collaborator, Friedrich Engels, were the most famous exponents of the materialist explanation of social change. Marx disagreed with Hegel's emphasis on the role of human ideas in social change, believing, like Smith, that different types of economic activity drive social change. Marx argued that different forms of economic activity are accompanied by different forms of exploitation and conflict. He also believed that social conflict creates a dialectic which propels societies to higher stages. Marx identified several stages in the process of change which include primitive communism, oriental society, slavery, feudalism and capitalism. With the overthrow of capitalism, society moves into a more peaceful stage of socialism which ultimately evolves into the final, perfect stage of communism. The similarity between these ideas and those of Augustine are striking.

As has been noted already, theories of social change have had an important influence on the modern-day concept of social development. Today, social development is defined as a process of change which takes place in a linear fashion and results in the progressive improvement of society. It is easy to see how Western theories of social change have influenced this definition and facilitated its adoption.

The Idea of Social Intervention

Ancient social thinkers believed that change occurs through a higher force such as the influence of God or the planets. In more recent times, many have claimed that social change is caused by societal forces. As was shown previously, Ibn Khaldun believed that societies change through an ongoing process of war. Hegel believed that human ideas propel societies to higher stages. In turn, Marx believed that societies change because exploited groups rise up and overthrow their oppressors.

None of these theories attribute social change to a deliberate human decision to cause, plan or direct change. Instead, they contend that social change occurs 'naturally' as the result of forces located within the social fabric. It is, of course, true that social theorists such as Marx and Hegel come close to suggesting that social change is caused by deliberate human action. Marx's belief that revolutionary action by oppressed groups causes change certainly implies that human beings can change society. However, both Hegel and Marx believed that human action is directed by wider, impersonal social forces. Marx declared that human beings make their own history, but he qualified this statement by pointing out that they do so within the context of wider historical and social processes. He also believed that there are 'laws' of history that govern the way society operates. While human action is needed to change society, it is motivated by wider social and historical forces.

The idea that human beings can intentionally improve society and even create ideal societies was first advocated by a group of social thinkers known as the *utopians*. They made blueprints for what they thought would be perfect societies. Although often ridiculed, they were the first advocates of intervention and the modern idea of planning.

Utopian thought has a long history. Plato was one of the first utopians. He developed an elaborate plan for an ideal society. This society would be ruled by philosophers who would govern wisely and maintain social harmony. So that they would be incorruptible and fully committed to promoting social well-being, the philosopher kings, as he called them, would not be permitted to marry or have property. Plato did not like democracy, believing that ordinary people did not have the ability to govern themselves. In addition, he believed that democracy created divisions and conflict. In his utopia, the philosopher kings would rule, create harmony and promote the interests of all citizens.

There are many other examples of utopian thought. The term was actually invented by the English statesman Sir Thomas More in the early sixteenth century. More used the term to name an imaginary island which contained his own perfect society. He modified the Greek word *topia* (which means a place) by adding the prefix *u* which can be interpreted either as *no place* or as a *perfect place*. Some experts (Manuel and Manuel, 1979) believe that his pun was deliberate, and that it was intended to convey the idea that utopia as a perfect place does not exist.

By the nineteenth century, many utopian books, novels and tracts had been published and several practical proposals to create actual utopias had been implemented. One of the first was Robert Owen who converted his cotton mill in New Lanark in Scotland into a workers' cooperative. Later he went to Indiana in the United States to manage a utopian commune known as New Harmony. This project failed as the members bickered and refused to cooperate with each other. Owen, and others such as Charles Fourier and Etienne Cabet, who also proposed the creation of planned communities in the early nineteenth century, were known as utopian socialists. They were denounced by Marx and Engels for being idealistic dreamers whose plans to reform society would fail to bring about significant social improvements.

Some utopian socialists did not attempt to create organized communities but sought rather to persuade those in political power to introduce meaningful social reforms. Most argued that social improvements could be brought about by using scientific knowledge. They argued that trained social scientists should be employed to undertake research into social problems and formulate policies to remedy them. Among the first advocates of this idea were a French nobleman, Count Henri Saint-Simon, and his collaborator, Auguste Comte, both of whom were mentioned in the last chapter. Saint-Simon held progressive political opinions and unlike many other members of the nobility, he survived the French revolution. Influenced by Saint-Simon, Comte wrote a major book about the use of scientific methods to study society and solve its problems. He advocated the creation of a new science of society which he called *sociology*, and he proposed that sociologists be trained to change society for the better.

At the end of the nineteenth century, sociology was established as a new scientific discipline in many universities in Europe and North America but few sociologists agreed with Comte that sociology should seek to solve society's problems. The English sociologist, Herbert Spencer, was particularly opposed to this idea, arguing that attempts to interfere with the natural processes of social change would harm society and retard its evolutionary progress towards a higher level of civilization. Spencer believed that societies, like natural organisms, are subject to the evolutionary laws discovered by Charles Darwin. Under the influence of Darwinist ideas, Spencer and his followers (such as William Sumner at Yale University in the United States) even opposed charity and government welfare programmes, believing that they interfered with the evolutionary process of natural selection. Under natural selection, they argued, only the fittest survive. By helping the weak and degenerate to survive, society as a whole would be undermined.

On the other hand, some sociologists endorsed Comte's point of view. Lester Ward in the United States and Leonard Hobhouse in England both rejected the non-interventionist attitudes of their time, and believed that governments should intervene to promote the welfare of their citizens. As was noted in chapter 1, Hobhouse coined the term 'social development' to connote a process of planned change. This term was later augmented by Charles North's use of the term 'social planning'. Ward invented the term 'applied sociology' to connote the application of sociological knowledge for social improvement.

The idea that scientific knowledge could improve society was also advocated by the Fabian socialists in England. At the turn of the century, the Fabians exerted influence on the British government to introduce social programmes that would deal with pressing social problems. They believed that meaningful social change could be brought about gradually through persuasion and by 'permeating' the centres of power with progressive ideas. The Fabians developed close links with reform-minded liberals who were known as the New Liberals. The New Liberals rejected the extreme individualism of the time and argued for a moderate degree of government intervention. Hobhouse himself was a New Liberal. In the United States, New Liberals included the supporters of the Progressive Party, economists such as Thorstein Veblen, philosophers such as John Dewey and social workers like Jane Addams.

Like Spencer, most economists at the time also believed that governments should not interfere in the economy. However, economists had not always held this position. Indeed, the earliest economists, who were known as the mercantilists, advocated government control over trade and other economic activities. The mercantilist system of protection and support for domestic industry undoubtedly contributed to Britain's economic success. In seventeenth-century France, Jean Baptiste Colbert, Louis XIV's Finance Minister, successfully adopted mercantilist ideas, stimulating the growth of industry through government directives, organizing production and controlling imports.

In the eighteenth century, as Europe experienced the beginnings of industrialization, interventionist ideas were vigorously attacked. In his famous book, *The Wealth of Nations*, Adam Smith criticized the mercantilists, and Colbert in particular, arguing that government intervention in the economy should be kept to a minimum. The proper role of the state, he claimed, was to ensure national defence, keep law and order and provide only those services which could not be supplied through the market. Although Smith's ideas were widely accepted, not everyone agreed with him. In the United States, Alexander Hamilton urged the new federal government to subsidize and in other ways actively promote new industries. In the first half of the nineteenth century, Friedrich List in Germany offered a spirited defence of state intervention in the economy and particularly in matters of trade. The British economist John Eatwell (1982) has shown that List's ideas subsequently influenced German political leaders who adopted an approach to economic development which differed significantly from that of Britain and other industrial countries.

Smith's arguments were compatible with a group of French economic thinkers of the eighteenth century who called themselves the physiocrats. They included François Quesnay, Pierre Dupont and the Marquis de Mirabeau. The physiocrats believed that the economy was governed by natural laws and they used the term *laissez-faire* to advocate non-interference in the market. Together with Smith's ideas, the physiocrats' approach was extended in the nineteenth century by economists such as Stanley Jevons in England, Carl Menger in Germany and Leon Walrus in Switzerland. They believed that the economy is an autonomous, self-regulated system, and that government intervention seriously harms its smooth operation. Later in the century, Alfred Marshall at Cambridge University refined these ideas, and formulated a comprehensive account of the working of the market economy. Marshall and his followers believed in non-intervention, and their views dominated economic thought at the time. Only a few economists vigorously argued for more government involvement in the economy. Thorstein Veblen, who founded the institutional school of economics, was a leading American advocate of government intervention, while in Britain the neo-classical position was challenged by Marshall's student, John Maynard Keynes, whose ideas were subsequently widely adopted.

Veblen and Keynes, and sociologists like Hobhouse and Ward, believed in social intervention through planning. However, their ideas were not implemented on a significant scale in the Western industrial countries until after the Second World War. In fact, planning on a national scale was first adopted in the Soviet Union after the Marxist

Bolshevik Party took power in 1917. It is perhaps ironic that Marxists who reviled the utopian socialists should have been the first to adopt comprehensive planning, and to succeed in doing what the utopians could only dream about.

THE WELFARE STATE AND PLANNING IN THE INDUSTRIAL COUNTRIES

Social development today involves the idea that human well-being can be promoted through organized intervention. It rejects the notion that the provision of social services is harmful to society. As was noted earlier, the view that government involvement in social affairs damages society was propounded by sociologists such as Herbert Spencer, the *laissez-faire* economists, leading politicians and wealthy people in the nineteenth century. However, despite their opposition, there was a gradual trend in the late nineteenth and early twentieth centuries to expand government involvement in social welfare. This trend originated in the Poor Laws which were the first attempt by government to respond systematically to a pressing social problem. In the early nineteenth century, as cities grew rapidly, and as urban conditions became detrimental to people's health, governments began to introduce sanitation, clean drinking water and other public health measures. Towards the end of the nineteenth century, the pressure for education grew and, in time, public education was introduced in many industrial societies.

These developments paved the way for the creation of more extensive government social programmes, including social security, housing and comprehensive health care. The first modern-day social security programmes were established in Germany in the 1880s by the Chancellor, Count Otto von Bismarck, who believed that growing political support for the German socialist party could be countered if the government introduced its own social welfare measures. Although many aristocrats and business leaders opposed Bismarck's programme, he introduced social insurance schemes which provided workers with a variety of benefits.

Germany's example was copied by other industrial countries, and social insurance became a central programme of the emerging welfare states. Some countries used the social insurance approach to provide health care, maternity payments, child allowances and similar benefits and, in time, these programmes were extended to cover larger numbers of workers. Social insurance was accompanied by public education and health services, a growing public housing sector and increasing provision of government social work services.

At the height of the Great Depression, President Franklin Roosevelt of the United States declared a New Deal for American citizens. The

United States was the only major Western industrial country without government social insurance and health care programmes. As unemployment rose during the recession, and as many hard-working Americans fell into poverty, support for government intervention increased. Although the New Deal focused primarily on emergency relief and job creation, the introduction of the Social Security Act in 1935 is regarded by many experts as a historic milestone in the evolution of America's welfare state.

The publication in 1942 of the Beveridge report is also regarded by many experts as an important event in the history of social policy. William Beveridge had been invited by the British Prime Minister, Winston Churchill, to chair a committee to ensure that the social needs of the British population would be adequately met after the end of the Second World War. There was concern that soldiers returning from the war should find jobs and that the problems of poverty, low educational standards and other adverse social conditions should be addressed. The Beveridge report recommended that the social services, particularly social security and health care, be expanded and that all citizens be covered. The report was acclaimed because it carefully analysed the major social problems facing countries such as Britain, and proposed solutions based on comprehensive government intervention.

After the war, the British government under Prime Minister Clement Attlee adopted many of the recommendations of the Beveridge report. In addition to creating a centralized social security system, the government established the National Health Service, expanded public education and embarked on an extensive programme of public housing. Unlike the United States, the British government also introduced family allowances which paid cash benefits to families with children. These efforts fostered the emergence of a highly centralized and comprehensive welfare state which covered the whole population. Unlike previous social services which focused on the poorest groups in society, the British welfare state sought to cover all citizens.

At the time, the Beveridge report was widely regarded as a model for the rest of the world. Many European countries also introduced extensive social programmes. However, in some cases, they were fragmented and managed by local governments, or sometimes by trade unions and other organizations which catered for particular groups of workers. Despite the achievements of the New Deal, the American welfare state did not provide health care or family allowances, and it relied extensively on means-tested programmes.

Although it was generally accepted that the developing countries could not afford to introduce comprehensive social services, colonial administrators were also influenced by the emergence of the welfare state in the metropolitan nations. Indeed, many colonies attempted to expand government social services. In some territories, such as India and Ceylon, commissions of inquiry similar to the Beveridge Committee were appointed (Midgley, 1984b). For example, the Ardarkar Commission in India recommended the introduction of social insurance for industrial workers and this resulted in the creation of India's Employee's State Insurance Scheme in 1948. Although few developing countries were able to introduce sizable social insurance programmes for employees, the emergence of the welfare state and the idea that government should be responsible for promoting social welfare subsequently influenced the emergence of social development in the developing countries. In the industrial countries, on the other hand, the emergence of the welfare state gave rise to the social administration approach. As will be seen later in this chapter, the social development approach evolved out of attempts by colonial welfare officials to identify social service models that contributed positively to economic development.

The Adoption of Planning

Planning is an important element in social development. Today, many believe that social development goals can be realized through systematic planning. As was noted earlier, planning is an old idea. It was promoted by the utopians and particularly the utopian socialists of the nineteenth century. It was also a central element of Marxist economic policy and was first adopted on a significant scale in the Soviet Union.

Although the Soviet planning system was generally condemned in the West, the concept of planning gradually gained popularity in the Western industrial countries. Planning was first introduced in these countries in the form of town planning. Later, largely through the writings of Keynes, a less directive form of economic planning than the Soviet approach was adopted. In the European colonial territories, on the other hand, directive economic planning was thought to be conducive to economic development. Despite their reluctance to adopt economic planning at home, several European governments introduced economic planning in their colonies. Albert Waterston (1965) reveals that economic planning was first introduced in the Gold Coast (as Ghana was then known) in 1919 when a ten-year economic development plan named after the colony's governor, Sir Gordon Guggisberg, was implemented. Several other colonies adopted similar plans. In 1935, the American colonial authorities in the Philippines created a National Economic Council to prepare an economic plan for the territory's development. In India in 1936, the Congress Party established a committee to study Soviet planning and to prepare its own plan for implementation after independence. After the Second World

War, the Philippines and India were the first of many newly independent developing countries to adopt comprehensive Soviet-style national development plans, and to create centralized government agencies responsible for their implementation. Although these agencies were powerful, the purpose of planning was to direct rather than rigidly control the economy. Except for the communist developing countries, where state control was absolute, interventionism in most developing countries was qualified by the goal of creating a mixed rather than a command economy.

In the industrial countries, the acceptance of planning came about largely through adoption of urban rather than economic planning. Modern town planning originated in the rapidly growing cities of Europe and North America in the late nineteenth century when the problems of slums became increasingly visible. At this time, reformers began to exert pressure on city governments to ameliorate slum conditions. Also relevant were the garden cities which were built at the end of the nineteenth century by philanthropists such as Ebenezer Howard. The garden cities were intended to resettle people from the slums in new, planned communities away from the city centre and its problems. The writings of Lewis Mumford and Patrick Geddes helped foster the idea that the urban environment could be improved through planning, and that planning would enhance the quality of urban life.

However, it was only after the Second World War that urban planning was adopted on a large scale in the industrial countries. The damage caused by the war fostered massive slum clearance and rebuilding programmes which resulted in the construction of large high-rise public housing complexes and the creation of new, planned urban environments. Zoning was widely adopted as a planning tool and it ensured that residential and economic activities were located in different areas. New transportation networks were constructed and recreation and social needs were addressed. The construction of large public housing projects became a central feature of urban planning in many industrial countries. However, it was soon recognized that the new housing estates were generating new and unforeseen social problems.

Urban planning, which was primarily concerned with the physical environment, gradually expanded to encompass economic and social activities as well. Urban planning agencies began to address problems such as unemployment, crime and poverty and, as James Midgley (1984a) revealed, the term 'social planning' was gradually adopted to connote the social aspects of urban planning. Social planning emerged as a distinct field, and social planners were primarily responsible for undertaking demographic analyses, data collection and assessing the social impact of planning decisions. However, social planning was not given as much emphasis as physical and economic planning.

The growth of urban planning in the industrial countries was accompanied by regional planning which focused on larger geographic areas. Regional planning sought to combine physical, economic and social strategies for the improvement of these areas. Usually, the geographic localities selected for regional planning were both poor and economically underdeveloped. The development of infrastructure and the creation of investment opportunities were regarded as prerequisites for future economic growth. Comprehensive regional development projects were adopted in various parts of Europe and the United States, and many were widely publicized. They include the massive Tennessee Valley Project in the United States and the Highland Development Project in Scotland. Regional planning has also been introduced in developing countries as disparate as Brazil and Saudi Arabia. In Third World countries, region planning has often focused on particularly remote, underpopulated and particularly deprived regions.

In most Western countries, economic planning has not been directive or comprehensive but has involved the adoption of Keynesian policies which seek to plan the economy through the use of indirect measures that stimulate demand and foster economic growth. As was noted earlier, Keynes was a liberal who believed that modest government intervention was needed to guide and improve society. Like Beveridge, he advocated the expansion of the social services. Neither Keynes nor Beveridge agreed with the socialists who wanted to take full control over the economy.

Although governments in the Western industrial countries expanded their social services and sought to manage their economies through Keynesian prescriptions, these two activities were generally separated. Few countries attempted to integrate social and economic policies in a systematic way. As was shown in the last chapter, the social services in the industrial countries have long played a subsidiary role to the economic sector. With the exception of the Scandinavian countries, few Western governments have sought to harmonize their economic and social policies, and few have treated the economic and welfare sectors as interdependent and mutually reinforcing. It was primarily in the context of Third World development that the idea of integrating economic and social development evolved.

COLONIALISM AND SOCIAL WELFARE IN THE THIRD WORLD

Attempts to purposefully link social policies and programmes to an overall strategy of economic development are central to the notion of social development. This idea originally evolved in the context of Third World development. As was noted in the last chapter, the concept of social development emerged from the activities of colonial welfare administrators in Africa during the 1940s and 1950s.

Colonialism had long been concerned with the exploitation of the natural and agricultural resources of the colonies. The colonial governments were primarily concerned with insuring that private enterprise (in the form of plantations or settler farms) were able to function profitably. Colonial administrators were responsible for law and order, and for keeping the subjugated indigenous population passive. Colonial governments were also responsible for encouraging the indigenous population to provide labour for colonial enterprise. When this was not possible, labour was imported from elsewhere in the form of slavery or indentured workers. Colonial governments also imposed and collected taxes to cover their administrative costs, and to construct the infrastructure which the colonial economy required. The colonial governments, therefore, sought to provide a framework which facilitated economic exploitation by private enterprise. Generally, colonial administrations were not directly concerned with economic development.

This situation began to change in the early decades of the twentieth century when some colonial administrations introduced development plans designed to foster economic growth. As was noted previously, the first of these was the Guggisberg Plan for the Gold Coast. Another major development, which facilitated government involvement in the economy, was the enactment by the British government in 1929 of the first of a series of statutes, known as the Colonial Development and Welfare Acts.

These statutes were designed to stimulate trade with the colonies. Faced with low demand for manufactured products during the Great Depression, the British government sought to expand overseas markets. The Colonial Development and Welfare Acts were intended to open new markets in the colonies and provide funds for investments in agricultural, commercial or industrial ventures which would 'promote commerce with, or industry in the United Kingdom' (United Kingdom, 1960: 5). Subsequent Colonial Development and Welfare Acts appropriated funds for education and social projects as well. Similar legislation was enacted by the French metropolitan government for the Francophone territories.

The Colonial Development and Welfare Acts did not magically transform the colonial economies, but they legitimated the notion of economic planning and authorized the use of resources for economic development. The statutes also fostered the idea that the colonies were not only sources of raw materials for export, but potentially viable economic entities in their own right. This idea became a primary theme in the campaigns of the nationalist independence movements, and a major commitment of the independence governments.

Economic development was a dominant theme during the post-Second World War period. Colonial administrators and nationalist leaders alike believed that economic development offered the best hope of transforming the colonial territories into prosperous industrial nations. After independence, many Third World governments created central planning agencies which prepared comprehensive five-year development plans. The role of industrialization in planning was widely emphasized. Many newly independent countries sought to emulate the West and the Soviet Union by mobilizing domestic resources and securing international aid for industrial investments. In the postwar era, economic development offered the prospect of transforming impoverished traditional economies into advanced industrial states. Leading economists such as Paul Rosenstein-Rodan (1943) and Arthur Lewis (1954, 1955) formulated theoretical conceptions of how economic development could be promoted. It is hardly surprising that the idea of economic development was widely embraced by political leaders, intellectuals and ordinary citizens alike.

Colonial Welfare and the Origins of Social Development

In a climate dominated by economic development, colonial welfare officials were challenged to contribute to the development process. Many economists argued that the social services detracted from development and that social expenditures should be curtailed to provide resources for productive investments instead. On the other hand, many indigenous political leaders were impressed with the growth of the welfare state in the industrial countries and believed that the introduction of government social services was compatible with attempts to modernize their societies. Many urged that health care and education be expanded since these services had been available only on a limited basis prior to independence. Many who advocated expanding the social services were nationalists who wanted to promote the interests of their countries. Others held populist or socialist views. Whatever their motivation, the need to link the expansion of the social services with the overriding need for economic development was generally accepted.

Originally, the social services were not provided by the colonial governments but by missionary organizations or charities created by settlers or educated local people. These activities coexisted with ancient traditional welfare institutions. However, the situation began to change just before the war. As the colonial cities grew and as urban slums and new social problems emerged, solutions were required. Juvenile delinquency, begging, destitution, homelessness and similar social problems now preoccupied the colonial governments which recognized the need for specialized public agencies which could deal with them. As Lucy

Mair (1944) reports, the British government first appointed a committee to investigate the need for social work services in the colonies in the late 1930s, and this was followed during the war by the creation of the first colonial welfare departments which built reformatories for juvenile offenders, children's homes and other institutions for the elderly, mentally ill and destitute. Social workers were imported from Britain to manage these departments and to train indigenous workers who could staff the institutions and provide casework services (Midgley, 1981).

The welfare departments were often criticized for consuming scarce resources for unproductive welfare services. Arthur Livingston (1969) reports that some senior colonial officials saw little need for social work services. They argued that the colonies would be better served by economic development programmes that promoted the welfare of all citizens, rather than focusing scarce resources on a few beggars and other conspicuously needy people. In this climate, some colonial social welfare administrators sought to identify new programmes that would transcend the narrow remedial focus of their departments and cater for the larger community. It was also hoped that programmes of this kind would promote wider economic development goals.

In West Africa, some colonial welfare departments introduced youth services that were intended not only to prevent young people from engaging in deviant behaviour, but to foster their participation in community activities such as road construction, agriculture and organized recreation. Many created women's programmes which provided instruction in maternal and child health, nutrition, cooking and dressmaking. Yet others embarked on adult literacy programmes which were known at the time as mass education. Because these programmes attempted to transcend conventional remedial functions and to meet the needs of larger groups, they were all identified as examples of 'developmental social welfare'.

Mass education was adopted by the colonial welfare departments largely because the colonial education departments were too preoccupied with primary and secondary education to pay attention to the educational requirements of adults even though the need for non-formal adult education had been stressed by the Colonial Office in Britain. Mair (1944) revealed that a memorandum published in 1935 by the Colonial Office encouraged the introduction of adult literacy because it believed that schooling for children would be wasted unless the whole community appreciated the benefits of education. The memorandum also stressed the need to link literacy training to the activities which characterize people's daily lives. Literacy training, the Colonial Office believed, would not be successful if it taught reading and writing in isolation from the agricultural and other economic tasks of rural people. To this end, it proposed that para-professional workers be trained to

combine literacy instruction with agricultural extension, the introduction of village water supplies, sanitary projects and similar activities.

The failure of the colonial education departments to implement mass
education provided the welfare departments with an opportunity to use
the mass education approach to transcend conventional remedial services. Mass education helped the welfare departments to expand their
activities into the rural areas and to introduce programmes that were
clearly developmental in character. Mass education was most enthusiastically adopted by colonial welfare administrators in West Africa
and was regarded, as Peter Hodge (1973) noted, as an effective means
for promoting development among rural people who were untouched
by large-scale economic projects or the opportunities afforded by the
urban environment. Hodge, who actually served as a colonial welfare
officer in West Africa, reported that mass education emphasized self-
help and self-determination as two critical concepts for mobilizing
people's involvement.

The mass education programmes introduced in West Africa soon
attracted the attention of the Colonial Office in London. Impressed
with the West African innovations, the Colonial Office urged welfare
departments in the other colonies to adopt mass education as well,
and to use this approach to promote a developmental approach to
social welfare. However, the term 'mass education' was not generally
liked and, by the end of the Second World War, the term 'community
development' had been adopted instead. This new term covered literacy education as well as women's activities, youth services,
infrastructural development projects, health and sanitary services and
similar programmes.

At a major conference of colonial welfare administrators in
Cambridge in 1948, the term 'community development' was formally
adopted to replace mass education. The conference also formulated a
definition of community development which emphasized the importance of self-help and self-determination as basic theoretical concepts
in community development. This definition was widely adopted in the
developing countries (Midgley et al., 1986).

Under the guidance of the Colonial Office, community development
was extended to other parts of Africa and the British empire. In some
territories, the formative West African model was modified to suit local
conditions. In India, for example, community development drew extensively on the ideas of Mahatma Gandhi and Rabindranath Tagore.
British initiatives in community development were also emulated by
other colonial powers such as the French who introduced similar programmes, known as *animation rurale*, in their territories (Gow and
VanSant, 1983). In the American sphere of influence, community development ideas were infused with notions of self-reliance, participation

and self-determination. As David Brokensha and Peter Hodge (1969) revealed, community development not only gave expression to widely held American cultural values but was seen as an effective antidote to communist subversion in Asia and Latin America.

Although the British Colonial Office actively promoted community development, it recognized that remedial social work services were also needed, and it cautioned the welfare departments against neglecting these services. It was proposed that the departments adopt a dual approach in which remedial services would cater largely for the urban poor, while community development would serve the rural masses. This dual thrust, it was believed, would comprehensively promote the well-being of the population and effectively link social welfare and economic development objectives. At another important conference of colonial welfare officials held in Ashridge in 1954, the term 'social development' was formally adopted to give expression to this idea. As a combination of remedial social welfare and developmentally oriented community programmes, social development involved 'nothing less than the whole process of change and advancement of a territory, considered in terms of the progressive well-being of society and the individual' (United Kingdom, 1954: 14). As this statement reveals, social development sought to promote broad welfare goals within the context of economic development efforts.

THE UNITED NATIONS AND THE POPULARIZATION OF SOCIAL DEVELOPMENT

The contribution of the British to social development was decisive but it was complemented and subsequently expanded by the United Nations. Since its inception, the United Nations has played a major role in the promotion of both economic and social development. Article 55 of the organization's Charter commits it to promote 'higher standards of living, full employment and conditions of economic and social progress and development'. However, the organization did little in its early years to foster these wider goals. Instead it adopted a limited view of social welfare as comprising remedial social welfare and community development.

During the 1950s, the United Nations gave priority to family welfare, child care and youth work which it regarded as central to social development. It undertook several studies into remedial social welfare, and sought to promote the spread of social work in the developing countries. The United Nations placed so much emphasis on remedial social welfare at the time that a later review of its activities concluded: 'The general impression given is that social factors were regarded as residual to the overall process of development and that social policy would be designed to provide remedial or palliative measures rather than positive and dynamic activities in the social field' (United Nations, 1971a: 2).

However, by the mid-1960s, the United Nations had reassessed its original commitment to remedial social welfare and new approaches which were more directly focused on levels of living and the eradication of poverty. These approaches sought to end the compartmentalization of the social services from economic development. Instead, the United Nations advocated that social programmes should be fully integrated with economic planning in an effort to enhance social welfare in the broadest meaning of the term.

Social Planning and Unified Socio-Economic Development

The initiative for reformulating the United Nations' approach to social development was taken by the organization's Secretariat. The Secretariat had become increasingly aware of criticisms of the organization's narrow approach to social welfare and its emphasis on remedial social work. By the early 1960s, the narrow view was being challenged on the ground that it bore little resemblance to the wider mandate enshrined in Article 55 of the Charter. A lengthy re-examination of the United Nations' approach was undertaken and this culminated in the adoption in 1966 of General Assembly resolution 1139 (XLI) on Reappraisal of the Role of the Social Commission. The resolution mandated a far broader scope for the Commission, which was now renamed the Commission for Social Development, and for the Secretariat which was charged with providing support for new programmes that would refocus the organization's activities on development goals.

Several new activities emerged from these attempts by the United Nations to identify a new developmental perspective. One initiative sought to identify statistical indicators that would assist national planning agencies to measure the degree to which social development goals were being attained. The United Nations Research Institute for Social Development in Geneva was commissioned to investigate the question but as Nancy Baster (1972) revealed, the task was a complex one. While a great variety of statistical data about different countries had been collected, it was not readily apparent how these data should be combined to measure abstract concepts such as 'development', 'social progress' or 'welfare'. Eventually, UNRISD produced two competing systems of measurement which were based on the same data but differed in orientation. Although both were complex measures utilizing a large array of statistical information, they were not widely employed. Nevertheless, they stimulated a great deal of subsequent research and fostered the development of more manageable social indices of social development.

As was shown in the last chapter, the indicators formulated by D. M. Morris (1979) and Richard Estes (1985) have been particularly useful. The most recent is the Human Development Index devised by the United Nations Development Programme (1990).

The attempt to identify indicators of social development required extensive theoretical discussion about the links between social and economic development. At the time, most economic planners believed that economic growth would, of itself, raise the levels of living of the masses in the developing countries. Central planning agencies should, they believed, concentrate their efforts on maximizing investment and fostering rapid rates of economic growth. Social expenditures were to be kept to a minimum in order to free resources for productive investments. This view was increasingly challenged by a small group of economists and other social scientists who believed that governments should formulate policies to harmonize their economic planning activities with social policies and programmes.

As a result of their contribution, the notion of 'balanced' or 'unified' socio-economic development gradually emerged to connote the integration of the economic and social components of development. However, these concepts were poorly understood in both conceptual and policy terms. To clarify these concepts and make practical proposals for attaining unified socio-economic development, the United Nations convened meetings of experts in 1969 and 1971. One of the experts who made a major contribution to the formulation of the concept of unified socio-economic development was the Nobel Prize-winning Swedish economist Gunnar Myrdal. Myrdal urged governments to plan their economies actively, adopt social policies that enhance people's welfare and take steps to redistribute income and wealth. Other economists who supported this view included Hans Singer and Benjamin Higgins both of whom also served as United Nations experts.

The expert meetings resulted in the publication of a major policy document on the subject of social planning (United Nations, 1971a). A major practical recommendation was that social planning units should be established in the central planning ministries to formulate social sectoral plans, assess the social impact of economic and physical planning and focus the overall planning process on the attainment of social objectives. A number of important resolutions on unified socio-economic planning and related topics were adopted by the United Nations at the end of the 1970s. These fostered the widespread acceptance of social planning among the organization's Third World member states. However, while social planning was widely regarded as the best means of promoting unified socio-economic development, many questions about the nature of social planning remained unresolved (Apthorpe, 1970).

Other International Agencies and Social Development
In addition to the unified socio-economic development approach, other strategies for promoting social development soon emerged. They too were promoted by the international agencies. Although academic scholars were widely consulted and played a major role in formulating these approaches, the role of officials at the different agencies was decisive. Inspired by the example of the United Nations, they nurtured the formulation of new approaches and fostered their adoption.

Several international agencies including the World Health Organization, the United Nations Children's Fund, the World Bank and the International Labour Office contributed to the emergence of the new social development strategies. Several of these agencies, such as the World Health Organization and the International Labour Office, had been responsible for social policy since their inception, but all re-examined their conventional approaches in the light of new debates about the role of social policy in developing countries.

The World Bank's attempt to refocus its activities on social development in the 1970s attracted widespread attention. The Bank was established to provide financial support for conventional economic rather than social welfare projects. However, during the presidency of Robert McNamara, the Bank's lending policies focused on social issues and particularly on the problem of poverty and inequality. During this time, its disbursements for education, health, housing, water supply, rural development and similar projects increased noticeably (World Bank, 1975). Perhaps most surprising in view of the Bank's historical conservatism, was its sponsorship of a publication in 1974 that called for the adoption of measures that would redistribute income and assets in favour of the poorest groups (Chenery et al., 1974). Echoing Myrdal's earlier insistence that redistribution was a precondition for economic growth, the book concluded that egalitarian and developmental objectives were not antithetical but complementary.

Perhaps the most popular of the various social development strategies formulated in the 1970s was the basic needs approach. This approach was formally adopted at the International Labour Office's World Employment Conference in 1976. As a result of many years of research into the problem of unemployment in developing countries, the ILO and its expert advisers came to the conclusion that conventional economic growth strategies were unlikely to absorb labour into productive wage employment on a scale that would deal with the problem of mass poverty in the foreseeable future. The alternative was to harness available resources to tackle the poverty problem and its manifestations directly. As a strategy, basic needs seeks to mobilize resources for social development. By putting priority on education, village health services, safe water supplies, literacy and similar social programmes, it addresses the root social problems of underdevelopment. It also seeks to integrate disparate economic and social components of the development process (Ghai et al., 1977; Streeten et al., 1981).

Basic needs embodies many of the ideas about social development which had emerged both in official development agencies and in academic circles during the 1960s. Its central tenets were adopted not only by the International Labour Organization but by other agencies including the World Bank as well. The World Health Organization and UNICEF also applied what were essentially basic needs concepts in the Alma Ata Declaration (World Health Organization, 1981). Publications concerned with international trade and foreign aid such as the Brandt (1980) report also reflected the influence of these ideas.

Unified socio-economic planning, redistribution with growth and basic needs all rest on the assumption that governments should be responsible for promoting social development. These approaches also assumed that governments would promote social development efficiently and justly. However, some proponents of social development did not share the assumptions of the statist approach, and believed instead that social development could best be fostered through the efforts of ordinary people themselves. This criticism resulted in the formulation of the 'popular' or 'community participation' approach.

Proponents of the popular participation approach claim that governments have created large and inefficient bureaucracies, squandered scarce resources on wasteful projects, used government agencies to corruptly benefit politicians and senior civil servants, and generally neglected the needs of ordinary people. They believe that social development goals can best be attained if ordinary people are mobilized to establish projects that serve their local communities and if they are actively involved in these projects. Concepts such as 'community participation' and 'people's empowerment' became popular slogans, and many non-governmental organizations, both indigenous and international, championed their aims. While some proponents of popular participation advocated a combination of government and popular effort, others distrusted government and argued that non-governmental agencies should have exclusive responsibility for social development. Several also advocated the adoption of confrontational tactics designed to pressure state agencies to be more responsive to people's needs (Hollnsteiner, 1977, 1982; Marsden and Oakley, 1982).

Some international agencies which had originally espoused a statist development model also began to promote the community participation approach. The United Nations published several reports on the question of popular participation in the 1970s and these reflected the organization's earlier involvement with community development

(United Nations, 1971b, 1975). Agencies such as the United Nations Children's Fund, the World Health Organization and the World Bank also put more emphasis on the involvement of local communities in social development and particularly in small-scale, local development projects (Newell, 1975; World Bank, 1975; World Health Organization, 1981, 1982; UNICEF, 1982). In the 1980s, this focus was further modified to include a concern for the environment, and for the way the unrelenting quest for economic growth has damaged natural as well as human habitats. Sustainable development, as this approach became known, has since attracted extensive attention in development circles (Estes, 1993; Redclift, 1987).

Of particular interest to social workers are the efforts of regional United Nations agencies such as ESCAP (the United Nations Economic and Social Commission for Asia and the Pacific) to promote the adoption of social welfare policies that focus more specifically on development needs. The search for a 'development thrust' in social welfare and social work services began with the international meeting of ministers responsible for social welfare which was held in New York in 1968 (United Nations, 1969). At this meeting, criticisms of social work's excessive focus on remedial social work were expressed, and calls were made for the introduction of more appropriate interventions that would enhance the relevance of social welfare programmes to development. The report of the ministers' conference identified three approaches to social welfare, namely the remedial, preventive and developmental. Noting that most national social welfare agencies were primarily concerned with remedial services, the ministers urged that more emphasis be placed on prevention and new, developmentally relevant provisions.

Unfortunately, few concrete examples of developmental social welfare were provided by the delegates to the ministers' conference. Few governments were able to identify programmes that would meet critical social needs and, at the same time, contribute positively to development. Consequently, few governments were able to respond to the ministers' conference by implementing a developmental approach.

One exception is the Philippines which hosted the first regional meeting of Asian social welfare ministers in 1970 (Philippines, 1971). At this meeting, a number of developmentally relevant forms of intervention were discussed. They included the adoption of more effective social planning by welfare ministries, active support for family planning, the introduction of programmes that address the problem of youth unemployment, and a focus on the nutritional and educational needs of preschool children. In 1976, the Philippine government formally adopted a comprehensive developmental social welfare programme which had numerous innovative components. To reflect its new developmental approach, the Department of Social Welfare became known as the Department of Social Services and Development. Several of the department's traditional remedial programmes, such as its social assistance scheme, were modified to reflect a new developmental orientation, and new programmes for unemployed youth and preschool children were introduced. The department ensured that family planning became an integral part of its activities, and an emphasis was placed on community-based interventions. Particularly important has been its commitment to child care programmes which seek to enhance nutritional standards among preschool children. Programmes directed at women have also been expanded.

Social welfare ministries in several other Asian countries have emulated the Philippines, and it is now common to find social welfare programmes in the region that seek to contribute to national development effort through promoting nutrition services, family planning, micro-enterprises and similar activities. These ideas have also had a major impact on international agencies such as UNICEF which refocused its conventional approach to child welfare and is now extensively involved in the promotion of child health, nutrition and maternal services in the Third World. The other United Nations regional agencies have also sought to promote a developmental approach to social welfare but these efforts have not been as successful. Today, the Asian countries are perhaps best placed to offer guidance on the adoption of a developmental social welfare approach.

Social Development in the Industrial Countries

As has been shown already, the concept of social development emerged in the British colonial territories in the middle decades of this century. Although social development has been significantly influenced by Western ideas (such as utopianism and theories of social change), and by planning and the rise of the welfare state, the social development perspective has been formulated largely within the context of Third World development. The term has been used by the international agencies and by academic scholars primarily to refer to social initiatives within the context of economic development in the developing countries.

There are, of course, programmes in the industrial countries which share many features with the social development approach. For example, regional planning which has been adopted in Europe and in the United States has attempted to transcend the conventional concern in urban planning with planning the physical environment to promote economic growth and foster social improvements as well. However, the obvious link between regional planning and social development has been neither widely recognized nor articulated into a coherent perspective. Another factor is that regional planning has tended to focus on infrastructural development, placing less emphasis on social programmes. Also, in the face of the current anti-interventionist mood which pervaded the industrial countries in the 1980s, regional planning has been given low priority by many Western governments.

Although social development has been influenced by the sizable expansion of government social services in the industrial countries and by the emergence of the subject of social policy, the two are not the same. As a process, social policy formulation forms an integral element of social development. Obviously, social development goals can only be met through effective social policies that address pressing social problems and social needs. However, as has been shown already, social policies in most industrial countries are seldom linked to economic development. Social policy and the social services in these countries are compartmentalized from programmes designed to promote economic development, and usually the social services are believed to be subsidiary and dependent on the economy. In the conventional social administration approach, the economy is the provider which meets the costs of social welfare. At the same time, the welfare system is often regarded as a drain on the economy. Few governments of the industrial countries regard the social services as an equal partner with the economy or view the economy and the social services as mutually supporting and reinforcing.

A major exception is Scandinavian countries such as Sweden. While social policy in Sweden shares many common features with other European welfare states, it differs from most other European countries by seeking explicitly to integrate social and economic policies. The Swedish approach not only integrates economic and social policy, but specifically uses social policy to foster economic development through effective labour market policies that maintain high employment. The linking of social policy to economic development in Scandinavian countries such as Sweden is more in keeping with the social development than social administration approach.

The Swedish use of social policy as an integral element of its social development approach would be alien in industrial countries such as the United States. Yet, it is in the United States that the most systematic effort has so far been made to promote the goals of social development in academic circles. As was shown in the last chapter, the promotion of the social development approach in the United States has been fostered through the efforts of a group of American social workers who had worked with the international agencies or who had gained experience of Third World conditions.

Their activities can be traced back to the creation of the School of Social Development at the University of Minnesota under the leadership of John Jones in 1971, and the subsequent diffusion of the social development perspective to other social work programmes in the country. As Roland Meinert (1991) revealed, the creation of the Inter-University Consortium for International Social Development in the late 1970s brought together educators from several American universities, and led to the inauguration of a new journal, *Social Development Issues*, and the publication of several important articles and books on the subject (Paiva, 1977; Jones and Pandey, 1981; Sanders, 1982). The Consortium is now a sizable international organization with both institutional and individual members in many different countries. Although the organization has not yet exerted any significant influence on government social policy in the United States, the current climate is highly conducive to its efforts being recognized.

THE DEMISE AND RESURGENCE OF SOCIAL DEVELOPMENT

While significant efforts were being made to promote the social development approach in the industrial countries in the late 1970s, political events minimized the effectiveness of these efforts, and challenged the idea that governments should assume responsibility for promoting social development to enhance the welfare of citizens. The most serious opposition to state involvement in social welfare came from Radical Right-wing political movements which gained political power in Britain, the United States and other countries in the late 1970s (Glennerster and Midgley, 1991). The Radical Right was able to persuade many voters that governments were to blame for the high levels of unemployment, inflation and strikes by trade unions that characterized the period. The two oil crises of the 1970s had caused serious economic problems and despite attempts by governments to correct these problems through Keynesian economic planning, recession, inflation and unemployment continued.

With the election of Radical Right-wing leaders such as Mrs Thatcher as Prime Minister of Britain in 1979 and Ronald Reagan as President of the United States in 1980, the belief that governments should be responsible for social development was seriously challenged. Equally significant was the earlier military coup by General Pinochet in Chile which overthrew President Allende and resulted in the imposition of Radical Right economic and social policies. In addition, the International Monetary Fund which had long opposed government-sponsored social development was now given new opportunities to impose its monetarist policies as a condition for granting credit to indebted Third World nations.

The Radical Right resurrected the *laissez-faire* theories of the nineteenth century. Radical Right-wing governments oppose government intervention and believe that social development occurs naturally as a result of economic growth. They also believe that economic growth is fostered when governments refrain from planning the economy, and instead implements policies that reduce taxes and help entrepreneurs to maximize their profits and wealth.

The Radical Right did not abolish the welfare state in the industrial countries, but it has been weakened through cuts to social expenditures, privatizing or contracting out social services to commercial providers and creating for-profit social services. As government responsibility for social welfare has been curtailed, the centralized, comprehensive welfare state has been radically altered.

There have been similar developments in Third World countries. During the 1970s, when interest rates were low and credit was freely available, the governments of many developing countries borrowed heavily to fund a variety of economic and social development projects. With the ascendancy of the Radical Right in the industrial countries, interest rates soared and many developing countries were suddenly faced with a huge burden of international debt. Many were forced to borrow from the International Monetary Fund and the World Bank to finance their debt repayments, and most have been compelled to impose severe cuts on their social programmes (Cornia et al., 1987). Under these conditions, the thrust for social development which characterized the 1960s and 1970s rapidly evaporated.

As was shown in chapter 1, the problems of poverty and social deprivation have again reached serious proportions not only in the developing but in the industrial countries as well. Cutbacks in social investments, the privatization of social programmes, the abandonment of social planning and similar policy developments which accompanied the rise of the Radical Right have resulted in a significant increase in unmet social need. Increased international and civil conflicts, domestic violence and ethnic strife, political repression, de-industrialization in the West and economic stagnation in many countries have further exacerbated the problem. As the twentieth century draws to a close, the human condition seems desperate.

Fortunately, there are signs of a growing desire to address the pressing problems of the time in a systematic way. The most strident Radical Right-wing political leaders are no longer in office and, in many industrial countries, more voters are supporting political parties that promise to address social needs. At the international level, world poverty, hunger and similar social ills are again receiving extensive attention. Despite the anti-interventionist climate of the 1980s, the notion of sustainable development has gained currency in development circles to resurrect the idea that economic development of itself cannot solve the critical social problems facing humanity. Indeed, proponents of sustainable development have vigorously criticized the relentless pursuit of growth and profits for the damage caused both to the environment and to human beings. In 1990, the United Nations Development Programme published the first of a new series of documents dealing explicitly with social development. Although the organization used the neologism *human development* (perhaps in an attempt to placate those on the political right who have long denigrated the word *social*), human development is nothing more than a synonym for social development. The decision of the United Nations to convene the World Summit on Social Development in 1995 offers considerable ground for optimism. This event reveals that after a period of neglect, social development is again on the global agenda. With the support of the world's leaders, the prospect of revitalizing the social development approach is better than ever before.

3
Theoretical Debates

The last chapter showed that social development has been influenced by different historical events. The expansion of government social welfare in the nineteenth century, the creation of the welfare state, the adoption of economic planning and the efforts of colonial welfare administrators and officials at the United Nations in the 1950s and 1960s to link social policies with economic development all contributed to the emergence of the social development approach.

However, social development has also been significantly affected by theoretical ideas. Explanations of the nature and causes of social change, ideas about ways of intervening to guide the process of change, and beliefs about what comprises an ideal society have all influenced thinking about social development. These ideas form the basis of social development theory. Social development not only is a practical affair, involving the design and implementation of social programmes, but also invokes complex theoretical ideas and beliefs.

For this reason, a proper account of social development must pay attention to theoretical aspects and examine the way theory has influenced the field. Unfortunately, social development is not theoretically well developed. Social development has no easily recognizable 'grand theories' or models which can be analysed and debated. On the other hand, it cannot be claimed that social development is totally devoid of theory. Scholars who have written about social development have made extensive use of theoretical concepts and, by borrowing from other disciplines, they have infused the subject with conceptual terminologies, ideas and insights. Their efforts form a basis for promoting a theoretical foundation for social development which can provide useful insights into key questions.

This chapter examines different aspects of social development with reference to theoretical ideas. It begins by discussing the role of theory in social development, paying particular attention to the different types of theory used in the field. It then offers a simple, representational model of social development as a process. Using this model, the chapter then reviews a variety of theoretical debates in social development. As will be shown, social development theory is characterized by sharp differences of opinion on many important questions. By examining these controversies and contrasting different points of view, theoretical problems in the field can be better understood.

THE NATURE OF THEORY IN SOCIAL DEVELOPMENT

Like most other social science fields, social development makes use of different types of theory. Three different types of theory – representational theory, explanatory theory and normative theory – will be discussed. Representational theory seeks to describe phenomena; explanatory theory examines causal associations; and normative theory evaluates events in terms of specific criteria. By examining different types of theory, the nature and uses of theory in social development may be better understood.

Representational theory seeks to create conceptual images or representations of situations. This type of theory translates observable patterns or structures in the real world into abstract, mental pictures. These representations are often known as models. Representational theory is the most basic form of theory. It does not seek to explain why events take place, but rather to provide a conceptual framework which can facilitate the analysis of causal associations. Representational theories also classify phenomena and simplify complex realities by breaking them down into their constituent parts. Although this produces an artificial representation of reality, it promotes a better understanding of complex systems.

Representational theories are based on concepts. Concepts are standardized terms which are used to denote specific phenomena. Concepts standardize language, and this assists social scientists to understand each other and to develop theories which can be readily analysed. In social development, scholars such as Roland Meinert and his colleagues (Meinert et al., 1984; Meinert and Kohn, 1987) have attempted to identify the key concepts which are used in the field. This has helped to clarify many terms and ideas. However, much more work needs to be done to ensure that social development's concepts are clearly defined and standardized.

Representational theories organize concepts and the interrelations between concepts into more complex conceptual systems. This creates a shared conception of reality. Because they order and make sense out of reality, representational theories are very important. Without these theories it would be very difficult to come to grips with complex phenomena. Also, without representational theories, it is difficult to formulate explanatory theories which analyse causal links. However, social development currently lacks a substantive body of representational theory which organizes theoretical activity. While several attempts at constructing models of social development have been made in the past, the field is still poorly developed.

Explanatory or analytical theory is specifically concerned with causal associations. Explanatory theories often build on representational theories, but their primary purpose is to explain why particular events occur. These theories also organize concepts into hypotheses that can be tested empirically. The verification and refutation of hypotheses is a critically important part of the process of developing correct explanations of events.

Because explanatory theories seek to explain events, they are obviously important not only to academic social scientists but to professionals as well. If they are to formulate policies which will effectively direct or control events, professionals need to know why these events take place. For example, if professionals are to implement effective solutions to a social problem, they need to understand its causes.

Some social scientists, particularly in sociology, political science and economics, believe that a sharp distinction should be drawn between explaining causal events and applying research findings to improve social conditions. They believe that the task of finding solutions to social problems should be left to policy makers. Detachment from practical matters, they believe, ensures that social scientists retain objectivity and are untainted by political and other influences. This attitude is known in the social sciences as value or ethical neutrality. However, for obvious reasons, the notion of ethical neutrality is not widely endorsed in applied fields such as social work and social development.

Normative theory is concerned with the evaluation of events, and with the formulation of principles which will inform the policy making process. While analytical theory is limited to explaining events, normative theory assesses these events in terms of evaluative criteria. This process aids policy formulation. These criteria may be moral in character in that they assess events in terms of wider cultural beliefs about what is 'good' and 'bad' or, more usually, they may be related to performance criteria. Performance criteria are usually defined in terms of whether policies and programmes attain specified goals.

Normative theories are widely used in applied fields such as social work, social policy and social development and they are of obvious value in determining whether particular approaches are effective or not. Although the significance of normative theory is not always appreciated in 'pure' social science disciplines, it is indispensable in the applied social sciences. Whether they recognize it or not, professionals regularly use normative theories to guide and assess their work.

While it is possible to distinguish between the three different types of theory, they are actually interrelated. Representational theories often contain both descriptive and analytical elements, and they often provide a normative framework within which specific interventions are implemented. Despite the claim that explanatory theory is untainted by values, explanatory theory is often influenced by the personal preferences and beliefs of theoreticians. In applied fields such as social development, it is very difficult to distinguish clearly between analytical and normative theory.

The interrelation of the three different types of theory can best be seen in large-scale theoretical conceptions known as 'paradigms'. Although social scientists employ this term loosely, and quite differently from the way it is understood in the natural sciences, it is widely used to connote 'grand theories' or 'schema' which encompass a large body of social reality and which combine representational, analytical and normative elements. In the social sciences, paradigms allow competing interpretations of social reality to be articulated and compared. Marxism, structural functionalism and Keynesianism are all examples of what social scientists call paradigms.

Using Theory in Social Development

As was noted earlier, social development does not have a well-developed body of theory. Much of the field consists of small-scale or middle range theories which deal with specific phenomena. Despite previous attempts to define and standardize concepts, they are still used loosely. Representational ideas are often implicit rather than explicit. Another problem is that much theoretical activity in social development is dominated by normative considerations. While it is understandable that social development writers should be primarily concerned with practical issues, normative commentaries in the field are often highly idealistic and hortatory. Explanatory theory is particularly poorly developed in social development. Social development has not generated a set of well-defined hypotheses which have been empirically tested and organized into larger explanatory systems. Although academics who write about social development frequently reveal a preference for large-scale theoretical approaches such as Marxism or structural functionalism, no paradigms have yet emerged even though the bases for constructing paradigms do exist.

Although it is difficult to provide an overview of theory in social development, this chapter explores the field by examining some of the major *debates* which are taking place around key theoretical issues. Because of social development's preference for normative discussion, many of these controversies deal explicitly with values, ideologies and beliefs. Hopefully, an understanding of these key debates will provide some insights into important theoretical issues in social development today.

To organize the material, different theoretical viewpoints on key social development questions will be examined within a simple representational model of social development *as a process*. Most definitions of social development emphasize the idea that social development is a process, and most theoretical work has implicitly or explicitly invoked the notion of process to frame the discussion. In this chapter, the idea of process will be specifically utilized to conceptualize social development in representational terms and to organize debates that involve representational, normative and explanatory questions.

Viewed comprehensively, the process of social development may be divided into three stages. First, there is the pre-existing social situation which social development seeks to change. Second, there is the social development process itself. Finally, there is the end state or goal which the social development process seeks to attain. As will be shown, there are sharp differences of opinion about many aspects of these three components of social development. These differences are expressed both by scholars working in social development and by those in other fields who are critical of social development. Because these debates make extensive use of normative theory, they can usefully be examined with reference to the insights of political economy. Indeed, as will become clear, many key debates in social development today are argued within the language and framework of contemporary political economy.

THE CONDITION OF UNDERDEVELOPMENT

A discussion of theoretical issues in social development begins with an analysis of the pre-existing social situation which social development seeks to change. While this may seem to be an uncontentious topic, it has generated several controversial debates. Specifically, different viewpoints on three aspects of the subject will be examined. First, different conceptions of the nature of the pre-existing state or condition will be discussed. Second, different explanations of the causes of this pre-existing condition will be examined. Finally, different opinions about the need to change this condition will be reviewed. As will be seen, representational, analytical and normative issues have all been raised in these discussions.

The Nature of Underdevelopment

Many social scientists have employed the term 'underdevelopment' to connote the initial social condition which social development seeks to change. The term has been used in many different settings. It has been used to denote economically and socially deprived regions, and also to describe whole countries. In addition, it has been used to describe groups of countries or whole regions of the modern world.

The term 'underdevelopment' was widely used in the field of development studies in the 1950s and 1960s. In development studies, the notion of underdevelopment was abstracted from analyses of social and economic conditions in the colonial territories which were then in the process of securing independence from European imperial rule. Economists defined underdevelopment as an economic situation dominated by a large and predominant subsistence agricultural sector characterized by low productivity, under-utilized labour and a dependence on primary commodities. Although some underdeveloped regions had a small modern sector, it was usually operated by expatriates or settlers. Sociologists defined underdevelopment as a condition characterized by traditionalism and backwardness. Social workers and social planners emphasized the low levels of welfare of underdeveloped regions. For them, underdevelopment was characterized by low life expectancy, poor health conditions, inadequate housing, and limited literacy and educational attainments.

While this conception of the condition of underdevelopment may have been accurate, it was not always welcomed by nationalist leaders who were anxious to project an image of their countries as dynamic, emerging nations. In time, the use of the term 'underdeveloped' was softened, and more acceptable versions such as 'less developed' or 'developing' came into use.

The rise of nationalist sentiment in the former colonial territories was accompanied by the assertive adoption of the neologism *Third World*, by the leaders of the non-aligned movement in the 1950s. The term's origin has been attributed to French writers like Alfred Sauvy, and to Mao Zedong's theory of the Three Worlds which differentiated the newly independent countries of Africa, Asia and Latin America from the Western, industrial nations and from the Soviet Union and its satellites (Wolfe-Phillips, 1979; Worsley, 1984). Whatever its origin, the term's geopolitical connotation was intended to convey the new-found confidence of the independence leaders in their ability to forge a 'third force' in world affairs, and to promote the rapid economic and social transformation of their societies. In this conception, the original emphasis on economic backwardness and social deprivation as characteristics of underdevelopment was replaced by new notions of dynamism and growth.

The new imagery was not, however, universally accepted. In Latin America, a far more pessimistic view of underdevelopment gained currency. André Gunder Frank (1967) who had worked at the United Nations Economic Commission for Latin America in Santiago, Chile became a leading exponent of this alternative view, claiming that underdevelopment was neither a static condition of economic and social backwardness nor a condition which would soon be ameliorated by progress. Rather, he defined underdevelopment as a condition characterized by an ongoing process of retrogression. Frank and other social scientists such as Walter Rodney (1972) articulated the Neo-Marxist theory of dependency which claimed that the continued exploitation of the developing countries by the rich industrial nations was causing the underdeveloped regions to experience more underdevelopment.

While dependency theorists such as Frank and Rodney believed that the underdeveloped regions were becoming more underdeveloped, there was considerable empirical evidence to refute their claim. By the 1970s, development experts of widely differing political beliefs had recognized that many developing countries were recording significant rates of economic growth and that social conditions were improving. While this was not true of all Third World nations, many were experiencing development rather than underdevelopment.

However, the developing countries were not undergoing uniform economic and social progress. Nor was development taking place evenly within these countries. Urban areas were developing faster than rural areas, and some rural areas were developing faster than others. Despite serious problems, the urban areas of many developing countries provided incomes, opportunities and access to services which were unmatched in rural areas. The urban–rural imbalance was widely recognized as a major problem in underdeveloped regions, and some social scientists such as Michael Lipton (1977) even described urban bias as the single most urgent problem facing the developing world.

In addition, very different patterns of development began to emerge in different parts of the Third World. While several countries in East Asia, the Middle East and, to a lesser extent, Latin America were recording unprecedented rates of economic growth, many African and South Asian nations were making limited progress. This problem was exacerbated by the fact that while many countries were experiencing rapid economic development, social improvements were lagging far behind. The problem was particularly acute in Latin America where high rates of economic growth and prosperity were accompanied by persistent poverty, deprivation and squalor. By the 1980s, as the world debt crisis, recession and economic adversity deepened, the problem of poverty became even more acute.

These events fostered the realization that underdevelopment cannot be viewed theoretically as a static condition of uniform economic and social backwardness. In recognition of the disparities which exist within societies, the notion of *distorted development* has now come into use to connote the way economic development without concomitant social development creates a severe imbalance between economic and social prosperity. As was argued in the introduction, the problem in most countries today is not that there has been no economic development, but rather that economic development has not been accompanied by improvements in social well-being for the population as a whole.

Today, the notion of distorted development provides a conceptually more viable representation of the social situation which social development seeks to ameliorate. It is also empirically more accurate. In addition, the concept of distorted development has fostered a greater awareness of the problems of underdevelopment. While the notion of underdevelopment as a uniform state of economic and social backwardness focused attention on the developing countries of the Third World, it concealed the fact that many industrial countries are also characterized by a disjunction between economic and social development. As James Midgley (1994) argued, these distortions are often manifested quite dramatically in deprived regions of the industrial world.

The Causes of Underdevelopment

The different conceptual images of the nature of underdevelopment discussed above are accompanied by two major explanations of the origins and causes of the condition of underdevelopment. The first explanation posits that underdevelopment is an original, archetypal condition which has always existed and which will continue to exist unless external stimuli are introduced to initiate social and economic change. The second contends that underdevelopment is not an original state but that some event or events have caused previously satisfactory conditions to deteriorate. As will be recognized, the second explanation draws inspiration from retrogressive theories of social change which claim that society has declined from a previously higher state.

In the 1950s and 1960s, it was generally accepted that underdevelopment was a natural, original state of economic and social backwardness. This idea was central to *modernization theory* which offered various analyses of the causes of backwardness. These analyses highlighted both economic and sociological factors. Ragnar Nurkse's (1953) concept of the vicious cycle of poverty was one of the first to offer an economic explanation of the cause of underdevelopment. Nurkse believed that underdevelopment exists because people are too poor to break out of poverty, and that the only solution lies in introducing capital for investment from external sources. Other theories of the time recognized the existence of a small modern sector in the economies of the developing countries which could form the focal point for modern economic development (Boeke, 1953; Lewis, 1954, 1955; Higgins, 1956). These 'two sector theories' extended the work of Nurkse, but also conceived of underdevelopment as an original condition.

Using the modernization approach, sociologists and psychologists identified traditionalism as the primary cause of underdevelopment. For example, Daniel Lerner (1958) argued that traditional forms of authority in developing countries kept people backward and prevented change. William Goode (1963) claimed that another cause of underdevelopment was the extended traditional family which restricted labour mobility and required conformity to family traditions. Everett Hagan (1962), David McClelland (1964) and Alex Inkeles and David Smith (1974) all argued that traditional beliefs prevented people from being entrepreneurial and using initiative to improve their situation. Bert Hozelitz (1960) used the sociological theories of the Harvard sociologist, Talcott Parsons, to formulate a comprehensive analysis of traditional impediments to modernization which implied that traditional culture needed to be changed if conditions of economic and social backwardness were to be eradicated.

Although much of this research applied to the developing countries, similar ideas have been used to explain the causes of underdevelopment in the industrial societies. In the United States, for example, the theory of the 'culture of poverty' was very popular in the 1970s. Developed by the anthropologist, Oscar Lewis (1966), who had undertaken research in Mexico and other Latin American countries, culture of poverty claimed that people were poor because they held attitudes and beliefs which kept them in a state of backwardness. They tended to have large families, were fatalistic, lacked ambition and would only look for work if they were forced to. Culture of poverty was also adopted in Britain and other industrial nations. Although the term 'culture of poverty' is not widely used today, the ideas underlying the theory continue to influence popular attitudes about poor communities in both urban and rural areas.

As was noted earlier, the belief that underdevelopment is an original condition was vigorously challenged by Frank, Rodney and other dependency theorists who claim that the social and economic problems of underdevelopment were caused by European imperialism and the capitalist penetration of Africa, Asia and Latin America. They argue that before European colonialization, these regions were prosperous, advanced and self-sufficient. Their people did not even need to trade with the Europeans but they were deceived or overcome by brute force and brought into the world imperialist system. After the subjugation of these regions, the Europeans began to transfer their wealth to Europe. Vast quantities of gold and other treasures were removed from Latin America and taken to Spain. In addition, the native people were forced to work for the Europeans. Plantations and mines were established to exploit the rich natural resources of the colonies, and their products as well as profits were repatriated. In time, once prosperous societies became impoverished and, dependency writers claim, this process of exploitation created the conditions of underdevelopment which characterize the Third World today. To make matters worse, they believe that the process of underdevelopment continues today and will continue until the exploitative capitalist system is overthrown. For the dependency writers, underdevelopment is not a static condition but an active process of further retrogression.

The dependency approach is a good example of an explanatory theory that attributes underdevelopment to specific external causes. Although dependency theory was developed with reference to the Third World, Stewart MacPherson and James Midgley (1987) have argued that it can be used to explain poverty and deprivation in the industrial countries as well. However, it has not been extensively adopted. Nevertheless, other theories such as William Julius Wilson's (1987) account of the origin of the urban 'underclass' express similar ideas. Analysing social conditions in American inner cities, Wilson identified an underclass of poor people who are condemned to live in conditions of deprivation, violence and despair. Their situation, he argues, is not an original condition but the result of de-industrialization and economic decline. De-industrialization, he contends, reduced job opportunities in the cities, facilitated the emigration of middle-class families to the suburbs, and resulted in the gradual deterioration of urban services. It is conditions such as these that social development seeks to change.

The Need for Social Development
A third debate about the pre-existing condition of social development concerns the need to change this condition. While the proponents of social development believe that it is self-evident that there is a need to change conditions of underdevelopment, some writers question the need for change. While few of these writers will unequivocally argue for the perpetuation of poverty, squalor and deprivation, they are concerned that social change will harm the indigenous culture and destroy cherished customs, values and traditions. In addition, some scholars are concerned that the vigorous pursuit of economic and social development will damage the environment and result in other undesirable changes.

The assumption that social change will harm the existing culture is not a new one. Throughout history, people have sought to preserve their own culture and to prevent the dilution of traditional beliefs. In addition, there are many who believe that traditional cultures are superior to modern society. This idea can be traced back to Jean-Jacques Rousseau in the eighteenth century who extolled the virtues of traditional pastoral societies where he believed 'noble savages' lived peaceful and contented lives. Rousseau's writings influenced a group of nineteenth-century writers, artists and intellectuals known as the romantics. They glorified the past and often resurrected medieval themes and rustic images in their work.

A commitment to preserving traditional culture also characterizes the beliefs of conservatives who dislike change and wish to preserve the existing social and economic system. One of the first systematic expositions of conservative ideas was offered by the eighteenth-century English philosopher, Edmund Burke, who was appalled by the upheavals of the French revolution. Burke's writings defended the traditional English way of life and argued for its preservation. Today, conservative thought is widespread not only in non-Western societies but in the industrial countries as well. The resurgence of Islamic beliefs, the rise of nationalism in many parts of the world, and a greater pride in ethnic origin are examples of this trend. In the United States and Britain, traditionalist thinking has been actively promoted by New Right political movements that wish to curtail permissiveness and encourage family values, religious beliefs and traditional ideas (Midgley, 1991).

The influence of Westernization has indeed been felt in many societies and, at one stage, Westernization was actively promoted. Nationalists leaders such as Turkey's Kemal Atatürk believed that his country would only achieve a high level of economic development and gain international respect if it adopted Western culture. The Shah of Iran held similar views. In development theory, and modernization theory in particular, the spread of Western ideas and institutions was actively promoted as a way of fostering development. However, today, Westernization is being actively resisted and many societies are now stressing the importance of their own cultural values.

The adoption of inappropriate economic and social development policies under the guise of modernization has caused many problems in numerous countries. As many Third World societies reject Western influences and seek to heighten awareness of their traditional values and institutions, a greater sensitivity to cultural diversity and respect for indigenous beliefs are needed. There is evidence that social development scholars today are more sensitive to these realities. For example, the literature on international social work has been more aware of the need to adapt social work principles and methods to fit local cultural conditions (Midgley, 1981, 1989, 1990). On the other hand, few attempts have been made to incorporate non-Western conceptions into social development thinking. One exception is Affaf Dabbagh's (1993) account of an Islamic approach to social development.

The imposition of inappropriate economic and social development programmes has indeed had a negative affect on traditional communities. Many ethnic or tribal minorities have been displaced by the construction of hydro-electric schemes, irrigation systems, modern highways and other developments. Often their traditional habitats have been invaded or destroyed. As Michael Cernea (1985) showed, the need to protect these communities has become increasingly recognized in development circles.

Some critics are concerned about the negative impact that social and economic development will have on the environment, and on society as a whole. Critics of economic growth as the primary means for promoting human welfare have claimed that the remorseless drive for growth ultimately defeats the very purpose of social development. Many writers have argued that the relentless pursuit of economic growth depletes scarce natural resources and produces wastes which pollute and irreparably damage the environment (Meadows et al., 1972). In addition, writers such as Edward Mishan (1967), Fred Hirsch (1977) and Christopher Lasch (1991) suggest that the quest for economic growth fosters acquisitiveness and excessive consumption, weakens traditional values and undermines the moral basis of society.

These divergent views present a normative challenge to the proponents of social development who have not fully appreciated their importance. Future attempts to formulate a coherent body of social development theory will need to take these concerns into account. The need for a greater sensitivity to traditional cultural values and beliefs is obvious. Hopefully, future attempts at theory building will incorporate non-Western conceptions. However, there is evidence that the concerns of those who question the relentless pursuit of economic growth are being incorporated into social development theory. As Richard Estes (1993) revealed, the importance of sustainable development as a social development strategy is being increasingly recognized.

THE PROCESS OF SOCIAL DEVELOPMENT

The notion of *process* is central to the theory of social development. Most writers contend that social development is a process, and most formal definitions contain the phrase 'social development is a process of . . .'. There are, of course, different opinions about what the process of social development consists of. Nevertheless, it is difficult to conceive of social development as anything except a process which results in some type of change or improvement to the existing situation.

This section reviews theoretical debates attending the notion of social development as a process. Employing various representational, explanatory and normative theories, social scientists have debated different aspects of the social development process. One debate concerns the preconditions needed to initiate the process of social development. While several writers have argued that social development can only take place if certain prerequisites are met, others dispute this claim. Another debate concerns the direction of the process of social development. While advocates of social development believe that social development involves progressive change, some critics are sceptical of this claim, believing that conditions have deteriorated during this century. The need for intervention in the process of social development has also been debated extensively. While advocates of social development believe that improvements in welfare will only occur through the active intervention of governments and other agencies, some social scientists have claimed that interventionism has a negative effect on society. Finally, the idea that social development, as process, involves competing normative prescriptions for attaining social development goals has been very controversial. Although different social development strategies have been formulated, they reflect deeper ideological conceptions which need to be analysed. Hopefully, an examination of these different approaches will provide deeper insights into social development as a process.

Preconditions for Social Development

The notion of social development as a process also invokes theoretical debates about how the process can be initiated. As has been shown already, the proponents of social development do not believe that social development occurs naturally, but that it requires intervention by the state or some other external agency. In addition to advocating specific forms of intervention, some writers claim that more general preconditions must be met before the social development process can be successfully initiated. One expression of this view is the idea that social development can only occur if pre-existing impediments to social change are removed.

As was shown earlier, the idea that existing conditions must first be changed if the social development process is to be effectively initiated permeates modernization theory. Modernization theorists such as Ragnar Nurkse (1953) argued that economic growth can only occur if radical measures are introduced to help communities break out of the vicious cycle of poverty. Others have placed more emphasis on removing the strictures of the traditional culture which, they believe, impede progress. Indeed, as Raymond Apthorpe (1970) pointed out, much social development thinking in the 1950s and 1960s was concerned with how the 'bottlenecks' to progress could be dislodged.

To combat traditionalism, modernization theorists urged that formal education and literacy programmes be introduced to combat superstition and outmoded beliefs. Education would also inculcate new attitudes conducive to the creation of dynamic capitalist societies. While most governments did in fact expand education, few did so in a deliberate attempt to erode traditional values. Instead, most were motivated by the idea that education is an investment in human capital. Equally influential was the argument that the acquisition of skills and knowledge is a prerequisite for economic development.

A perennial theme in the literature on the impediments to social development is the population question. Echoing the earlier warnings of Thomas Malthus, writers such as Paul Erlich (1969), Donella Meadows and her colleagues (1972) and Lester Brown (1974) claim that rapid population growth poses a major threat to the social well-being of the world's people and its environment. Unless population growth is curbed, no meaningful social improvement can be achieved. As the 1994 United Nations World Population Conference revealed, concerns about the seriousness of population growth and the need to control it continue to be expressed today.

Many development experts have also been troubled by the rate of migration from rural to urban areas which they regard as an impediment to progressive social change. Many studies showed that urban growth in the developing world has been unprecedented and that cities in many countries are growing very rapidly. Some experts argue that rapid migration is putting serious pressure on jobs. To deal with the problem, some economists such as Paul Bairoch have urged that steps be taken to limit migration. Bairoch's (1973) study for the International Labour Office encouraged governments to invest more heavily in agriculture, create improved social services in rural areas, help schools to promote skills suited for agricultural employment and, as a last resort, adopt enforceable migration controls. Like population policy, migration control was another attempt to promote social development by removing an obstacle to employment creation.

However, it is now apparent that anti-migration measures have had little effect and that attempts to curb migration are doomed to failure. Even countries such as China and South Africa that have used the criminal law to punish migrants who entered cities without permission have not been able to stop the flow (Hardiman and Midgley, 1982, 1989). Nor do all social scientists regard migration as a problem. Indeed, some view migrants as rational economic actors who reveal their entrepreneurial potential by moving to the city in order to promote their economic interests. Despite the fact that jobs are limited, they come to the city and somehow find work or otherwise establish themselves in self-employment. As Otto Koenigsberger (1976) argued, this contributes to the dynamism of the urban economy and promotes economic development.

Today, as social change has affected many traditional communities, concerns about the traditional obstacles to social development are seldom expressed. Instead, it is much more common to read about government intervention being a major impediment to social progress. Mark Lusk (1992) has argued that government is a primary obstacle to social development. Writing specifically about Latin America, he claims that bureaucratic inefficiency, complex rules and regulations, and political corruption have stifled social development efforts. If social development is to succeed, government controls must be eased and people must be freed to pursue their own interests. A similar critique is offered in Hernando de Soto's (1989) best selling book, *The Other Path*, which attacks the 'mercantilist' tradition in Latin America for impeding development.

An opposite argument which views unrestrained capitalism as an obstacle to social development was popular in the 1960s and 1970s. Development writers such as Gunnar Myrdal (1970), Dudley Seers (1972), Keith Griffin (1976, 1978), Michael Lipton (1977) and James Midgley (1984b) believe that entrenched inequality is a major obstacle to change. These writers claim that feudal land ownership inhibits production and economic growth, that the subjugation of women and minorities prevents their participation in development, and that the practice of debt bondage and servitude hinders the effective use of labour. In addition, they have condemned the concentration of power and wealth in the hands of the few since this perpetuates rigid hierarchies and oppressive social structures which are inimical to social progress. They urge the adoption of egalitarian development strategies to combat exploitation, wealth concentration and oppression in impeding progressive social change.

One group of writers who have discussed the preconditions for successful social development argue that change can only be initiated through an *apocalyptic event*. These writers usually emphasize the need for the revolutionary destruction of the existing social system. From the time of Jean-Jacques Rousseau in the eighteenth century, advocates of the apocalyptic view have claimed that meaningful social change can only take place if the prevailing social system is overthrown. Rousseau's advocacy of a new social contract required the destruction of the *ancien régime*. It also required the use of coercion in the new society. As Robert Nisbet (1980: 241) noted, Rousseau justified the use of coercion to ensure that all remained equal and free under the 'General Will'. As Rousseau put it: 'This means nothing more than [human beings] will be forced to be free.' It is not surprising that Rousseau's ideas inspired the leaders of the Jacobin party, and radical revolutionaries such as François Babeuf and his followers during the French revolution.

The apocalyptic requirement has, of course, been most systematically advocated in Marxist thought, and particularly in the writings of Lenin, Trotsky and Mao. But it is not only given expression in Marxist thinking. For example, the French philosopher, Georges Sorel, who was mentioned earlier for his attack on the idea of progress, advocated the use of violence as a precondition for meaningful change. The apocalyptic idea has also found expression in development thinking, particularly in the work of dependency writers such as André Gunder Frank (1969) who believes that all attempts to improve economic and social conditions in the developing countries are doomed to failure unless the capitalist system is overthrown through revolutionary action. This belief has been echoed by many radical left-wing writers on development questions over the years.

The Idea of Progress in Social Development

Social development is today defined as a progressive process which results in a steady improvement in social conditions. As was shown in the previous chapter, this belief is based on ancient ideas about the nature of social change. Since the time of Augustine, most explanations of social change in Western thought have been progressive, optimistically claiming that society moves steadily along an upward slope to higher states of prosperity.

The idea of progress in social development is closely linked to the concept of modernity. Inspired by the ideas of the Enlightenment, many nineteenth-century sociologists studied the way the process of change produced alterations to existing economic activities, attitudes, social relations and social institutions. Originally, the concept of modernity dealt exclusively with the industrializing societies of Europe and North America but in the 1950s the analysis of modernity focused on the newly independent developing countries of the Third World. As was noted earlier, the notions of progress and modernity were given forceful expression in the theory of modernization. The idea of development also gives expression to the idea of modernity. Combining the elements of economic growth and social change, the concept of development has gained currency throughout the world. Today, the study of development has produced a substantive body of analytical and normative theory designed to foster social progress. Both development and social development may be viewed as products of progressivist thought inspired by the Enlightenment.

While the proponents of social development all believe in progress, this view is not universally shared. Despite technological advance and significant improvements in social conditions, the idea that Western society is experiencing progress has been challenged by numerous scholars. One of the first modern thinkers to offer a systematic critique of the idea of progress was the French social philosopher, Georges Sorel, who attacked the notion that Western society had improved or that it could be improved through natural processes of social change. Another important critic was the historian Oswald Spengler (1926), whose book *The Decline of the West* claimed that, far from progressing towards a higher state of civilization, the industrial countries were retrogressing into a state of decline. This book, which was published in Germany in 1918 and translated into English in 1926, soon became a best seller. As Robert Nisbet (1980) has shown, many literary figures during this century including T. S. Eliot, James Joyce and W. B. Yeats have also challenged the idea of progress. Eliot's poems exude a deep sense of despair about the decadence, vulgarity and meaninglessness of modern life.

Some modern-day social scientists have also concluded that social change in the West has been regressive rather than progressive. The Critical Theorists of the Frankfurt School such as Theodore Adorno and Max Horkheimer (1944) challenged the belief that Western capitalist societies had reached a high level of progress, and they were pessimistic about social and political conditions in these nations. As was noted earlier in this chapter, dependency thinkers such as Frank and Rodney have argued that conditions in the Third World have deteriorated because of the spread of global capitalism. A similar pessimism characterizes the work of many writers on social policy. While many have previously claimed that Western welfare states exemplify high levels of social progress, others have argued that welfare states are experiencing a crisis of major proportions (O'Connor, 1973; Habermas, 1976; Mishra, 1984).

In a recent article, the American political scientist, Gerhart Niemeyer (1993), epitomized the sense of despair which characterizes some social science thinking. Niemeyer described the twentieth century as one of the worst in human history. Despite the claims of the proponents of progress, he believes that this century has had more destructive wars, oppressive ideologies, totalitarian forms of government and achieved a more complete enslavement of the human spirit than any other. Christopher Lasch (1991), another American writer, has criticized the very idea of progress as nothing more than naive American middle-class optimism which fails to recognize the extent to which massive pollution, resource depletion and ecological destruction have been caused by 'progress'.

Social development advocates will need to respond more vigorously to criticisms of the idea of progress. While most proponents of social development take the notion of progress for granted, the argument that social change has been retrogressive rather than progressive needs to be addressed. This is particularly important in the 1990s, as economic conditions in many parts of the world remain unsatisfactory, as ethnic conflict escalates, as poverty and social deprivation remain _widespread and as discrimination, hatred and oppression continue to characterize the human condition.

The Concept of Intervention
Social development is fully committed to the principle of intervention-ism. All social development thinkers believe that societies can be improved through directive action. As was noted previously in this book, this belief has been inspired by utopian thought and the concepts of 'guided' or planned change which were advocated by sociologists such as Lester Ward, Leonard Hobhouse and Charles North earlier in this century. Indeed, Hobhouse's use of the term 'social development' was explicitly intended to give expression to this idea. It has also been informed by the writings of economists such as Thorstein Veblen and John Maynard Keynes who believed that planning could foster social well-being on a large scale. The widespread adoption of planning, and the emergence of the welfare state in the industrial countries, appeared to enshrine interventionism as an everyday feature of modern life.

While interventionist ideas were gradually accepted and imple-mented during the twentieth century, they have not been universally welcomed. As was shown in chapter 2, interventionism was vigorously opposed by Herbert Spencer and William Sumner and by neo-classical economists in the nineteenth century. Despite the contribution of Keynes, the idea that government intervention harms the economy has now been popularized by monetarist and supply-side economists. Surprisingly, the idea that government intervention harms society has also been advocated by Marxist writers such as Bill Warren (1980) who believes that attempts by well-meaning reformers to introduce statutory social services interfere with the 'laws of history' discovered by Marx. Intervention, Warren argues, retards the dynamic of capital-ist development, perpetuates feudal modes of production and delays the revolutionary transformation of capitalist societies to socialism.

Modern-day exponents of non-interventionism not only claim that intervention harms the social system, but contend that intervention is immoral because it requires coercion. One of the most important expo-nents of this idea was Friedrich von Hayek (1944), the Nobel Prize-winning Austrian economist who claimed that attempts by gov-ernment to plan the economy and provide social welfare require the use of government power if these plans are to be implemented effectively. While the government's efforts may be well intentioned, it results in the diminution of liberty and the beginning of a process that leads ulti-mately to serfdom.

Hayek's ideas were extended by Milton Friedman (1962, 1980), another Nobel Prize-winning economist, who argues that economic activities can take place through only two institutional arrangements, namely voluntary cooperation between individuals or totalitarian rule by government. The former arrangement, he contends, is both morally preferable and economically efficient. Societies which have promoted markets to permit the voluntary exchange of goods and services have a high degree of personal freedom and economic development. Friedman believes that freedom and efficiency can best be preserved if governments limit their role to maintaining law and order and ensuring that the market operates without monopolistic restriction. They should also provide care on a limited basis for those who cannot meet their own welfare needs through the market and mitigate the social costs that arise when it is not possible to arrange for injured parties to be directly compensated. Intervention beyond these bounds, Friedman argues, diminishes freedom and harms economic growth.

In addition to the idea that intervention diminishes freedom, many critics have claimed that it is not practically possible for human beings to direct society. Hayek (1949) contends that societies comprise millions of individuals who function independently of each other. No individual, he believes, can know all there is know about the way society operates. Each individual can only know a little about a small part of society, and comprehensive attempts to direct it are bound to result in massive errors. Even if individuals collaborate with each other to plan society, their limited knowledge will still prevent them from formulating and implementing comprehensive plans.

This idea has been restated by the American political scientist, Charles Lindblom (1959), who claims that planning requires that planners are omniscient (in that they know all there is to know about society), and that they are omnipotent (in that they have the power to implement their plans). Since they are neither omniscient nor omnipotent, comprehensive planning is simply not possible. Instead of trying to introduce comprehensive planning, politicians and administrators should adopt a 'muddling through' approach which makes small, incremental changes and seeks to bring about small, step-by-step improvements.

The famous philosopher of science, Karl Popper (1945, 1957), reached a similar conclusion but his argument is more complex. Popper believes that all attempts to plan society are based on a utopian vision. All planners are utopians in that they want to change society to create a future, perfect society. However, since it is actually impossible to predict the future, they have no assurance that their vision of the future will be attained. For this reason, they seek to make their vision of the future come true. Usually, along the way, the effort to force change on society changes their vision. This has happened in communist societies where the utopian vision of attaining socialism has been betrayed by oppression, corruption and the naked use of power. Popper believes that all attempts to introduce comprehensive planning to improve society are doomed to failure. Instead, Popper prefers what he calls a 'piece-meal' approach to social change which is not governed by unattainable historicist predictions, and which does not negate the principles of the 'Open Society'. Proponents of social development have not adequately responded to the critique of interventionism. Nor have they articulated an adequate theoretical conception of what intervention entails. It is important that a coherent theory of interventionism in social development be formulated since the notion of intervention is fundamental to all social development endeavour. Such a theory needs to justify interventionism, give proper recognition to the role of human agency in social development, and ensure that individual rights are safeguarded. It also needs to explicate a clearer notion of who will be responsible for social development, and under which auspices social development strategies will be implemented. A clearer motion of what social development entails as a strategy for social improvement is also needed. The final chapter attempts to initiate a discussion of this kind.

The Economic Dimension
The idea that social development is inextricably linked to economic development characterizes the definition of social development offered in this book, and distinguishes the social development approach from other approaches for promoting people's welfare. However, the issue has been much neglected in discussions on social welfare and, in addition, there are several aspects of this idea that are controversial and which offer competing theoretical points of view.

In the literature on social policy, much of the discussion on economic aspects focuses narrowly on the differences between social and economic policy (Boulding, 1967; Titmuss, 1974; Piachaud, 1989) or deals only tangentially with the economic implications of social programmes that promote what Richard Titmuss (1963) called 'occupational welfare'.

Titmuss has probably written more on the subject than other scholars in the field. In one paper (1968), he criticized the assumption that continued economic growth would, of itself, eradicate poverty and bring prosperity to all; and in his work for the government of Mauritius (Titmuss et al., 1961), he was careful to ensure that proposals for the expansion of the island's welfare system were compatible with economic realities. However, Titmuss's analysis of the models of social policy (1974) comes closest to analysing the relationship between social and economic policies. His account of the industrial 'achievement–performance' model observed that certain social programmes were closely related to occupation efficiency and productivity. He noted that in the Soviet Union and Germany, the value of retirement pensions and similar benefits are often linked to the worker's length of employment, rank and work performance. However, instead of regarding the link between employment performance and social welfare as a positive one, Titmuss criticized the way these approaches were used to maintain differentials between workers and exacerbate inequalities. He also criticized the notion that social policy should function to serve wider economic interests. This 'handmaiden model', which relegated the social services to the status of an adjunct to the economy, offended his commitment to an institutional approach which redistributed resources, reduced inequality and fostered social solidarity.

Titmuss's views on occupational welfare and the 'handmaiden approach' to social welfare probably inhibited a full examination of the contribution that the social services can make to economic development. However, as social service programmes have come under increasing pressure in the face of recession, structural unemployment and economic difficulties, social policy experts such as David Piachaud (1989) have called for new approaches which transcend the conventional perspectives of the social administration approach and directly address economic concerns. In addition, economic issues will become more prominent in social policy debates as many more economists become involved in the study of social policy. Unlike earlier times when social policy was regarded as a 'soft' welfare activity, economists are now extensively engaged in research into the social services, the costs of social programmes and the economic effects of social investments (Birdsall, 1993).

In view of the need to address economic aspects, social policy writers would do well to learn from the social development approach which explicitly relates social interventions to economic considerations. However, there is little evidence that mainstream social policy research is cognizant of the social development approach or of the work which has been done in developing countries to integrate social and economic interventions.

Another matter for debate in social development concerns the best way of integrating social and economic policies and programmes. As will be shown in the final chapter, there are three ways of fostering this goal. These include the creation of organizational structures that promote integration, the formulation of economic policies that enhance social well-being, and the implementation of social development strategies that mobilize human and social capital and engage needy people in productive activities that contribute positively to economic development.

Finally, there are differences of opinion about whether the purposeful implementation of integrated social and economic policies does, in fact, enhance the welfare of the population. As was shown earlier in this chapter, many opponents of interventionism claim that attempts to improve people's welfare through the implementation of economic and social policies does more harm than good. However, there are many economists who reject this doctrinaire *laissez-faire* position. Over the years, many distinguished economists have argued convincingly that the judicious intervention by governments in economic and social affairs not only raises standards of welfare but enhances the efficiency of the economy. As Nancy Birdsall (1993) has shown in a recent study, investments in social programmes have brought real returns and fostered economic development. On the basis of her analysis she concludes that 'investing in social development is good economics' (1993: 19).

Of course, the task of implementing an effective social development process is not an easy one. In addition to harmonizing social and economic components, there are many disagreements about the best strategies for attaining social development goals. Attempts to formulate a theoretical conception of social development as a process that harmonizes social and economic concerns involve the articulation of specific strategies. This requires that specific policy and programmatic proposals be formulated and implemented. Despite the theoretical and practical problems of developing such strategies, it will be shown in the next chapter that a variety of policy proposals for linking social and economic development have been devised. These draw on a variety of ideological antecedents which offer competing prescriptions for improving society and which need to be examined in more depth.

Ideological Roots of Social Development Strategies
The analysis of social development as a process also requires an examination of the different practical projects, policies and programmes that have been adopted to attain social development goals. These projects, policies and programmes will be designated in this book as social development strategies. They are at the very core of the social development process. As will be shown in the next chapter, a number of social development strategies have been formulated. While these strategies are essentially practical in character, they are not devoid of theoretical content. Underlying these different strategies are different beliefs about the best way of promoting social development. These beliefs invoke different representational images about what social development as a process involves. They also involve different sets of values which contrast and evaluate different strategies. For this reason, a discussion of different social development strategies is heavily dependent on normative theory. As was suggested at the beginning of this chapter, normative theory plays a major role in an applied field such as social development.

Although social development is permeated with normative ideas, it is only recently that an attempt has been made to analyse social development's normative basis and to identify and classify the major ideological roots of social development strategies (Midgley, 1993). Ideologies, Midgley notes, are major normative perspectives consisting of values, beliefs and preferences for different social arrangements. Proponents of different ideologies believe that their prescriptions for organizing society are the best and most likely to promote human happiness and social well-being. It is not surprising that ideologies have influenced social development. As will be shown in the next chapter, the three major Western ideologies of *individualism*, *populism* and *collectivism* have all affected the way the social development process has been defined in normative terms.

Individualist or liberal ideology teaches that the ideal society is one in which the individual is accorded primary importance. This ideology prescribes that individuals are at the centre of the social universe and that they are endowed with natural rights, freedom, rational choice and the ability to determine their own future. Individualism is a powerful theme in Western culture, particularly in Britain and the United States, and it has recently enjoyed a resurgence as Radical Right-wing political parties have secured power in many countries. Individualism also characterizes the capitalist economic system which is today a global rather than a Western system.

Individualism evolved as a protest against feudal absolutism, finding formative expression in the Protestant reformation. It found further expression during the Renaissance as rationalism and scientific knowledge increased. The English civil war, the French revolution and the American war of independence powerfully reinforced the spread of individualism, legitimating the Enlightenment ideals of reason, liberty and self-determination. In the nineteenth century, individualism evolved into diverse doctrines including utilitarianism, *laissez-faire* or classical liberalism, romanticism and the softer New Liberal approach which, as was shown in chapter 2, emerged during the later decades of the century. In addition, the rise of industrial capitalism as an economic system fostered the individualist world-view and was, in turn, sustained by its teachings.

Normatively, individualism accords primary importance to individual choice, freedom and personal rights. Individuals are responsible for their own destiny and capable of acting independently in the economic market to promote their own well-being. While individuals exist within the wider context of society, society is little more than aggregations of individuals. Accordingly, governments should refrain from imposing controls on individuals and curbing their rights. Individuals have inalienable rights to act independently of collective constraint. Collective constraint is permitted only when individual action threatens the welfare of others or requires unusual sacrifices to protect the welfare of all.

As will be shown in the next chapter, individualist themes have exerted some influence in social development circles. Some social workers have advocated an individualist approach by arguing that society can be improved through individual self-betterment or through measures that enhance the capacity of individuals to cope effectively and to enhance their relationships with others. In so doing, they improve society. Another expression of individualist thought in social development is the advocacy of entrepreneurial attitudes which stress the importance of individual initiative, self-responsibility, choice and the pursuit of self-interest. Proponents of this approach believe that social development can best be promoted when individuals are encouraged to enter the economic market and operate effectively in the market as rational economic actors. However, they do not suggest that individuals should be left to themselves to succeed or fail in the market. Instead, they advocate the adoption of measures that promote effective market participation. These include policies that foster the emergence of an enterprise culture, the creation of institutions that support entrepreneurs and commercial ventures, policies that promote 'informal' sector activities and specific programmes that assist low-income and needy families to become economically independent.

Populist ideology claims that the best society is one in which an ambiguously defined entity, *the people*, is accorded primary importance. Although the notion of the people is elusive, populists extol the virtues of ordinary people, their lifestyles, beliefs and institutions. Many populist leaders have effectively advocated the 'people's interests' to secure political power, and once in power, have introduced social and other programmes to consolidate popular support. Populist leaders often secure electoral support by being anti-establishment. They attack 'big business', corruption in government and intellectuals who they claim are out of touch with people's needs and sentiments. Populism champions the cause of ordinary people against the establishment, seeks to serve their interests and represent the popular will.

Many populist writers place emphasis on the community as a locus for people's activities. They believe that communities form the basis of society and that the enhancement of community life offers the best opportunity for promoting people's happiness, a sense of belonging and identity. Writers such as Amitai Etzioni (1993) who stress the importance of community life are known as communitarians. However, communitarianism is not the same as populism. Populism transcends communitarianism and includes political beliefs and programmes that focus on societies as a whole. Indeed, writers such as Gavin Kitching (1982) have argued that much Third World development is populist in character. Using the term broadly, he characterizes any development strategy that opposes industrialization and seeks to promote local interests as populist. From this perspective, the policies of both Mao Zedong in China and Julius Nyerere in Tanzania are classed as populist. Nor is communitarianism the same as collectivism. As will be shown later, collectivist ideology prescribes the common ownership of resources. Communitarians, on the other hand, believe in private ownership but nevertheless stress the need for cooperation among neighbours and a greater degree of caring and sharing among community members.

Populist and communitarian ideas have been very influential in social development and have found expression in different community-based interventions. These interventions include conventional community development strategies and the more radical community action approach. These strategies have been adopted in both the developing and the industrial countries. The implementation of communitarian forms of social development is usually the responsibility of individual community workers, or change agents as they are sometimes known. These workers are usually employed by public or private agencies responsible for promoting community-based interventions.

Collectivist or socialist ideology teaches that the best society is one in which the collectivity is accorded primary importance. Collectives are made up of associations of people who own resources collectively and share authority to make decisions. Examples of collectives include communes and similar anarchist communities, cooperatives and trades unions. The ultimate collective is the state, which is regarded as the most comprehensive mechanism for representing the common interests of citizens. In the democratic socialist version of collectivist thought, governments offer a basis for collaborative social effort and for expressing basic human needs for altruism, solidarity and cooperation. Collectivists believe that the state is the most effective means for organizing economic and social affairs, and for meeting people's social needs.

Socialist thinkers have often claimed that collectivism is an ancient idea. Examples of collectivism, they believe, are to be found in small preliterate tribal societies, in biblical teachings and in the medieval guilds. However, socialism only flourished after the French revolution and its major proponents were significantly influenced by its ideas and events. The early socialists, who are known as the utopian socialists, had ambitious plans for creating ideal societies in which the means of production, distribution and exchange would be collectively owned. As was noted in the last chapter, they were derided by Marxists who believed that socialist societies could not be created through planning but could only emerge as a result of revolution propelled by historical forces. In Europe, socialist ideas were most effectively promoted by the labour movement and by the creation of political parties that represented the interests of workers and advocated government involvement in social affairs. The success of these democratic socialist parties was a major factor in the emergence of the modern European welfare state and the extensive involvement of governments in economic and social planning.

As will be shown in the next chapter, collectivist ideas have been widely adopted in social development, particularly in those strategies which advocate the active involvement of governments in promoting social welfare. Collectivist ideas have significantly influenced the formulation of various social development strategies by the international agencies. These include unified socio-economic development, redistribution with growth, and basic needs. These approaches have been influenced by the idea that the state should take primary responsibility for social development.

Although collectivist ideas are, of course, at the centre of Marxist theory, Marxism has not provided a normative basis for the formulation of a coherent social development strategy. However, some writers have used Marxism to criticize other approaches for failing to bring about 'real' social change. Others have extolled the virtues of communist societies or communist institutions such as the commune, and have advocated revolutionary action to attain social development goals.

As will be shown in the next chapter, the three ideologies of individualism, populism and collectivism provide a normative basis for different social development strategies. Advocates of these strategies are usually influenced by ideological beliefs and normally they oppose strategies based on other normative ideas. These differences will become clearer when the major social development strategies are more closely examined.

THE GOALS OF SOCIAL DEVELOPMENT

The final element in a comprehensive theory of social development concerns the goals of social development. Many writers view social development as a process that culminates in a desired end state. However, this 'end state' is not always described in detail, and often references to the goals of social development are implicit rather than explicit. Nevertheless, references to the goals of social development are frequently made in the literature. As will become apparent, the failure to define these goals in tangible terms is a function of the utopian nature of much thinking about the ultimate ends of social development effort.

As was shown in the last chapter, utopian ideas have played a major role in social development thinking. These ideas have fostered the implicit belief that social development inevitably fosters social improvements. Influenced by utopianism, many social development writers take it for granted that their proposed interventions will improve society. However, this is not self-evident, and there is a need to define goals more clearly. On the other hand, some claim that it is not possible to define 'social improvement' or 'social betterment' precisely and that a degree of ambiguity about goals is appropriate given the complexity of the field.

To better understand the issue of goals, the influence of utopian ideas in social development needs to be examined in more depth. Discussions of the influence of utopianism in social development also involve debates about the wider question of whether social development goals can in fact be attained. As has been noted earlier in this chapter, critics of interventionism have blamed utopianism for advocating unattainable ideals. They have also presented objections to the idea that social development can improve society. These objections involve criticisms of intervention which were mentioned earlier, as well as pessimistic forecasts about the possibility of achieving any meaningful social progress at all.

Different Utopian Influences
In formulating conceptions of the goals of social development, most social development writers have drawn inspiration from utopian ideas. Some are *radical utopians* in the sense that they believe in the complete reorganization of society according to some comprehensive blueprint, but most are *moderate utopians* believing in the possibility of attaining a steady improvement in social conditions through purposeful action. As has been shown already, the utopian belief that society can be improved through intervention is inspired by the work of moderate utopians such as Henri Saint-Simon and Auguste Comte rather than the radical utopianism of Charles Fourier or Robert Owen. While Fourier, Owen and others created actual utopian communities, Saint-Simon and Comte believed that scientific knowledge can be applied through planning to foster social progress. It is in this tradition that late nineteenth-century writers such as Ward, Veblen, Hobhouse and the Fabians gave expression to utopian ideals.

As has been shown already, utopianism has been extensively criticized. Critics such as Friedrich von Hayek and Karl Popper believe that utopian goals cannot be realized without the use of coercion. This criticism is directed at the essence of the utopian paradox, namely that the goal of utopianism, societal perfection, cannot be attained. Since a state of perfection cannot be attained, utopians must either abandon their goal or use force in a desperate attempt to attain it.

While this criticism may apply to radical utopians who do in fact try to create ideal, perfectly planned societies, it does not apply to those who have a much looser conception of the end state of social development. Moderate utopians do not define the end state of social development as an objective, millennialist condition but rather a loosely conceived 'improved' society in which certain welfare criteria have been met. For many of these writers, more emphasis is in fact placed on the process of improvement rather than the attainment of any final, ideal goal. However, as was suggested earlier, this results in an unsatisfactory situation in which the goals of social development are not properly defined.

Moderate utopians also believe that improvements can take place by gradual modifications to an existing social, economic and political system rather than by the destruction of this system and its replacement with an 'ideal' society. This point of view was actively promoted by the Fabians and the democratic socialists who rejected the idea that an apocalyptic overthrow of existing society is required to bring about meaningful social change. Instead, social improvement can be promoted through what the Fabians called gradualism and permeation. However, the Fabian belief in gradualism was vigorously attacked by Marxists and Leninists who believed that the Fabians had betrayed socialist ideals.

It is not surprising that moderate utopians seldom make use of the episodic technique which identifies distinct stages in the development process. Writers who use the episodic technique are far more likely to define the final stage of social change as one of perfection, and to require radical prescriptions to attain it. Moderate utopians who view social change as an evolving process do not see the need for a prescriptive conception of social development's final state, but place more emphasis on an ongoing progressive process.

Although most social development writers today are moderate rather than radical utopians, the radical influence is still strongly felt. Radical utopianism characterizes the work of Marxist writers who often cite countries such as China or Cuba as examples of what effective social development can achieve. In particular, the Chinese Commune was widely extolled in the 1970s as an example of socialist perfectibility. While this type of Marxist writing is not very consequential in social development today, the influence of radical utopian ideas can still be seen in the advocacy of community participation and similar forms of social activism.

Different Conceptions of Social Development Goals

Although contemporary social development theory does not have a precise definition of an end state, it does have specific conceptions of what improvements in social conditions entail. Despite a degree of ambiguity about these goals, end state conceptions can best be understood by examining the way they are defined by the proponents of different social development strategies. Conceptions of goals are also closely linked to the way social development is defined as a process. Different social development strategies not only recommend different means of improving social conditions but contain at least some conception of what this improvement involves. In the individualist strategies discussed earlier, the goals of social development are conceived differently from those advocated by collectivists or populists.

Attempts to define the end state of social development invariably invoke debates about the desirability of attaining *material* versus *ideational* goals. In keeping with the political economy definition used in this book, the social development strategies which will be described in the next chapter focus on material welfare goals. However, ideational definitions of social development are also popular and are promoted by different exponents of social development. As was shown in Chapter 1, social development has been viewed in sociology as a process of 'guided' social change which promotes modernity. Similarly, some social workers have defined social development as a process of personal growth and self-actualization. These social workers have drawn on psychological ideas and the individualist traditions of American social work to argue that individual betterment results in improved social relationships between people and that this, in turn, improves society as a whole. Political scientists such as Robert Putnam and his colleagues (1993) stress the need for increased human rights, political participation and social integration in social development. Also relevant is the idea of cultural rights and respect for the beliefs of others. Social development thus involves the adoption of policies that facilitate cultural expression and create opportunities for people to enjoy their cultural heritage. Another ideational approach emphasizes the concepts of social justice and peace as desirable social development goals. These various topics featured prominently at the 1995 World Summit on Social Development in addition to materialist concerns.

In the materialist conception, progress towards the attainment of social development goals is measured in quantifiable terms. In this approach, social indicators are widely employed to determine the extent to which material needs are satisfied (Baster, 1972; Estes, 1985). On the other hand, ideational conceptions of the goals of social development are seldom defined by using quantifiable indicators. Instead, these goals are described in abstract terms and involve descriptive, normative accounts that invoke qualitative notions about human interaction, the meaningfulness of life and participation in decisions.

While the conception used in this book is primarily materialist in nature, it does not suggest that non-material elements are unimportant.

Although there is a distinct preference in the literature for either materialist or ideational views, this dichotomy is an artificial one. The satisfaction of material needs should be linked to the promotion of non-material ideals such as peace, social solidarity, tolerance and cultural richness. Indeed, human welfare is enhanced not only through meeting material needs but through promoting the cultural, relational, political and other qualitative aspects of life.

The Prospect of Social Development

A major topic of debate about the goals of social development concerns the issue of whether these goals can, in fact, be realized. While social development proponents appear to have no doubt on this issue, there are many who criticize and even ridicule social development writers for being starry-eyed idealists whose faith in the possibility of human betterment through planned intervention is not only naive but preposterous. By challenging the idea that social development can improve society, these writers not only criticize social development's ability to attain its goals but seek to undermine the entire basis of social development. Their views may, accordingly, be regarded as a critique of the social development approach as a whole.

There are different aspects to the claim that social development goals cannot be attained. First, as was shown previously, it has been argued that social development goals can only be attained through the use of coercion. However, this argument is negated by the experience of many societies. During this century, the Western European welfare states achieved high standards of living for the mass of their populations without creating oppressive totalitarian political systems. Unlike China and the Soviet Union, Western Europe's great historical achievement was the ability to foster economic and social development within a liberal democratic climate. Indeed, few totalitarian societies have so effectively promoted the attainment of social development goals. Instead, many have been characterized by poverty and poor social conditions.

The second aspect of the claim that social development goals cannot be realized relates to the technical problems of planning. As was noted earlier in this chapter, writers such as Lindblom and Friedman have argued that planning requires knowledge, skills and an ability to direct complex systems that are beyond human ability. Consequently, they argue that social intervention is doomed to failure. However, this argument can also be negated by experience. Despite serious technical problems, many countries have successfully adopted planning to promote both economic development and the social well-being of their populations. Contrary to the claims of ideologues on the Radical Right, the record of economic and social planning has not been an unmitigated disaster. Indeed, planning has enhanced the quality of life for millions of people. Just one example of the effective use of planning is Jennie Hay Woo's (1991) account of educational planning in Taiwan. Pointing out that educational planning is today often denigrated for being a failure, she demonstrates that educational planning in Taiwan has been remarkably successful, and that it has played a critical role in the nation's economic and social development.

This is not to deny that there have been failures, but failures should not doom renewed efforts. An air crash disaster does not justify the termination of air travel but results instead in the adoption of improved safety measures. Similarly, the problems of poorly conceived social policies should not result in the conclusion that all interventions in human welfare are ineffective. As in any other field of human endeavour, social development's failures do not negate its efforts but instead require renewed resolve, more research into efficacy and greater competence in implementation.

While social planning faces formidable technical problems, social scientists are now more able to formulate and implement technologies that increase the chances of success, assess the effectiveness of interventions more accurately and make better forecasts. There are many useful social planning techniques which address the technical obstacles to successful intervention (Conyers, 1982; Midgley and Piachaud, 1984). Similarly, while futurology is in its infancy, there is evidence to show that the initial efforts of futurologists such as Toffler (1971, 1983) and Kahn (1979; Kahn and Wiener, 1967) and to project the likely outcomes of present-day actions will be significantly enhanced.

Third, there are some who believe that the notion of social development is incompatible with current social and political realities. These critics claim that the social and political climate is antithetical to large-scale remedies which require centralized planning. This criticism is inspired not only by individualist thought which rejects centralized forms of intervention but by postmodernist theorists who believe that the modern age which began with the Enlightenment has come to an end (Keller, 1990; Turner, 1990; Smart, 1992).

Postmodernist writers note that the project of modernity which emanated from the Enlightenment fostered the emergence of large-scale normative theories about the organization of society. Marxism, liberalism and similar ideologies all gave expression to intellectual themes which are consonant with modernity. Advocates of postmodernism believe that their usefulness is now exhausted. As cultural and social realities change, new ideas are needed. The collapse of communism, the demise of industrial society and the fragmentation of established institutions are all symptomatic of the coming of the postmodern age. They claim that the obsolescent 'grand' structures of modernity are gradually being replaced with small-scale social systems, decentralized authority, more participatory forms of social organization and a renewed pride in ethnic and national identity. As a result of these changes, there is little room for social development in the postmodern world.

While postmodernist thinking is currently in vogue in intellectual circles, the claim of some of its exponents to offer new emancipatory prescriptions are highly questionable. Many will be sceptical of the postmodernist claim that their evocation of local, small-scale solutions to massive social ills can replace the 'grand narratives' which provide systematic analyses of the causes of social problems as well as comprehensive solutions. It is difficult to see how the critical social needs of millions of people can be effectively addressed through ambiguous proposals of this kind.

Another criticism of social development on the ground that it is out of touch with current realities concerns the issue of the globalization of economic life. There has been much discussion in both academic and popular circles about the global economy and its apparent ability to negate the efforts of local and national governments to promote economic development (Bluestone and Harrison, 1982; Lash and Urry, 1987; Reich, 1991). A good deal of research is now available to show that local economies are substantially integrated into the world economy and that they are significantly influenced by events and decisions in other parts of the world. Analysts of the global economy have predicted that policies designed to enhance economic development at the domestic level will have little effect if they do not specifically address the challenges of the global economy. Some experts have urged that relaxed trade controls, measures to attract multinational investments and above all efforts to enhance local competitiveness be introduced. These policy prescriptions have, however, been criticized on the ground that they invariably result in lower wages, reduced employment opportunities and similar negative adjustments.

A recent and rather depressing account of the way economic globalization affects national and local development efforts is provided by Noam Chomsky (1994) who argues that a new *de facto* world government comprised of the International Monetary Fund, the World Bank, the Group of Seven countries (G-7) and the General Agreement on Tariffs and Trade (GATT) is emerging. This world government is designed to promote the interests of international capitalism rather than those of individual nations or communities. Critical economic decisions with wide-ranging consequences are being made by these international bodies without any concern for the interests of particular nation states. National governments, and particularly those of the developing countries, have very little influence over these decisions which often nullify national development efforts and negatively affect the well-being of local people. In this adverse international climate, local and national social development efforts are likely to have little impact.

The globalization of economic endeavour does pose a direct challenge to social development. Critics argue that social development's socio-spatial focus and its concern with localities, regions and nation states are ignorant of the worldwide trend towards globalization. Also, because globalization overrides local effort, social development is an ineffective means of promoting people's welfare. Because social development's focus is inward rather than global, its interventions are applied in isolation of wider international, economic realities.

While it is true that social development writers have not paid adequate attention to the global economy, there is no reason that domestic development efforts cannot be cognizant of the global economy and responsive to the challenges it poses (Karger, 1992). Social development's socio-spatial focus and domestic concerns do not preclude an appreciation of the impact of international events or an attempt to cope with them. Indeed, there is evidence to show that governments which have successfully promoted social development have done so with full awareness of global realities and have taken these into account as they have sought to formulate strategies that foster the integration of social and economic policies within the context of a comprehensive developmental approach. Similarly, while some writers imply that the global economy invariably reduces local and domestic economies to a passive state of paralysis and stagnation, there have been successful efforts to meet the challenges through active government intervention and appropriate policies. The use of incentives to attract multinational investors into local economies is hardly a recent innovation, and negotiated trade agreements that bring benefits to both local communities and international investors have been effectively adopted in the past. Similar policies can be introduced to make social development a realistic option for progressive domestic change within the context of the global economy. Also, it has been possible for developing countries to organize in the past to promote their interests against those of the more powerful industrial nations. As dissatisfaction with the international agencies rises, it is likely that international collaboration to resist their influence will increase.

Another set of criticisms are not primarily concerned with whether social development goals can be attained, but with the desirability of seeking to attain them. These criticisms were discussed earlier in this chapter where it was shown that many different views about the need for social development have been expressed. Some writers have criticized social development for seeking to change traditional societies which, they believe, would be better off if they were left alone. Instead of welcoming social development, these writers advocate the preservation of traditional values and institutions. As was noted previously, the opposition to Westernization and the resurgence of traditionalist and fundamentalist beliefs in many parts of the world poses a challenge to social development. Social development's modernist proclivities, it can be argued, are at variance with traditionalist conservative views in many parts of the world (Midgley and Sanzenbach, 1989; Dabbagh, 1993).

A related expression of this view has been stated on many previous occasions in this book. It has already been shown that many writers oppose social development on the grounds that it involves governmental and other forms of 'interference' in social and economic affairs. Proponents of *laissez-faire* ideas ranging from Spencer to Hayek believe that societies operate according to natural processes which are responsible for the well-being of all. These writers are implacable critics of social development because they believe that attempts by well-meaning but misguided social development planners to direct these processes are harmful to the common good because they impede the smooth functioning of the natural social and economic system. While these critics are often called conservatives or neo-conservatives, their ideas are in fact informed by the radical individualism of liberal thought.

The criticisms of social development by the opponents of economic growth have also been mentioned earlier in this chapter. In an excellent summary and analysis of the ideas of 'anti-growth' writers, H. W. Arndt (1978) suggests that social development's commitment to material progress through continued economic development has formidable opponents. However, the linking of social development to the notion of sustainable development offers an accommodation which many will find acceptable. As many proponents of both sustainable and social development now claim, progressive change can be fostered without destroying the planet or mortgaging the well-being of future generations.

Lastly, some writers have criticized social development's attempt to promote social welfare for all by arguing that current conditions are so bad that nothing can be done to improve the situation. They contend that nothing can be done to reverse the decline of recent decades and they argue that in the present climate of decadence, decline and corruption, it is absurd to seek to attain social development objectives. As was shown earlier, critical theorists such as Adorno and Horkheimer (1944) as well as leading literary figures such as Eliot were extremely pessimistic about the prospect of improving society. The critical theorists conclude that all forms of opposition to the oppressive realities of modern life have been neutralized, that human beings have been reduced to objects, that alienation is widespread and that the Western culture industry has enslaved the masses. Although they hoped that critical theory would foster emancipation, they thought that this was highly improbable. Other critical theorists such as Herbert Marcuse (1964) and David Gil (1985) are less despairing but their work is hardly hopeful in tone.

Pessimistic and even nihilistic assessments of the prospect of social development should not be dismissed out of hand. There are indeed legitimate grounds for being dejected about the human condition. However, there are also grounds for optimism. While the need for social development remains critical, it should also be recognized that the improvements in social conditions which have taken place during this century for hundreds of millions of ordinary people are historically unprecedented. Despite pessimism, history has shown that progress is possible. Many social development advocates will understand why despair is a common attitude in intellectual circles today, but they also believe that hopelessness is not a tenable position. There is no alternative, they believe, to declaring a faith in future progress through rational intervention and concerted action. This attitude gives ultimate expression to social development's utopian proclivities and its hope for a better world.

4
Strategies for Social Development

The previous chapter reviewed a variety of theoretical issues in social development. This chapter goes beyond theoretical discussion to examine the different programmes, policies and strategies which have been adopted over the years to promote social development. While theory is of obvious importance in the field, social development is primarily a practical affair involving tangible programmes, policies and strategies for achieving specific goals. These practical activities need to be discussed in some detail.

However, it must be recognized that theory and practice in social development cannot be separated. Theory has shaped social development practice and the experiences of those who implement social development programmes have, in turn, informed theoretical thinking. The link between theory and practice is particularly clear when the normative bases for social development are examined. As was shown in chapter 3, social development strategies are based on different ideological approaches which emphasize different beliefs and values. The taxonomy of ideologies provided in the last chapter offers a useful basis for classifying the various strategies and it will be employed here.

Using this taxonomy, three major types of social development strategies will be discussed. First, the chapter examines social development strategies that place primary responsibility for promoting social development on individuals. It then discusses strategies that stress the role of local communities in fostering social development. Finally, the chapter concludes with an examination of those strategies that rely on governments to promote social development.

When discussing practical proposals for social development, this chapter uses terms such as 'policies', 'plans', 'programmes', 'projects' and 'strategies' loosely. While these terms have precise meanings, they will be used interchangeably. The term 'strategy' will be used most frequently to organize the major programmatic approaches which have emerged in the field. It refers to those projects and programmes that share similar ideological orientations and advocate similar interventions.

While the various strategies offer different prescriptions for attaining social development goals, all subscribe to the view that people's welfare can best be promoted within the context of a comprehensive process of economic development. The strategies to be discussed in this chapter are, therefore, concerned not only with welfare issues but with harmonizing social interventions with economic development activities. It will be seen that some of these strategies are more explicitly focused on economic activities than others, and that some are more successful in the way they link social interventions with economic development endeavours. Nevertheless, all are distinguished from other approaches for promoting social welfare by their association with economic development.

SOCIAL DEVELOPMENT BY INDIVIDUALS

As was shown in the previous chapter, the view that social welfare can best be promoted when individuals independently pursue their own self-interests (and thus their own welfare) is a fundamental tenet of Western individualist ideology and the basis of the modern capitalist economic system. Proponents of this approach believe that the welfare of the whole society is enhanced when individuals strive to promote their own welfare. This normative position also underlies the *individualist or enterprise approach* to social development.

However, individualist ideology has not been popular in social development circles. Most advocates of social development have placed more emphasis on government- or community-based forms of intervention. Most believe that the individualist approach is incompatible with social development's commitment to improve society through intervening in economic and social affairs. They reject the idea that social development goals can be attained by simply requiring people to take responsibility for their own welfare.

However, there is a difference between an extreme *laissez-faire* approach and the idea that steps should be taken to help people to become self-reliant and participate effectively in the market. While the former approach dogmatically asserts a non-interventionist position, the latter urges the adoption of measures that enhance individual functioning, create a more vibrant enterprise culture and facilitate the productive use of the market by ordinary people.

This latter approach has become more popular in social development circles in recent times. Its proponents do not believe that welfare results *automatically* from the pursuit of economic self-interest, and they argue instead that specific interventions by governments and other organizations are needed to promote social development within the context of a market economy. It is this belief in specific interventions that characterizes the individualist approach to social development today.

Different policies and programmes have been advocated to promote the individualist approach. These include large-scale interventions that create an enterprise culture which is conducive to individual success, as well as small-scale interventions that assist low-income families, small-business proprietors and those in the so-called informal sector to operate effectively in the market place. As has been noted previously in this book, some social workers have also promoted an individualist approach by seeking to help individuals to enhance their functioning and interpersonal relations within the context of an enterprise culture.

Fostering an Enterprise Culture to Promote Social Progress

The individualist approach can only be effective if there is a vibrant economy which permits individuals to function as rational economic actors. Individuals can only meet their own needs and those of their families and dependants if there are jobs, opportunities for self-employment and sound prospects for investment. Since they cannot enhance their welfare in a stagnant or shrinking economy, every effort must be made to ensure that the economy is buoyant and that people can participate effectively in productive economic activities.

For this reason, advocates of the individualist strategy argue that a positive culture of enterprise should be created by governments and other agencies to support individual effort. Although most people have an inherent capacity for entrepreneurship, this capacity cannot be realized if the market does not work properly or if opportunities for enterprise are blocked. Therefore, action is needed to maximize opportunities for individuals to participate and function in the market.

The modernization approach discussed in the last chapter requires governments to create a dynamic capitalist economy and address the causes of underdevelopment and economic backwardness. Modernization theory urges governments to mobilize all available resources for investment in industry and other modern sector enterprises in order to stimulate economic growth, create jobs and, through a strategy of employment creation, raise the income of the population. Its advocates recommend that consumption be deferred and that government spending be curtailed so that resources can be released for productive investment. Writers such as Walt Rostow (1960, 1963) believe that governments that mobilize sufficient investments for industrial development will experience a 'take-off' into sustained economic growth. This will create wage employment on a large scale and, as a result of increased employment opportunities, people in the subsistence agricultural sector will find work in the new factories and other modern enterprises. Through wage employment, their incomes will rise, they will spend more on the goods and services produced by the modern economy, and this, in turn, will create more demand and foster the further expansion of the economy.

The modernization approach was adopted in many parts of the developing world in the 1950s and 1960s. Modernization theory was, in fact, abstracted from the experiences of the Western industrial nations which had undergone economic transformation as a result of industrialization. The successful postwar reconstruction of Germany and Japan also depended on policies that mobilized capital for industrial investment and fostered rapid economic growth. The Soviet Union and the Eastern European communist countries also stressed the need for continued industrial expansion although here, of course, centralized planning rather than the market guided the process of industrialization.

While most Third World governments adopted the modernization approach, they did not implement it in the pure form recommended by its proponents. Few Third World governments were able to mobilize the capital they needed from their domestic economies, and most borrowed heavily on international markets to finance development efforts. Few curtailed consumption and instead many sought to expand education and other social services (Hardiman and Midgley, 1982, 1989). Most governments also adopted planning in an attempt to direct the development of their economies. Few created the vibrant free market systems recommended by the advocates of modernization. In the 1980s, as a result of substantial interest rate increases, many developing countries were faced with a massive burden of debt. At the behest of the International Monetary Fund and the World Bank, many have been compelled to introduce structural adjustment measures to deflate their economies, reduce government intervention and finance debt repayments. As result, many have suffered real setbacks in economic and social development.

However, proponents of the individualist approach have applauded these developments, claiming that structural adjustment policies are recreating the vigorous capitalist dynamic needed for development. They point out that the retrenchment of state involvement in the economy, denationalization, deregulation and privatization are fostering a new climate of entrepreneurship and growth in many developing countries. Similarly, the collapse of communism in the former Soviet Union and Eastern Europe, as well as economic liberalization in China, is releasing the creative potential of billions of people. In the West, where large-scale manufacturing industries are in decline, a new optimism in the resurgence of small enterprises and self-employment opportunities is emerging. Advocates of the individualist approach argue that the dynamic expansion of the East Asian economies demonstrates that a culture of enterprise can transform backward societies. They claim that the adoption of policies which foster entrepreneurship, competition and initiative can bring dramatic change to all low-income societies and communities.

These ideas have been widely advocated in recent years by the international agencies. For example, the United Nations Development Programme has placed considerable emphasis in its *Human Development Reports* on the role of markets, individual initiative and self-determination in fostering social welfare. In one report, the United Nations Development Programme defined social development as a process of widening people's choices to decide 'what people should have, be and do to insure their own livelihood' (1990: 10–11). The World Bank has also stressed the need to promote an enterprise culture to bring about social development. In a report, *The Challenge of Development*, the Bank (1991) argued for the adoption of 'market friendly' development strategies that restrict government intervention in the economy, ease regulations, promote competition, encourage investment and foster integration with the global economy.

However, this anti-statist position is not shared by all proponents of the individualist approach. Some have argued that governments have a critically important role to play in creating conditions that foster enterprise, job creation and rapid economic development. As was noted earlier, most proponents of economic modernization believe that governments should guide or direct the process of economic growth. In addition, many believe that governments should create the institutions needed to foster an enterprise culture. The concepts of 'institution building' or 'institutional development' have been widely used to connote this idea.

The concept of institutional development has been used in development circles for many years but it is still poorly defined (Paiva, 1977; Matthews, 1986; Israel, 1987; North, 1991; World Bank, 1991). Some writers use the concept to refer to the capacity of local people to organize themselves by creating small-scale associations that meet their needs and enhance opportunities for interaction. Others use the term to connote the emergence of formal organizations that promote economic modernization. Yet others define the term as the emergence of skills associated with management and organizational operations. More recently, the term has been used with reference to Eastern Europe to describe the need for modern economic institutions that support a free market. These include legislative provisions for promoting trade, enforcing contracts and recognizing property ownership. Also included are the creation of banks and other credit institutions, the establishment of stock exchanges, the adoption of standard weights and measures and the development of agencies that register commercial firms, award patents and provide a host of services needed for the operation of a market economy.

It is in this latter sense that the term 'institution building' is most frequently used by proponents of the individualist approach. They argue that individuals will only be able to promote their welfare as independent economic actors if governments create institutions which will facilitate their efficient use of the market. This requires the emergence of institutions that support the market and enhance its ability to function effectively.

Promoting Small Enterprises for Needy People

Supporters of the individualist approach also believe that governments should create conditions conducive to the emergence of small-scale enterprises which provide opportunities for poor people to generate the resources they need to meet their own social needs. This approach differs significantly from the economic modernization approach discussed previously. As was noted earlier, the modernization approach relies on mobilizing capital for large-scale industrial development and thus for employment creation. It is through employment that people earn the income they need to meet their social needs.

Proponents of small-scale enterprises are critical of many aspects of the modernization approach. They point out that low-income countries cannot create wage employment on a scale needed to raise the incomes of the poor. The emphasis on industrial development, they point out, is highly inappropriate to the needs of developing countries. Ernst Schumacher (1974) and George McRobie (1981) have argued that not only has industrial development failed to raise levels of living in most developing countries but that it has been responsible for widespread environmental pollution. They also contend that the debt problem can be avoided through local small-scale enterprise development. If sufficient individuals create small enterprises, the economy will grow endogenously and expand through local effort rather than external investments. It will also support the emergence of a dynamic entrepreneurial culture. Advocates believe that this approach offers the best prospect for the poor to participate effectively in the market and enhance their welfare through their own efforts.

The current interest in small enterprise as a mechanism for social development began with the identification of what is often referred to as the 'informal sector'. By the 1970s it was widely recognized that, contrary to the teachings of modernization theory, jobs were not being created in the developing countries at a sufficiently rapid rate to absorb labour from the subsistence sector. In most developing countries, the modern sector was simply not expanding fast enough. In others, a lack of investment, widespread corruption, bad planning and excessive government regulation meant that the modern sector was not growing at all. In some developing countries, this was accompanied by inappropriate employment and labour market policies which resulted in the creation of a small wage labour force in the modern sector, protected by unions, government regulations, the patronage of the ruling political party and social insurance programmes which cater only for those in regular wage employment. While this 'labour aristocracy' enjoys many benefits, the bulk of the population has no access to gainful employment and continues to toil in the subsistence sector in both the urban and the rural areas.

At the end of the 1960s, the International Labour Office became concerned about the employment problem in the Third World (Plant, 1983). Under its World Employment Programme, the agency commissioned a series of in-depth country studies to investigate the problems of labour utilization, poverty and underdevelopment, and to make recommendations for fostering productive employment. Three countries, one in each of the major world regions were studied: Colombia, Sri Lanka and Kenya. The Kenya study (International Labour Office, 1972) challenged the premises of modernization theory and its assumption that the creation of wage employment in the formal sector offered the best prospect of promoting social development.

The Kenya study found, for example, that the unemployment rate was extremely high when defined as the proportion of those of working age who were not in regular wage employment. Clearly, only a small proportion of the labour force in Kenya had steady jobs. But this did not mean that unemployed workers were idle or drawing unemployment insurance while waiting to find jobs. Apart from the fact that there was no unemployment insurance, most 'unemployed' workers were economically active, not as employees, but as workers in an 'informal' sector of small enterprises ranging from backyard repair shops to vending stalls in street markets. Many such enterprises are owned and operated by families and have few if any employees. Others are highly productive and employ larger numbers of workers. Most are labour intensive and make use of adapted technologies, many are unregulated and some are illegal. Nevertheless, the ILO claimed that informal sector enterprises offer promising opportunities for individuals to apply their entrepreneurial skills, generate income and enhance their welfare.

The Kenya study argued that these informal sector operations contribute more to the economy than has been recognized. As it noted: 'the bulk of employment in the informal sector, far from being only marginally productive is economically efficient and profit making' (International Labour Office, 1972: 5). The report urged the Kenyan government to view the informal sector as a positive resource for development, and to adopt policies that support and foster its growth.

Following the publication of the Kenya report, many accounts of the informal sector and its contribution to development have been published (Hart, 1973; Mazumdar, 1976; Bromley and Gerry, 1979; International Labour Office, 1985; Portes et al., 1989; Thomas, 1992). The informal sector is also known as the 'unofficial economy', 'unregulated sector', or 'underground' or 'black' economy. As was noted earlier, the informal sector consists of a great variety of enterprises which include easily recognizable services such as those mentioned earlier, as well as less prepossessing activities such as begging and garbage picking (Birkbeck, 1979; Ruiz-Perez, 1979). Many studies have shown that the informal sector is sizable. Estimates by Mazumdar (1976) found that between 50 per cent and 70 per cent of the urban labour force in many Third World cities work in the informal sector. More recent estimates by the International Labour Office (1985) for African cities range from a low of 44 per cent for Abidjan to a high of 95 per cent in Benin.

A particularly optimistic account of the informal sector is offered by Hernando de Soto (1989) who criticizes Latin American governments for using the power of the state to favour only a small section of the population. Since those in power ignore the needs of the majority, ordinary people have to rely on their own resourcefulness to meet their needs. Writing specifically about Peru, de Soto shows how the 'informals' have succeeded in providing for themselves and their dependants despite the restrictions imposed on them by the state. In addition, their activities have succeeded where the state has failed. While the government constructed public housing for only a small proportion of the population, 42 per cent of Lima's citizens have been housed by private informal sector entrepreneurs. Some 91,000 street vendors dominate the city's retail trade and are able to support over 300,000 dependants. Despite the government's attempts to provide public transport, 93 per cent of the transport fleet is owed by informal sector entrepreneurs. Their activities comprise a dynamic alternative to the state's mercantilist economy and form the basis for future economic growth.

Initially, research into the informal sector concentrated on urban areas but, more recently, the existence of a sizable rural informal sector consisting of services, processing and small-scale industrial enterprises has also been recognized (International Labour Office, 1984). It has been shown that informal sector activities are to be found in the Western industrial countries as well, particularly among low-income and immigrant communities (Sassen-Koob, 1989; Stepick, 1989). In addition, as Sergio and Dellagio (1987) revealed, informal sector activities were widespread in the former communist countries despite a prohibition on these activities. With the demise of communism, these activities have become even more common.

Since the 'discovery' of the informal sector, some social scientists have argued that the growth of small enterprises offers the best prospect for development. This argument has been made with reference to both the developing and the industrial nations. In industrial countries such as the United States, the importance of small-scale enterprises in the economy has been emphasized in recent years. Various writers have argued that the large manufacturing and service corporations have lost jobs, while the small-scale sector has grown. Peter Drucker (1985) claimed, for example, that the largest Fortune 500 Corporations lost between four and six million jobs in the 1970s and 1980s, while small and medium-size businesses created between 35 and 40 million new jobs. Many proponents of small-scale businesses also believe that small businesses contribute more to sustaining a dynamic enterprise culture than large corporations, and that they offer the best hope for economic prosperity in the future (Drucker, 1985; Birch, 1987; Case, 1992).

On the other hand, some writers have cautioned that the informal sector should not be regarded as a panacea for the world's economic problems. Some believe that the transformation of subsistence economies will not be accomplished without massive investments in modern industry and the creation of wage employment on a large scale. Others do not regard the informal sector as a viable locus for social development effort. Bromley and Gerry (1979) have shown, for example, that many informal sector jobs are poorly paid and extremely demanding, and that they do not offer ready opportunities for advancement. Many informal sector activities such as domestic service, housework and scavenging are economically unproductive and often exploitative. This assessment differs significantly from accounts which optimistically view the informal sector as providing the best prospect for promoting a market economy in the developing world.

Nevertheless, proponents of the individualist approach have urged governments to adopt measures which support and strengthen small-scale enterprise to foster not only economic but social development as well. The small enterprise sector, they believe, provides excellent opportunities for the poor to engage in productive economic activities. In underdeveloped areas, it is far cheaper to promote these activities than to mobilize capital for large-scale industrial development and job creation. In view of the tendency for large-scale enterprise to replace labour with technology, the informal sector is more labour intensive and likely to create more employment. It is also more likely to foster a sustainable economy in the longer term, and to adapt to changing local needs and circumstances.

One recommendation is that governments ease the restrictions currently placed on the informal sector. Many studies have shown that governments suppress rather than promote small-scale enterprise. Many developing countries have laws and regulations which make much informal sector enterprise illegal. In addition, governments seek to control informal sector enterprises because they avoid taxes, licensing regulations, laws governing employment and working conditions, social security payments and wage regulations. Nevertheless, following the publication of the ILO Kenya study in 1972, numerous governments have either eased these restrictions or refrained from enforcing them. Many others have adopted policies designed to promote informal sector activities. On the other hand, some governments have continued to repress informal sector activities and rigidly enforce restrictions.

In addition to advocating policies that ease restrictions on small-scale enterprises, a number of specific measures that foster the growth of these enterprises have been advocated (Weeks, 1975; World Bank, 1978; Portes et al., 1989). Most experts urge governments to improve credit facilities for small businesses, to build infrastructure such as industrial estates and markets which can support these enterprises, to train entrepreneurs in small-business management and to provide extension services to help small businesses with product design, marketing, financial planning and similar routine activities. The need to integrate the small enterprise sector with the larger formal sector is particularly important. Experts urge governments to increase the services and goods they purchase from the informal sector and to encourage large firms to subcontract to this sector as well. Instead of avoiding them, commercial banks and private sector business firms should be urged to interact and provide services to small businesses.

Today, many more governments are actively fostering the creation of micro-enterprises among poor people, including those who apply for government social assistance. The Philippines has been a leader in this field, using an enterprise approach to support small producers in both urban and rural areas and helping them enhance their skills (Andersen and Khambata, 1981). The international agencies are also promoting this approach. Since its sector policy paper on small enterprises was published, the World Bank (1978) has also promoted the development of informal sector activities among the poor through its lending and technical assistance programmes. Other international agencies such as the Inter-American Development Bank have also sought to promote this approach and some successes have been recorded. For example, the Inter-American Development Bank (1988) revealed that it had lent more than US $72 million for the development of small enterprises during the preceding decade. This had resulted in the creation of no less than 162 successful enterprises by low-income people in the agricultural, industrial, retail, crafts and fishing sectors. These activities are highly compatible with the individualistic approach to social development. They are compatible with the 'market friendly' strategies currently being promoted by both the World Bank (1990, 1991) and the United Nations Development Programme (1990, 1993).

Promoting Social Welfare by Enhancing Individual Functioning

Proponents of the individualist approach believe that if people are to promote their own welfare, they must be able to function effectively, and operate confidently within the context of an enterprise culture. Strategies that create an enterprise culture and generate opportunities for small-scale enterprises can only be effective if ordinary people utilize these opportunities. Unfortunately, many individuals are not able to function competently in the capitalist system. Many lack confidence, have low self-esteem or are simply overwhelmed with personal problems that impede their capacity to cope. Others are poorly motivated or prefer non-legitimate alternatives to those prescribed by the dominant individualist culture. For this reason, steps must be taken to assist these individuals, and remove the factors that impede effective functioning. Supporters of the individualist approach believe that social work is well placed to provide assistance of this kind, and it is in this context that they have advocated social development strategies that rely on social work interventions.

During the nineteenth century, when *laissez-faire* ideas were predominant in Europe and North America, it was widely believed that the pressing social problems of the day could be attributed to problems of individual malfunctioning. Poverty was generally attributed to individual malfunctioning. It was generally accepted that the solution to the problem of poverty lay in restoring the capacity of individuals to utilize the economic market productively. As was noted in chapter 1, social work emerged from the efforts of the Charity Organization Society to remedy the causes of malfunctioning among the 'deserving' poor. The women volunteers who became the first social workers sought to counsel the poor and help them become economically self-sufficient. Initially, they tried to help their clients find work or to deal with the material problems which impeded their ability to operate in the capitalist economy. In time, however, they placed more emphasis on dealing with the psychological factors that impeded their clients' functioning.

By the middle of this century, social work was heavily committed to a psychotherapeutic approach that attributed all social problems, including poverty, to individual malfunctioning. While social work was not exclusively concerned with treating the causes of individual malfunctioning, the therapeutic approach predominated.

The promotion of social development within social work circles in the 1960s was intended to counteract the heavy emphasis on remedial intervention that characterized the profession. However, despite these efforts, the individualist approach continues to exert considerable influence in the profession. This influence has been felt even in social development circles where some social work advocates of social development have defined social development in ways that are highly compatible with the profession's individualist commitment. As was noted in chapter 1, some social workers such as Henry Maas (1984) believe that social development goals can best be promoted when people learn to function competently and when they establish effective relationships with each other.

While many social workers who have written about social development in individualist terms do not specifically relate their approach to economic activities, others such as Frank Paiva (1977) have addressed this aspect. Paiva was one of the first social workers to formulate a comprehensive conception of social development which drew on the United Nations literature and at the same time applied social work's individualistic approach to social development. He believes that it is through helping individuals to improve the quality of their lives that social development goals can be attained. Indeed, Paiva defines social development as a process of enhancing the capacity of individuals 'to work for their own and society's welfare' (1977: 332). This approach, as Chandler (1982) notes, implies that social workers can promote social development by teaching capacity building and functioning skills to individuals.

The idea that social workers can be employed to teach poor people to function effectively as economic actors in the market is today being promoted in some developing countries. In these countries, social workers are being used to help poor clients establish small enterprises which generate income and help them meet their needs. The Philippines has actively promoted this approach and, as James Midgley (1981) reported, its government social work programmes make extensive use of social workers to create micro-enterprises. Although these efforts are not always successful and can be criticized for fostering what Angela Reidy (1981) calls an inappropriate market-based welfarist approach, it offers opportunities for social work to address the problems of the poor in tangible, material ways.

Social workers in the industrial countries have not become extensively involved in creating micro-enterprises among poor clients even though this idea is not a new one. In the 1970s, when culture of poverty theory (Lewis, 1966) was widely used to explain the causes of poverty, it was sometimes suggested that social workers should be employed to counsel the poor and change their attitudes and lifestyles. However, few social workers actually became involved in activities of this kind. More recently, social workers in Iowa have introduced programmes that help recipients of social assistance establish their own businesses and become self-sufficient (Else and Raheim, 1992).

Although social work makes extensive use of counselling and psychotherapy, a coherent approach for counselling poor people to function more effectively in the market has not yet emerged. Apart from the examples given earlier of social work involvement in small-scale enterprise development, direct social work practice has not formulated specific approaches to 'treat' the poor. The prospect for formulating an approach to social development which uses clinical social work techniques has, however, been fostered in publications by Judith Lee (1988) and Mark Stern (1990), both of whom have examined the role of direct practice interventions with poor people. Although these publications do not cover the issues comprehensively, they offer a basis for formulating a treatment approach which is compatible with an individualist approach to social development.

SOCIAL DEVELOPMENT BY COMMUNITIES

The view that social development can best be promoted by people themselves working together harmoniously within their local communities forms the basis of what may be called the *communitarian approach* to social development. Advocates of this strategy believe that people and communities have an inherent capacity to organize themselves to ensure that their basic needs are met, their problems are solved and opportunities for advancement are created. In order to achieve these goals, they need to cooperate with each other and share a common purpose. In this way, they are able to exert greater control over local resources and local affairs. They are also better placed to secure external resources to promote social development at the local level.

As was shown in the last chapter, the communitarian approach is strongly influenced by populist ideology. The proponents of community-based social development strategies make frequent use of the term 'the people' in their writings and all advocate the adoption of social development strategies that seek to promote people's welfare within the context of community life (Gran, 1983; Korten, 1983; Korten and Klaus, 1984; Cernea, 1985; Oakley, 1991; Burkey, 1993).

As was noted in the last chapter, communitarian populism is different from collectivism. While collectivism also encourages cooperative endeavour, it requires that resources be jointly owned and managed. Communitarianism does not require common ownership but instead urges people to collaborate with others to promote their own interests within community settings. Communitarian populism also differs from collectivist statism. Unlike statists, communitarians oppose the idea that governments should be responsible for development. Instead, they believe that the most effective and enduring development programmes are those that are created and managed by local people themselves.

The communitarian approach to social development has been exceedingly popular in social development circles and different strategies for promoting social development in community settings have been formulated. Three strategies will be discussed in this section. The first is community development which, as was shown in chapter 2, initially emerged in colonial times to mobilize the participation of rural people in economic development. The second is community action which is a much more radical and activist approach. The third focuses on gender issues and on the contributions women make to social development. As a 'community', women's needs and perspectives have been much neglected in development thinking and, throughout the world, they remain marginalized and oppressed. However, women's groups have become much more active in social development in recent years. They have formulated a gender-based approach which addresses women's concerns and contends that social progress can only occur if women are fully involved in social development endeavours.

Community Development and Social Development
The history of social development described in chapter 2 pointed out that the term 'social development' was invented by the British to connote two elements in colonial social policy: namely, remedial social welfare and community development. It also showed that community development was promoted by colonial social welfare administrators so that their welfare departments could contribute positively to economic development.

Although community development was a primary strategy for social development in the 1940s, it had older roots. Before colonization, many indigenous societies had well-established traditions of cooperative endeavour, and communal ownership was widespread. Traditional forms of government were rooted in the local community, and this was generally recognized by the colonial governments. In many cases, traditional authority was formally incorporated into the colonial system of political control. Village headmen and chiefs were given limited powers by the colonial authorities and they were, in turn, expected to serve colonial interests. The colonial authorities also made use of communal labour for development purposes and particularly for the development of infrastructure. As Peter Mould (1966) revealed, roads and other projects were often constructed with the help of local labour assigned by chiefs and headmen. The advantages of using local resources for development purposes was also recognized by missionaries who used villagers to help them build churches, schools and clinics.

Nor were the British experiments in West Africa in the 1940s entirely original. Before community development was formalized in West Africa, colonial administrators in India such as F. L. Brayne had advocated that similar programmes be introduced. In addition, Indian leaders such as Rabindranath Tagore and Mahatma Gandhi both created utopian communities based on Indian village life which they claimed offered a basis for organizing society as a whole (Bhattacharyya, 1970). It is not surprising that, after independence, these ideas had a significant influence on India's community development programme.

In the 1940s, the British colonial authorities in London actively promoted community development throughout the Empire. The French also encouraged the adoption of community development in the form of *animation rurale* (Gow and VanSant, 1983), and it was also fostered in countries in the American sphere of influence. For example, the United States actively promoted community development in Latin America during the 1960s as a part of the aid programmes introduced under the Alliance for Progress (Brokensha and Hodge, 1969).

Although community development programmes in different parts of the world have common features, David Brokensha and Peter Hodge (1969) note that they evolved in different ways in different countries. For example, there are major differences in the administrative structure of community development in different parts of the world. In some countries, community development is closely linked to local government. This approach emphasizes local political organization and cooperative endeavour managed by local leaders with the support of the central government. In other countries, community development is directly associated with agricultural extension. Here, community development personnel are usually employed by government agricultural departments. In other territories where the social welfare model which had emerged in West Africa was adopted, community development stresses the creation of village-level economic and social projects.

In most cases, community development has adopted a materialist approach which encourages the construction of community centres, schools, clinics, roads and sanitary and water supply projects. However, in other cases, more emphasis has been placed on non-material or ideational aspects. These include enhancing community identity, strengthening democratic participation and fostering self-help and self-determination. These ideas feature prominently in community development theory, and are often emphasized by expatriate community development personnel such as American aid workers who have placed great stress on ideational aspects (Brokensha and Hodge, 1969).

Community development programmes also vary in their geographic coverage. As Ronald Dore and Zoë Mars (1981) reveal, many countries have organized community development on a national basis and these programmes are administered by central and provincial bureaucracies. Some are closely identified with the ideologies and political activities of ruling political parties. Examples include the Chinese system of communes, and the Tanzanian *ujamaa* villagization programme. Others are local in scope and focus primarily on a particular community. This is especially true of community development programmes established by non-governmental organizations and by local people themselves. Some of these, such as the Commilla Project in Bangladesh, have attracted international attention. In addition, while most community development programmes operate in rural areas, others serve urban areas, particularly slums and squatter settlements.

Whether administered by governments or non-governmental organizations, community development programmes share common operational features. They generally rely on trained para-professional personnel to mobilize local participation, organize activities and link the community to external resources. These personnel are employed by community development agencies and often they come from outside the community. However, community development programmes also use local workers who have been trained for the task. Most programmes also rely extensively on local participation. Community development is invariably defined as a partnership between external agencies and local people. Usually, local people contribute their labour and other local resources while technical expertise and external resources are provided by the community development agency. Today, there is an extensive literature on community development which not only defines the techniques used by community development personnel but articulates the theoretical principles in community development work. As was noted earlier, two of these principles, self-determination and self-help, have featured prominently in community development theory.

Although community development has not always realized its potential, it offers an effective means for promoting social development within the context of economic development. Local community development projects have made a significant contribution to raising the levels of living of ordinary people. They have contributed extensively to the formation of physical infrastructure. Many rural communities have constructed networks of feeder roads that not only enhance communications but increase access to markets and more readily import materials and technologies. Similarly, the construction of irrigation projects, land clearance and the cooperative weeding and fertilizing of crops have also fostered local economic development.

Community development programmes have also enhanced productive activities. Many communities have established cooperatives which support production, assist with storage, facilitate marketing and retail produce and goods. The role of these cooperatives in promoting local development has been quite extensive. In addition, community development has supported economic development through the creation of social infrastructure and social programmes that enhance human and social capital formation. Community development programmes throughout the world have resulted in the construction of schools, clinics, drinking water supplies and sanitary projects which have improved people's productive capacities and added to the formation of social capital.

Although community development emerged in the context of Third World development, it also has relevance to the industrial countries. Indeed, social work in the West has long advocated community intervention and, in many countries, community-based programmes which are similar to community development in the Third World have been introduced. For example, the 'War on Poverty' programmes of the 1960s in the United States made extensive use of a community-based approach in an attempt to reduce the incidence of poverty. However, as James Midgley and Peter Simbi (1993) have pointed out, community development in the industrial countries is seldom concerned with economic development. They suggest that the industrial nations can learn from the Third World experience and usefully adopt an economic development focus.

Community Action, Participation and Development

Despite its undoubted achievements, there was widespread disillusionment with community development during the 1970s. Many critics claimed that community development bureaucracies had become large and inefficient, and that indifference and even corruption were widespread. In the late 1970s and 1980s, as fiscal difficulties became severe, many governments reduced community development expenditures and, in many countries, community development programmes did little more than extol the virtues of self-help while failing to provide resources for projects (Midgley and Hamilton, 1978). In many low-income developing countries, the only resources allocated to community development projects were for staff salaries. Consequently, many began to doubt the value of government community development projects, and community development's capacity to promote social development obviously suffered.

Another criticism concerns the motives of government community development programmes. During the 1970s, it was widely believed that governments used community development as a means of exerting political control over the population. David Brokensha and Peter Hodge (1969) have shown that community development programmes were indeed promoted by some governments to contain communism and combat insurgency. Community development has also been perceived as a way of reducing discontent in rural areas. As Ignacio Cosio argues, this motive characterized the Mexican community development programme which offered 'concessions which do not tackle the underlying causes of backwardness and poverty' (1981: 350).

Other writers do not impugn conspiratorial motives to governments but nevertheless claim that community development became a means of imposing central government policies and programmes on local people. Although community development is based on the belief that people themselves should determine the nature and pace of development, they claim that most community development programmes impose government policies on the community. Reviewing *animation rurale* in African francophone developing countries, David Gow and Jerry VanSant (1983) note that these programmes are incompatible with the centralized administrative tradition which the francophone nations inherited from the French. They are, in fact, a mechanism for implementing central government directives. Samuel Mushi (1981) reached a similar conclusion about the Tanzanian *ujamaa* programme. Although it was supposed to foster local decision making, cooperation and participation, it had really become an arm of central government administration.

It was in this climate that the alternative community action or community participation approach emerged. Unlike community development, this approach is overtly anti-statist, rejecting government sponsorship of local development and calling instead for the empowerment of local people. Instead of depending on governments to provide much-needed technical expertise and resources, proponents of the community action approach urge local people to take full control over community development activities and rely on their own initiative. In addition, they encourage local people to adopt an adversarial approach towards government. Instead of being the passive recipients of government aid, local people should politicize their activities and actively organize to demand the services to which they are entitled.

The radicalized community participation approach became popular in social development circles in the 1970s and 1980s, but it had older roots. Some community activists drew inspiration from the Marxist and Maoist revolutionary tradition. Arguing that capitalism was to blame for the problems of poverty and deprivation in the Third World, they claimed that community action would mobilize the masses, result in the overthrow of capitalism and create popular institutions such as the commune which would ensure the well-being of all its members.

While many community activists are inspired by revolutionary ideas, the community action approach owes more to radical populism than socialism. Much of the literature reflects the ideas of the American community worker, Saul Alinsky (1946, 1971), who had organized successful community action campaigns in Chicago and whose writings had been widely disseminated. Many proponents of community action are also inspired by the work of the Brazilian writer, Paulo Freire (1972), whose theory of *conscientization* offers practical proposals for raising the political awareness of poor people and for organizing them to take control of their own affairs. Armed with these ideas, proponents of community action have sought to transform community development into a more politicized and activist approach.

However, community participation shares many similarities with conventional community development. Like community development, community participation relies on trained workers who are responsible for motivating local people to participate in development projects and for teaching them the tactics of community action. However, unlike community development personnel, community action workers are overtly activist and they emphasize the importance of political action, confrontation and campaigning in reaching community goals. For this reason, terms such as 'organizers', 'change agents', 'conscientizers' or *animateurs* are preferred.

Unlike community development, the community action approach attempts to target the poorest and most powerless groups. While community development works through existing power structures, community action seeks to bypass the local elite and empower the impoverished. However, the proponents of community action claim that, as a result of years of oppression and deprivation, the poor are fearful, apathetic or indifferent and that they may be reluctant to participate. For this reason, it is necessary to raise self-awareness of their condition. Conscientization is, therefore, a major component of community participation. As Marie Hollnsteiner notes, community organizers seek to make local people 'aware of their life situation, why it is so and what alternatives they have or can create to redress its deficiencies' (1982: 48). This often involves the use of confrontational tactics: as Hollnsteiner comments, organizers must persuade, suggest, challenge, analyse and agitate.

Conscientization results in a greater desire to address the inequalities and oppressive conditions which cause poverty and deprivation. Successful conscientization fosters the emergence of local institutions and organizations that can campaign for improved conditions. Mass meetings, group discussions and similar activities that enhance participation are essential elements of the 'community building' process. Although community participation seeks to strengthen community leadership, leaders are held accountable and are required to consult regularly with the rank and file. The local organizations that emerge from community building efforts also help to establish links with progressive development agencies in the non-governmental sector and with political movements that support their endeavours. Together they form an alliance that challenges government and agitates for improved services. The process of building effective local organizations is facilitated by adopting particular projects which have a high probability of success. Success promotes further community involvement and strengthens resolve for future activities.

Although community action is ostensibly anti-statist, it has been championed by the international agencies and by many governments as well. Indeed, as was noted in chapter 2, the United Nations became an active supporter of community participation after its unified social planning approach had been subjected to criticism in the 1970s (1971b, 1975). UNICEF, the United Nations Children's Fund, has been particularly enthusiastic about community participation and has made it a key component of its maternal and child health programmes. The agency has shown that the community action approach has been very successful in reaching women and in helping them to organize to improve their health and that of their children (UNICEF, 1982).

The proponents of community action claim that local communities can effectively organize to identify and implement programmes that enhance their economic and social well-being. While community action often results in the adoption of similar economic and social development projects that are like those prescribed by the proponents of community development, its advocates believe that community action is a far more effective means for attaining social development goals. While community development imposes them from above, often with government resources, community action fosters their emergence from within. This permits community ownership, maximum participation and more enduring achievements. However, while many proponents of community action sincerely believe that their approach can introduce significant social change, Midgley and his colleagues (1986) have argued that this belief is based more on rhetoric and ideological commitment than a careful analysis of the effectiveness of different forms of community involvement.

Women, Gender and Social Development
Social scientists have long been interested in the way different societies define the roles of men and women. The term 'gender' is widely used in social science circles to connote these culturally determined roles. Gender relates not to sexual characteristics but to the social distinctions based on these characteristics. As anthropologists and sociologists have shown, there are enormous variations in the roles of men and women in different societies (Mead, 1962; Oakley, 1972).

These variations are particularly marked when the work men and women perform in different societies is compared (Murdoch, 1937).

Despite these variations, gender roles are seldom egalitarian. There are exceptions, but in most societies the division of labour by gender is highly differentiated and unequal. In many societies, the division of labour is related to the phenomenon of domestication. As Barbara Rogers (1980) points out, the dominance of patriarchal ideology in many cultures relegates women to play the gender role of mother, housewife and nurturer. This role is not only arduous, monotonous and devoid of satisfaction but, Rogers argues, inferior to the gender roles of men. Indeed, domestication is accompanied by discrimination not only in the domestic sphere but in the wider society as well. Educational opportunities for women are restricted on the grounds that education is wasted on girls whose future lies in bearing and rearing children, and in providing comfortable homes for their husbands. Similarly, employment opportunities are limited because women are not expected to seek work in the labour market. Women who do find employment in the labour market are often compelled to work in low-wage, exploitative conditions. In addition, culturally determined gender roles restrict women's freedom, choices and rights. In many societies today, women are denied freedom, discriminated against and oppressed simply because they are women.

In view of institutionalized discrimination against women, it is not surprising that women have long been neglected in development. As Rogers points out, women are seldom employed in government development agencies or in international organizations concerned with development issues. Development policies, plans and projects have conventionally been designed to serve the interests of men, and have seldom recognized the existence of women let alone their special needs and insights. The patriachal structures which exist in many cultures have, therefore, been reinforced by development strategies. This omission not only neglects women but has contributed to a deterioration in their living standards. Julia Cleves Mosse (1993) reports that global recession and the harsh effects of structural adjustment policies have had an especially deleterious effect on the incomes of poor women and their families. As was suggested in the introduction to this book, the disadvantaged position of women in many societies and communities today is a major manifestation of distorted development or as Vandana Shiva (1989) puts it, of 'maldevelopment'.

Attempts to address the situation of women in the context of development have gained momentum in recent years. One of the first to initiate a discussion of these issues was Ester Boserup (1970) whose pioneering work drew attention to the paradoxical fact that women, and particularly rural women, made a major contribution to development while deriving few benefits from development effort. Contrary to stereotypic beliefs, women were actively engaged in productive labour in agriculture and related activities. However, this fact was ignored by development experts who formulated economic models that focused on the deployment of male labour and designed development projects that would bring benefits primarily to men.

Boserup's critique had a major effect in drawing attention to the role of women in development. As Heleen van den Hombergh (1993) pointed out, Boserup's writing facilitated a greater awareness in the international development agencies of the need to recognize the role of women in development. Her work contributed directly to the decision to mark 1975 as the International Women's Year and to declare 1975 to 1985 as the United Nations Decade for Women. However, while these events undoubtedly heightened awareness of the need to integrate women in development, they did not bring about greater equalities for women (van den Hombergh, 1993).

Caroline Moser (1989) has reviewed the various approaches which have emerged over the years to address gender issues in development. The first approach, which she calls the *welfare approach*, views women as passive recipients of special development programmes designed to address their needs as mothers and homemakers. In many developing countries, Ministries of Social Welfare have established women's programmes to promote domestic activities or otherwise provided maternal and child welfare services to help women in need. The second approach, the *equity approach*, seeks to enhance the status of women and foster greater equality with men through access to employment, equal pay and greater opportunities. However, this approach has not been very successful in developing countries partly because it is viewed as threatening and an inappropriate import of Western feminist ideas. The third approach is called the *anti-poverty approach* because it seeks to foster productive self-employment among low-income women. This approach defines the low position of women as a consequence of economic underdevelopment and not as a result of subjugation. By creating small-scale income-generating projects among poor women, it suggests that women can enhance their status through economic development. The fourth approach is known as the *efficiency approach* because it seeks to enhance the involvement of women in development on the ground that women are a useful productive resource for economic growth. It encourages the participation of women in development because of the positive contribution they can make to development. The final approach, known as the *empowerment* approach, has been articulated by women themselves. It attributes women's subjugation not only to patriachy but to imperialism and neo-colonialism. It contends that the position of women can only improve when women become self-reliant and exercise full control over decisions that affect their lives. To achieve this objective, women must mobilize through a bottom-up strategy of campaigning and organizing. To be fully empowered, they must collectively oppose all forces that perpetuate their oppression.

For obvious reasons, this last approach has had enormous appeal among women's groups and among organizations that seek to enhance the status of women. One group that has attracted international attention for its efforts to promote the empowerment approach is DAWN (Development Alternatives with Women for a New Era). DAWN was established just prior to the World Conference of Women which was held in Nairobi in 1985. As Moser reports, the organization has adopted both long-term and short-term strategies. Long-term strategies seek to change laws and civil codes that negatively affect women, modify discriminatory property rights and change cultural institutions that support male dominance of society. Short-term strategies seek to increase women's ownership of economic productive activities through self-employment and women's cooperatives, enhance educational opportunities for women and increase the productive capacity of women who derive their livelihood from agriculture.

The empowerment approach advocated by DAWN has been adopted by many local women's groups and organizations throughout the world. As Moser suggests, these groups have used various strategies to further their aims but, of these, organizing and social action have been the most popular. Moser reports that Gabriella, an alliance of women's groups in the Philippines, has been successful in securing national attention for its campaigns for increased rights. In Bombay, women's groups have organized effectively for improved housing conditions, for changes to inheritance laws and for decisive government action against rape and bride burning. In Ahmadabad, a group of low-income self-employed women have successfully organized to defend themselves against harassment and exploitation by middlemen and they have established a bank, several cooperatives, skills-training programmes and informal social security schemes. As Arline Prigoff (1992) reveals, women have successfully organized in many parts of the world to promote their well-being within the context of a gender-based approach to social development.

These and countless other women's groups around the world have effectively used techniques compatible with the communitarian approach to social development. They have adopted both community development and community action tactics to promote their aims and to enhance their solidarity as women. However, while their notion of a community may be derived from a common gender status, their goals are more wide-ranging. As DAWN's charter reveals, the organization seeks to create a world where 'inequality based on class, gender and race is absent from every country and from the relationships among countries' (Moser, 1989: 75). Ultimately, women may use their gender-based social development approach to create a community in which all are truly equal.

SOCIAL DEVELOPMENT BY GOVERNMENTS

The belief that social development can best be promoted by governments, their specialized agencies, policy makers, planners and administrators forms the basis of the *statist approach* to social development. Drawing on collectivist ideology, advocates of the statist strategy believe that the state embodies the interests of society as a whole and that it has a responsibility to promote the well-being of all citizens. Statists believe that government is collectively owned by its citizens and represents their interests. The state is, therefore, the ultimate collective.

However, statists recognize that governments do not always act in ways that do, in fact, promote the welfare of the people. They are not naively unaware of the way the power of the state has been used in the past (and is still used today) to oppress the masses. Nevertheless, they believe that many governments are committed to furthering the welfare of their citizens and that they are able to mobilize resources to achieve this goal. Governments also have the authority to ensure that social development policies are implemented, and that social and economic policies are harmonized.

The statist approach has played a critical role in development during this century. The idea that economic growth and social welfare can be fostered through government planning have been implemented in many countries. It has found expression in the Western liberal democracies, in the centrally planned communist countries and in the Third World. During this century, government intervention has increased significantly. Although vigorously attacked during the 1980s by the Radical Right, the idea that governments can promote positive social change has not been invalidated. Despite ideological opposition and budgetary cutbacks, many governments today continue to exercise responsibility for both economic and social development.

This section discusses the role of governments in promoting social development. It begins with an examination of the unified socio-economic development approach which was widely adopted in the developing countries in the 1970s. Then there is a review of the strategies that emphasize the redistribution of resources as a basic requirement for social development. There follows a consideration of the basic needs approach which charges governments with the responsibility of ensuring that the social needs of all citizens are met. Finally, the sustainable development approach which calls on governments to promote policies that protect the environment and safeguard the interests of future generations is discussed.

Promoting Social Development through Unified Planning

The contribution of planning to the emergence of social development was discussed at length earlier in this book. Planning gives expression to the idea of intervention, and it is a central notion in social development. Drawing on utopian ideas, and on sociological theories of 'guided' change, advocates of planning contend that social and economic processes can be directed through rational intervention to improve society. Planning was widely adopted after the Second World War in the newly independent developing countries where attempts to promote rapid economic growth and modernization were actively fostered by both governments and international agencies such as the United Nations. Proponents of modernization theory urge that all available resources be allocated to investment in industry and other modern enterprises and that consumption be deferred. They argue that social expenditures should be curtailed, and that the creation of a dynamic economy be given priority.

The advocacy of planning by the United Nations in the 1950s reflected this view. While the United Nations advocated the adoption of economic planning to foster rapid growth, it also promoted what James Midgley (1984d) has called a residualist approach to social welfare in which minimal government services catering to the needs of the most desperate sections of the population were created. This approach not only minimized government responsibility for social development, but fostered the compartmentalization of social policy from economic development.

The residualist approach was not, however, widely adopted. The nationalist governments of most developing countries were eager to expand the social services, believing that social programmes were an integral part of the process of becoming a modern society. Many allocated sizable resources to education and health. Social security, housing and social work services were also introduced, although on a smaller scale. The residualist approach was also criticized for failing to contribute to the overriding need for development. In the colonial period, welfare administrators had sought to identify social interventions that would support economic development initiatives. The emphasis on residualism contradicted this idea and viewed social welfare as a drain rather than a resource for progress. By the 1960s, as criticism of the residual approach intensified, the United Nations began to reassess its original approach.

The reassessment of the official United Nations' position on development was discussed earlier in this book, where it was shown that experts such as Gunnar Myrdal, Hans Singer and Benjamin Higgins urged the organization to adopt a new approach which transcended the narrow emphasis on economic growth and sought to integrate economic and social planning. This approach was known as *unified socio-economic development planning* and as was shown previously, the United Nations (1971a) adopted numerous resolutions on the subject which facilitated the spread of social planning among the organization's member states. It also facilitated much more research into social issues, encouraged the development of new approaches to social welfare in the context of development, and resulted in the identification of social indicators.

As Marshall Wolfe (1980) has shown, experts at the United Nations also began to question the economic planning models which were adopted in the 1950s. Most development plans at the time were exclusively concerned with economic factors such as investment, trade and the development of economic sectors. They seldom made reference to social conditions or to the emerging social sectors. The central planning agencies were exclusively staffed by economists who believed that social welfare would increase automatically as a result of employment creation. In the 1960s, these assumptions were increasingly criticized.

As a result of these developments, many Third World countries began during the 1970s to expand the scope of their central planning agencies to incorporate social planning. New divisions concerned with social sectoral planning were created, more sociologists, anthropologists and other social scientists were recruited to work closely with economic planners, and there was a new attempt to define development in social rather than narrow economic terms. Training courses for social planners were created both in the developing countries and at institutions of higher education in the industrial nations such as the London School of Economics (Hardiman and Midgley, 1980). Gradually, a new body of literature emerged to define the roles of social planners and to provide a conceptual basis for their work (Apthorpe, 1970; Conyers, 1982; Hardiman and Midgley, 1982, 1989; MacPherson, 1982).

During the 1970s, national plans began to define development in terms of reducing poverty and raising levels of living. Social indicators were increasingly used to complement economic indicators. Plans also began to include chapters dealing with sectoral fields such as education, health, rural development, housing and social work services. In some countries, social planners sought to identify the obstacles to improving people's welfare. While some were concerned about the social impediments to economic modernization such as traditionalism and population growth, others focused on the role of exploitation, wealth concentration and oppression in preventing progressive social change. Many were also committed to mobilizing investments for human capital formation. Based on the ideas of Gary Becker (1964), Frederick Harbison (1967, 1973), George Psacharopoulos (1973, 1981, 1992) and other writers, many economists began to accept that government investments in education, health and other social programmes foster economic growth. These ideas were widely used as a rationale for social sectoral planning. By the 1980s, considerable progress had been made in linking social and economic planning and promoting a unified approach to development.

During the late 1970s and 1980s, as a result of two major oil shocks and dramatic increases in global interest rates, many developing countries fell into debt, and many governments were compelled to seek additional aid to meet their credit obligations. This resulted in the imposition by international agencies such as the International Monetary Fund and the World Bank of 'conditionality' or structural adjustment policies. These policies sharply reduced government intervention in the economy, curtailed social expenditures and limited social planning. As a result, the social planning initiatives which were adopted in the 1970s have been impeded and, in some cases, discontinued.

However, some developing countries have managed to maintain their commitment to unified socio-economic planning. Central planning has not been universally abandoned and, in many countries, there has been a renewed commitment to social intervention. As the costs of structural adjustment have been recognized, some lending agencies have taken a softer approach and permitted the adoption of programmes that seek to reduce the worst excesses of conditionality. In 1990, the World Bank surprised many social development experts by publishing a comprehensive report on world poverty. Although the ideological approach used in this report was quite different from the one used by the World Bank in the 1970s, a commitment to poverty alleviation signalled a new concern with social issues. It suggests that social planning may again be accepted as a viable approach for promoting social development.

The unified approach to development planning requires that government economic and social plans be carefully harmonized. The unified approach gives equal emphasis to economic growth and social progress, and requires that economic and social planners share a common commitment to improving the well-being of the population. It requires that planners be properly trained for the task and that they acquire the technical expertise needed to formulate and implement effective social and economic policies. It also requires that governments make a commitment to promoting economic growth and fostering social welfare. It depends on state intervention, technical expertise and political will. While unified socio-economic planning may be criticized for being top-down and technocratic, current social and political conditions may well prove to be conducive to the revival of this approach and its adoption.

Although unified socio-economic planning was formulated with specific reference to the developing countries, it has relevance to the industrial nations as well. In most industrial countries, social policies are based on the social administration approach described in chapter 1, and social programmes are quite separate from economic development efforts. Often social policies are formulated without reference to economic policies even though they are dependent on the economy for funding. Part of the problem is that few industrial nations have centralized planning agencies which are responsible for both economic and social planning. For this reason, the unified approach has obvious relevance to the industrial nations.

Economic Growth, Welfare and Equality
The unified approach evolved out of a dissatisfaction with the economic models which characterized early development planning. The models assumed that growth would create large-scale employment, absorb labour into the modern sector, increase income and eventually eradicate poverty. Unified planning challenged this assumption. It claimed that growth is an insufficient basis for promoting social welfare. Accordingly, proponents of unified planning urged governments to set specific social goals for development, and to channel resources to the population through social plans that target low-income groups, expand education, health and other social programmes. Because unified planning requires that sizable government resources be allocated for the social sectors, it involves the redistribution of resources. However, the redistributive implications of the unified approach were not articulated.

By the 1970s, many advocates of a statist approach to social development began to draw attention to the issue of inequality. They claimed that the economic growth models which had been implemented in many developing countries had produced impressive results but that this had not eradicated poverty and deprivation. Rates of economic growth in most underdeveloped regions had indeed been high. Reviewing growth trends for 100 developing countries between 1960 and 1980, the World Bank (1982) found the great majority of these nations had recorded rates of GNP per capita growth in excess of 3 per cent per annum. Economists of very different political persuasions agreed that the developing countries had performed very well when judged by economic growth criteria. Peter Bauer (1976), a conservative economist, criticized the pessimistic attitude which characterized development economics at the time, pointing out that most developing countries had experienced rapid economic advance and material progress. The Marxist writer, Bill Warren agreed, claiming that growth had been 'outstandingly successful' (1980: 90). Similarly, the liberal economist, Michael Lipton, exclaimed that 'the past twenty five years has seen more growth in output per person than the previous twenty centuries' (1977: 29). However, despite these achievements, all recognized that poverty, hunger, homelessness and other social ills in Third World countries remained critical.

The fact that economic growth had not made a major impact on the problems of poverty and social deprivation convinced many social development experts that the benefits of growth had been unequally distributed. Economic growth, they claimed, had not raised the levels of living of the poorest groups but had instead enriched the business, political and administrative elite. Many agreed with the dependency writers who claimed that, despite decolonization, the developing countries were still being exploited by the industrial nations. Others noted that landowners, the rural upper class and those with traditional authority had benefited disproportionately from economic growth and that they continued to exploit the rural masses. Many felt that the unified approach did not deal adequately with these problems. Some drew attention to the fact that social investments were being concentrated in urban areas and that the poorest groups were simply not being reached by the expanded social programmes which had been introduced.

In the 1970s, some writers began to argue that development planners needed to address the problem of inequality directly. Gunnar Myrdal (1970) was a major proponent of the new emphasis on egalitarian development, claiming that entrenched inequalities were an impediment to economic modernization. Dudley Seers (1972) criticized conventional growth models of development, arguing that the problem of poverty could not be resolved through economic growth alone. In 1974, the results of a major study which specifically addressed the issue of redistribution and economic growth were published. The study was undertaken jointly by senior World Bank staff and academics at the Institute of Development Studies at the University of Sussex (Chenery et al., 1974). It dealt with the question of whether growth and equality are antithetical objectives. The authors rejected the claim that growth and equity are incompatible and argued that it is possible for governments to promote economic growth while at the same ensuring that the resources generated by economic growth are equitably distributed. Developing new economic planning models, they proposed a variety of policies and programmes that would specifically reduce inequality and direct resources to the poorest groups.

Developing these ideas, Keith Griffin (1976, 1978; Griffin and James,

1981) contends that progressive governments need to implement redistributive policies expeditiously to counter the entrenched interests of elites who oppose egalitarian social change. Griffin (1976) is particularly concerned about the perpetuation of feudal structures and the concentration of land ownership in many Third World countries and believes that this problem has to be dealt with through radical means. Michael Lipton (1977) has focused attention on the urban–rural imbalance, arguing that urban bias represents the most blatant and severe form of inequality in the Third World. More recently, the oppression of women has become an important concern among proponents of an egalitarian approach to social development. As was noted previously, many feminist writers have shown that the oppression of women is not only morally abhorrent but a major impediment to progressive social change (Moser, 1989; Shiva, 1989).

A variety of proposals have been formulated to address the problem of inequality in development. These include the adoption of more progressive taxation policies that can mobilize resources to fund services for low-income groups as well as the removal of regressive measures that place an unfair burden on the poor. Many proponents of egalitarian development have called on Third World governments to reduce their excessively large military budgets and wasteful expenditures on conspicuous monuments, conference centres, sports complexes and other symbols of national prestige that bring few benefits to ordinary people.

Others egalitarian writers have urged governments to increase spending on social services and to address the educational, health and other social needs of the population. Many have argued for investments in infrastructure that enhance the productive capacities of the poor. Some have stressed the need for measures that deal with the structural conditions that perpetuate inequality and oppression. These structural conditions include land concentration and feudal systems of production which survive in many rural areas in the Third World. Also relevant are entrenched religious, ethnic and class-based systems of oppression which stifle initiative and development. They also include marked urban–rural and regional differentials in access to resources, and the exclusion of women and other groups from participation in political life. If economic development is to benefit the population as a whole, these problems must be dealt with.

Proponents of egalitarian development are acutely aware that political factors are of critical significance if their approach is to be effectively implemented. They acknowledge that few governments will enthusiastically embrace an egalitarian approach, and they recognize that those that do will face determined opposition from entrenched domestic as well as international interests opposed to progressive social change. Indeed, with the ascendancy of the Radical Right in the 1980s, the weakening of the Third World in geopolitical affairs, and the fall of Soviet and Eastern European communism, the influence of the egalitarian approach has declined significantly. Whether the egalitarian approach continues to exert influence in social development circles remains to be seen. Nevertheless, as inequalities have become more marked and as social conditions have deteriorated, its insights remain highly relevant today.

Social Welfare and Basic Needs
The concern with equality in social development circles in the 1970s was not universally shared. While some experts were sceptical about the possibility of governments implementing an egalitarian social development strategy, others questioned the need for a strategy of this kind. Some such as Paul Streeten (Streeten et al., 1981) have argued that it is more important for governments to address the basic problems of poverty and deprivation in developing countries than to redistribute resources. These writers also claim that there is simply not enough wealth to be redistributed. Because the incidence of poverty is so great, redistributing the income of the rich will not make much difference to the incomes of the poor. Others argue that an egalitarian social development strategy will have a negative effect on economic growth. They reject the econometric models of the Redistribution with Growth theorists which had claimed that the apparently antithetical goals of growth and redistribution could be harmonized. Instead, they argue that a trade-off between growth and equity is inevitable, and that an egalitarian development strategy will retard growth and harm the poor (Friedman, 1962; Bauer, 1976).

It was in this climate that the basic needs approach emerged. Its proponents agree that economic growth of itself will not eradicate mass poverty in developing countries, and they are sceptical of conventional economic models that stress the role of wage employment in raising levels of living. While these models accurately describe the economic transformation of the Western industrial nations, they do not fit the circumstances of Third World societies. Indeed, despite rapid rates of economic growth, jobs are not being created on a sufficient scale to absorb labour from the subsistence sector. In addition, while wage employment in the modern sector is regarded by many economic planners as the goal of development, the rapid growth of an urban informal sector of self-employed workers in many developing countries suggests that conventional economic development models need to be re-examined. The problem of employment and labour utilization is of particular interest to the International Labour Organization which championed the basic needs approach in the 1970s.

As was shown earlier in this chapter, the International Labour Organization began in the 1960s to question the viability of employment creation strategies in developing countries. After undertaking detailed studies in three developing countries, the organization's World Employment Programme concluded that the prospects of creating full employment along the lines suggested by modernization theorists was limited (Plant, 1983). Instead, the organization urged governments to support informal sector self-employment, and take steps to raise levels of living for the population through expanding the social services and raising the productive capacities of the poor. This latter recommendation evolved into the basic needs approach.

The basic needs approach was formally adopted at the ILO's World Employment Conference in Geneva in 1976 (International Labour Office, 1976, 1979; Ghai et al., 1977). Attended by representatives from 121 countries, the conference agreed that the problems of poverty and deprivation in Third World countries required immediate solutions. While the goal of full employment was a desirable one, it was unlikely to be achieved in the foreseeable future. It was, therefore, more important for governments to address the problem of poverty directly rather than waiting for poverty to be resolved through the expansion of employment. Instead of hoping that economic growth would eventually create sufficient employment to eradicate social deprivation, governments should adopt measures to meet the immediate basic needs of their citizens.

The basic needs approach urges governments to use their existing social planning and human service programmes to address the pressing unmet needs of the poorest groups in developing countries. These unmet needs consist, first, of basic survival needs such as those for nutrition, safe drinking water and shelter. A second group of needs are not necessary for bare survival but are regarded as social rights which society guarantees for all citizens. They include the need for education, health care and social security. Finally, there are non-material needs such as the need to participate in the political process, to be protected against discrimination and to have equal opportunities for advancement.

Although the proponents of basic needs recognize that there are great differences among countries in the extent to which these various needs have already been met, they stress the importance of ensuring that at least the basic survival needs of all people are satisfied in the near future. Paul Streeten and Shahid Burki (1978) estimated that the basic survival needs of about 1,200 million of the world's people had still not been met. While considerable progress had been made, the problems of hunger, inadequate shelter and unsafe drinking water remained critical. They estimated that about 50 per cent of the world's poor had insufficient daily calorie intake; about two thirds had insufficient daily protein intake and approximately the same proportion had no access to safe drinking water. About 42 per cent lived in homes that were unsafe or inadequate. Given the extent of the problem, they urged governments to take immediate steps to address the basic needs of these extremely poor people.

The adoption of the basic needs strategy involves a number of policies and programmes. First, governments should undertake needs assessment studies to determine which needs are the most pressing, and to prioritize basic needs strategies. Second, basic needs requires the identification of target groups. Proponents of the basic needs approach believe in targeting resources to the most needy sections of the population rather than saturating the whole population with services. By targeting specific interventions on needy groups or on geographic areas, proponents of basic needs seek to remedy the tendency for existing social services to cater disproportionately for urban dwellers and those who are relatively well off. Third, basic needs involves the development of specific programmes that are low cost, appropriate to local conditions and participatory in that they involve needy people in the delivery as well as the consumption of services. In many developing countries, social services have been based on a Western model which is both expensive and ineffective. These programmes need to be modified to fit local conditions. In addition, if services are to reach a large number of poor people, costs have to be reduced. This can be done by involving local people in the design and delivery of services. Involving people in these programmes would also enhance uptake and the responsiveness of local communities to new social programmes. Finally, basic needs requires a firm commitment from national leaders, planners and administrators as well as the international agencies and Western governments if it is to be successful.

Streeten and Burki's 1978 estimates of the cost of implementing a basic needs strategy concluded that between US $30 billion and US $40 billion per year would be needed to create the infrastructure and meet the recurrent costs of delivering a bundle of basic needs services (including nutrition, water and sanitation, housing, health care and education) to the poorest developing countries between 1980 and the year 2000. This represents between 12 per cent and 16 per cent of their average GNP and between 85 per cent and 110 per cent of all their public revenues. As these estimates reveal, the poorest developing countries cannot meet their own basic needs without substantial external aid.

As was noted previously, the oil shocks, increasing indebtedness and the rise of the Radical Right in the late 1970s and 1980s severely impeded the implementation of statist social development strategies such as basic needs in the developing countries. As many developing countries were compelled to adopt structural adjustment policies and severely reduce their social expenditures, programmes designed to meet basic needs were abandoned (Stewart, 1985). Instead of helping to fund a comprehensive basic needs strategy, Western financial institutions and governments extracted even more resources from the Third World. By the mid-1980s, aid flows to the developing world had fallen significantly, reducing the prospect of funding a basic needs approach at an adequate level. It is not surprising that social conditions in many developing countries, particularly in Africa, Latin America and low-income Asian nations, deteriorated at this time.

On the other hand, the basic needs approach has been widely accepted as a potentially effective means of promoting social development in the poorest nations. The idea of targeting resources on the poor by focusing on low-income areas has gained widespread support. The need to modify social services programmes to fit local needs and conditions has also been accepted. Despite the negative influence of conditionality policies, some international agencies such as the World Health Organization and UNICEF have promoted basic needs within particular social sectors. The advocacy of primary health care and the focus on maternal and infant health by UNICEF have resulted in the widespread adoption of specific strategies which have produced significant results in many low-income countries. The successful implementation of these strategies suggests that the basic needs approach is workable. Hopefully, current changes in the international political and economic climate will result in its future adoption and enhance the levels of living of the poorest groups.

Sustainable Development
Although there can be little doubt that economic growth produced spectacular results in the developing countries in the decades following the Second World War, some began to question the importance accorded to growth in development circles. As was noted earlier, economists such as Gunnar Myrdal (1970) argued for a redefinition of development that took social factors into account and it was through his involvement with the United Nations that unified socioeconomic planning was widely adopted. Others writers such as Edward Mishan (1967) argued that the relentless pursuit of economic growth in the industrial countries had generated costs which were detrimental to society as a whole. Some such as Ernst Schumacher (1974) criticized the emphasis on industrialization in development policy and urged the adoption of a 'people-friendly' approach which mitigated the dehumanization that accompanied large-scale development. Some writers such as Barbara Ward and René Dubos (1972) stressed the negative impact of a high-growth economic development

strategy on the physical environment. Echoing a growing public awareness of the problems of pollution and environmental degradation, they argued that the relentless pursuit of economic growth creates severe environmental problems. Perhaps the most comprehensive statement on this issue was a report published by a group of experts at the Massachusetts Institute of Technology for the Club of Rome (Meadows et al., 1972). The report warned that unless steps were taken to manage the process of development, control population and limit the impact of economic growth on the environment, there would be serious consequences for all humankind.

Since the 1970s, awareness of global environmental problems has increased significantly and there is a greater appreciation of the need for government action to limit the effects of pollution, erosion, deforestation, the destruction of species and other forms of ecological damage. As in many other fields, the United Nations has played an important role in fostering an awareness of these issues. The 1972 Stockholm Conference on the Human Environment and the creation of the United Nations Environment Programme resulted in the adoption of many conventions and treaties by member states which have addressed environmental concerns. This has, in turn, heightened awareness of the need for action. Many development plans have introduced policies to respond to environmental problems, and there has been an increasing awareness of the importance of incorporating specific programmes to protect the environment in development projects. Social forestry and community-based environmental projects have begun to feature much more prominently in government development programmes. This has facilitated a greater concern for the environment in development circles.

A concern for the environment also began to emerge as an important theme in development debates that were not primarily concerned with environmental problems. Instead of compartmentalizing environmental issues, discussions on development began to integrate development and ecological issues. This resulted initially in the formulation of the *ecodevelopment approach* (Farvar and Glaeser, 1979; Sachs, 1980; Glaeser, 1984) which subsequently fostered the emergence of the concept of sustainable development. Although the idea of sustainable development deals explicitly with environmental issues, it seeks to link these issues to other critical development concerns such as economic growth, urbanization and population.

Michael Redclift (1987) points out that the concept of sustainability has long been used in forestry and agriculture to describe efforts to replenish natural resources through careful resource management. Although the term appeared in several reports and publications dealing with economic and social questions during the 1970s, it was formally adopted and popularized by the Brundtland Commission in the 1980s. The Brundtland Commission (officially known as the World Commission on Environment and Development) was appointed by the United Nations in 1983 under the leadership of Mrs Gro Harlem Brundtland, the Prime Minister of Norway, to examine the relationship between the environment and economic and social development. The Commission consisted of twenty-two members and held public hearings in different parts of the world. It published its findings in 1987 (World Commission on Environment and Development, 1987), and urged the adoption of *sustainable development* as a new development strategy.

As defined by the Brundtland report, proponents of sustainable development urge that all development activities seek to meet current human needs without compromising the ability of future generations to meet their own needs. Sustainable development is, therefore, development that lasts and ensures that the interests of the next generation are secured (World Bank, 1992: 34). Defined specifically in an ecological context, sustainable development creates a process that ensures that natural resources are replenished, and that future generations continue to have the resources they need to meet their own needs. This approach to development invites people to make use of the earth's resources but to ensure that future generations continue to have access to these resources.

The successful adoption of sustainable development requires that governments make a definite commitment to protecting the environment and, at the same time, commit themselves to promoting the well-being of their citizens. Proponents of sustainable development emphasize that they are equally concerned with the welfare of people and the protection of the environment. They are also concerned with population issues, the eradication of poverty and the promotion of appropriate social services programmes.

While sustainable development is environmentally sensitive, it is not narrowly concerned with environmental protection. In many poor countries, the introduction of punitive environmental regulations cannot be enforced because they would harm the livelihood of millions of ordinary people and, if enforced, would simply punish the weakest sections of the population. For this reason, governments need to formulate policies and programmes that promote the economic and social welfare of the population in ways that do not harm the environment. On the other hand, governments should take immediate steps to regulate polluting industries and other large-scale economic projects that cause environmental damage. They should incorporate appropriate regulatory policies and ensure that their development plans are more environmentally sensitive. They should also link environmental policies to local development initiatives through expanding environmental education, creating incentives and promoting a sense of ownership of environmental resources.

Although the concept of sustainable development has indeed been popularized in development circles, the claim by some of its proponents that it forms a new 'development paradigm' can be questioned. Despite its wider concern about poverty, population growth and related social issues, it is substantially focused on the environment, and emphasizes the importance of ecological considerations in development. It is still poorly defined and requires more theoretical refinement if it is to serve as a unifying development concept (Estes, 1993). On the other hand, its advocacy of environmental issues is critically important and forms a key element of an integrated approach to development which harmonizes economic and social perspectives.

5
Achieving Social Development: The Institutional Perspective

The primary purpose of this book has been to provide a comprehensive overview of the field of social development. It has offered a definition of social development within the framework of different approaches for promoting human welfare, traced the history of social development, examined key theoretical debates in social development and described the major social development strategies. The book has also shown that there are wide differences of opinion on many social development questions. Social development has been defined in different ways in different disciplines; different people and groups of people with different interests have contributed to the historical evolution of social development; theoretical issues are approached from different points of view; and different social development strategies have been formulated.

While this book has sought to provide a broad overview of the field, it will not confine itself to surveying the subject but will seek to integrate the material by offering its own strategic view of social development. This final chapter will attempt to formulate a coherent strategic approach to social development which seeks to combine the diverse strategies discussed earlier. Although it is unlikely that its attempt at a synthesis will be universally accepted, it articulates an approach to social development which will be called the *institutional perspective* and which, it will be argued, offers a workable set of prescriptions for promoting social development goals.

The institutional perspective seeks to mobilize diverse social institutions including the market, community and state to promote people's welfare. It is inspired by an ideological position that accommodates diverse beliefs and by social science theories that harmonize different social development approaches. It contends that the social development strategies discussed in the previous chapter are not mutually exclusive, but that they can be integrated to promote the attainment of social development goals in conjunction with a dynamic process of economic development. However, it will be argued that governments must play a leading role in harmonizing these different strategies and in managing social development effort. For this reason, the institutional perspective is characterized by an activist administrative style known as *managed pluralism*.

The chapter begins by describing the features of the institutional perspective, and by tracing the ideological and theoretical ideas on which it is based. It then considers how the institutional perspective can be implemented. It pays particular attention to the organizational arrangements needed to implement the institutional perspective, and examines ways in which economic and social policies can be linked within specific socio-spatial contexts. Finally, the chapter presents some illustrative examples of the successful implementation of an institutional social development perspective. It shows that it is possible to harmonize diverse strategic approaches to social development within the context of wider efforts to promote development. Although the institutional perspective is articulated in this chapter, it will become clear that it has already informed the previous chapters, and particularly the definition of social development provided in chapter 1.

THE INSTITUTIONAL PERSPECTIVE

As noted earlier, the institutional perspective contends that different social institutions including the state, market and community can be mobilized to promote the attainment of social development goals. It argues that the different strategic approaches to social development discussed in the previous chapter rely on only one of these institutions and that they do not, therefore, utilize the full range of possible interventions conducive to human well-being. Proponents of the institutional approach believe that these strategies should not be regarded as competing but as compatible. They seek to harmonize these different strategies and facilitate their implementation in ways that are compatible rather than competitive. The institutional perspective may be seen, therefore, as a strategic approach that seeks to combine the different social development interventions discussed in the previous chapter.

To foster the synthesis of these different strategies, the institutional perspective requires that governments play an active role in managing and coordinating the implementation of strategies. Governments should actively direct the process of social development in ways that maximize the participation of communities, the market and individuals. In addition to facilitating and directing social development, governments should also contribute directly to social development through a variety of public sector policies and programmes.

The institutional perspective requires the creation of formal organizations that can assume responsibility for managing social development effort and harmonizing the implementation of different strategic approaches. These organizations exist at different levels but they should ultimately be coordinated at the national level. They also make extensive use of specialist personnel who have the training and skills to foster the achievement of social development goals.

The institutional perspective draws on an ideological position that promotes pluralism and accommodates diverse beliefs. It is also inspired by the theoretical ideas of social scientists who have argued for a 'middle-way' compromise between the different ideological polarities of Western political thought. Their work has resulted in the emergence of established conceptual approaches in the social sciences such as Keynesianism, welfarism and institutionalism. It is this last term, which is associated with the work of Thorstein Veblen, Richard Titmuss and Gunnar Myrdal, that will be used in this book to connote an attempt to synthesize diverse approaches to social development and foster a coherent conception for achieving social development goals.

Ideological Roots of Institutionalism
The institutional perspective is based on an ideological position that transcends the major ideologies in Western political thought. Instead of asserting the value of only one belief system, it advocates tolerance for other positions and seeks to accommodate their diverse insights. The institutional position, therefore, recognizes that different ideologies have validity, and that their diverse insights can be harmonized.

The institutional perspective in social development has its roots in attempts to promote the toleration and coexistence of different beliefs. In modern Europe, this idea can be traced back to the Renaissance when scholars such as Sir Thomas More and Desiderius Erasmus first pleaded for religious tolerance. Indeed, as D. J. Manning notes, More's *Utopia* not only permitted people to hold and express their religious beliefs but allowed them to try and convert others to their opinions provided they did so 'peaceably, gently, quietly and soberly, without lusty and contentious rebuking and inveighing against others' (1976: 35).

In time, the notion of religious toleration evolved into proposals for the toleration of diverse political ideas. The writings of John Milton, John Locke and Voltaire, as well as the cataclysmic upheavals of the English civil war, the French and American revolutions, and the Napoleonic wars all shook the feudal foundations of Europe and fostered the articulation and expression of new political beliefs. It was during the nineteenth century that the notion of political pluralism gained support. Although disliked by those in power and imperfectly implemented, the idea that rationally articulated political beliefs should compete for electoral advantage was gradually accepted, and today forms the basis for modern democratic political systems. Ideological pluralism also paved the way in the nineteenth century for the emergence of political beliefs that sought to reconcile the extremes of unfettered capitalism and totalitarian socialism. These centrist ideologies have informed the institutional perspective.

Attempts to reconcile *laissez-faire* liberalism and revolutionary socialism began when factions within the socialist and liberal movements sought to formulate a compromise between these two polar positions. In Britain, progressive members of the Liberal Party such as Joseph Chamberlain campaigned for free public schools, for easing the harsh provisions of the Poor Laws and for increased rights for workers. Similar policies were proposed by the leaders of the Progressive and Populist Parties in the United States. In Europe, many socialists accepted the concept of pluralism and used the electoral process to campaign for greater government control of the economy. In Britain, the Fabians adopted the strategies of gradualism, permeation and persuasion to promote socialist goals. However, those who advocated a compromise position were under constant attack and some were vilified as traitors to their cause. Lenin maligned the Fabians and, in Germany, Eduard Bernstein's democratic ideas were furiously assailed by Rosa Luxemburg and others in the mainstream Marxist movement for abandoning the necessity of revolution.

Nevertheless, within both the liberal and the socialist movements, conciliatory groups became more influential. The New Liberals emerged within the liberal camp to promote greater government involvement in social affairs. In the socialist movement, democratic socialists successfully argued for the pursuit of socialist goals through electoral rather than revolutionary means. By the 1950s, many believed that a workable ideological comprise had been forged and the notion of ideological convergence gained popularity. However, despite the claims of writers such as Daniel Bell (1960) and Francis Fukuyama (1992), the notion of ideological convergence remains controversial. Nevertheless, the emergence of a centrist position which combines the insights of capitalist and socialist ideology within the framework of a pluralist political system has validity and inspires the institutional perspective in social development.

Theoretical Origins of the Institutional Approach
The articulation of a centrist ideological position in Western political thought facilitated the formulation of social science theories that embody a compromise position between *laissez-faire* capitalism and communism. Scholars who articulated these theories are closely aligned with political groups at the centre of the ideological spectrum, but their writings transcend ideology and offer more sophisticated theoretical accounts conducive to the formulation of practical policies and programmes.

The term 'institutionalism' is primarily associated with the work of the American economist, Thorstein Veblen, who was one of the first to attack the claim of neo-classical economists that the market is the only viable institutional mechanism for achieving prosperity. Veblen rejected this view and drew attention to wider social motives and forces in society that shape economic behaviour. He contended that the pursuit of economic interest is only one of many factors that influence human motives. He believed that the values and wider institutions of society are as important as the market in determining economic behaviour. It is Veblen's emphasis on wider social institutions rather than narrow economic considerations that led to the use of the term 'institutionalism' to describe his ideas.

Veblen attacked the *laissez-faire* beliefs of his time and was an unrepentant critic of big business. His most famous book, *The Theory of the Leisure Class* (1899), derided the values and lifestyle of the business community, and introduced stock phrases such as 'conspicuous consumption' and 'captains of industry' into the English language. This book reveals Veblen's debt to Marx but unlike Marxists he did not advocate revolutionary action. Instead, Veblen favoured a technocratic approach by which expertise could be harnessed to serve wider social interests. Although he did not go as far as the Fabians in advocating technocratic government, his sympathies were clearly in that direction.

Veblen's writings were not well received in academic circles in the United States. However, they inspired many younger economists who later helped to formulate the policies of the New Deal. In the United States, the institutional approach is today associated with John Kenneth Galbraith who is probably Veblen's best known successor. Galbraith's many books have reiterated the interventionist critique of *laissez-faire* liberalism, exposed the power of large corporations and decried the poverty and squalor that continue to coexist side by side with affluence and prosperity (as in Galbraith, 1958).

The institutional approach has also been influenced by the work of John Dewey and William James. Dewey and James were advocates of a philosophical approach known as pragmatism. Pragmatism emphasizes an empiricist approach to knowledge. This approach is based on the idea that human beings do not know the world passively by absorbing information through their senses but that they test the veracity of acquired knowledge through experience. Pragmatism fosters a practical and flexible approach which contrasts sharply with the more dogmatic theoretical positions of *laissez-faire* liberalism and Marxism. Pragmatism appealed to the Fabians and inspired their empiricism. The Fabians and other European democratic socialist organizations believed strongly in the need to collect and use factual data to support their political campaigns.

Another influence on the emergence of the institutional approach is the solidaristic theories of the French sociologist, Emile Durkheim, who criticized the extreme individualism of the late nineteenth century and argued for measures that enhance feelings of belonging and interdependence. Durkheim believed that modern societies are characterized by a decline in solidarity and that this creates feelings of anomie and alienation. He urged that social institutions that foster integration should be encouraged. As will be shown, this idea is powerfully restated in the writings of R. H. Tawney and Richard Titmuss, leading proponents of the institutional approach.

Veblen's work shares similarities with the writings of John Maynard Keynes who is not, of course, known as an institutionalist but whose name is today used eponymously to describe his theories and those of his followers. Unlike Veblen, Keynes was less concerned with criticizing capitalism than with moderating the excesses of the capitalist system. However, Keynes challenged the orthodoxy of *laissez-faire* economics, rejecting the idea that the economy is a self-regulating system. He argued that government should intervene to manage demand and thus to maintain high employment and steady incomes. Keynes did not believe that the state should nationalize the economy or introduce centralized Soviet-style economic planning. Instead, his 'middle way' called for indirect planning through fiscal and monetary control as well as a judicious programme of public works.

Although Keynes's writings influenced the creation of the welfare state, the rise of welfarism is usually associated with William Beveridge who was responsible for preparing proposals for the introduction of comprehensive social services in Britain after the Second World War. As was shown in chapter 3, the recommendations of the Beveridge report were generally adopted after the war and resulted in the creation of comprehensive health care, social security, education and housing programmes.

Both Keynes and Beveridge were members of the British Liberal Party, and both were influenced by New Liberal thinkers such as Leonard Hobhouse who, as was shown earlier in this book, had used the term 'social development' to advocate the use of planning to direct the process of social change. Hobhouse's (1911) exposition of New Liberal ideas was generally regarded as the definitive statement of this approach. While both Keynes and Beveridge believed that governments should play an active role in managing the economy and creating social services to ensure that minimum standards of welfare are maintained, neither believed that the state should take full control of the economy or that state interventionism should replace capitalism. Both thinkers remained individualists rather than collectivists.

The Influence of Statism

Some institutionalists have been more influenced by collectivist ideology and statist interventionism than the reformist liberal tradition. They include R. H. Tawney, Richard Titmuss and Gunnar Myrdal to name only a few. Although these writers are usually identified with democratic socialism rather than the ideas of Veblen, there are similarities between their work and that of Veblen. Both Tawney and Titmuss emphasized the importance of wider values and institutions in social life, and both were vigorous critics of the competitive attitudes that characterized what Tawney (1921) called *The Acquisitive Society* and Titmuss (1960) described as *The Irresponsible Society*. Their work is also marked by an emphasis on solidaristic values. Like Durkheim, Tawney argued that both economic and social activities should be planned by governments with the deliberate intention of enhancing solidarity and minimizing the class and other divisions which inhibit the expression of people's common humanity. In *The Gift Relationship* (1971), Titmuss made a similar plea. Social policy, he argued, should encourage social solidarity and foster altruism, fraternal values and anonymous helpfulness between people. The ethical themes in these writings are clear. While Tawney and Titmuss strongly advocated state intervention, statism was not merely a mechanism for managing the economy or providing social services, but a means of promoting higher social and moral values.

Titmuss was one of the first institutionalists to become involved with the Third World. He led a mission to Mauritius in the 1950s and completely overhauled the country's social welfare system. He also helped plan Tanzania's health care system. In addition, he supported the creation of the social planning courses at the London School of Economics which were designed to train professional personnel for social development. Directed by Margaret Hardiman and James Midgley (1980), these courses advocated a statist approach and, in keeping with the institutional perspective, the courses prepared social scientists to assume responsibility for social policy development, programme implementation and social administration in both central planning agencies and sectoral social service ministries in developing countries.

Perhaps the best known institutionalist in development studies is Gunnar Myrdal who, as was shown earlier in this book, played a key role in formulating the United Nations' unified approach to development planning. Because of his vigorous advocacy of the institutional position, Myrdal is often described in the literature as the leader of the neo-institutionalist movement. Myrdal acknowledges his debt to Swedish democratic socialism and its commitment to equality, solidarity and other central socialist values. Like other socialists, he advocates an activist role for the state in economic and social affairs. However, Myrdal is pessimistic about the ability of Third World countries to implement the statist agenda. In 1970, he formulated the concept of the 'soft state' which alluded to the apparently widespread problems of administrative inefficiency, corruption and laxity which he believed characterized public administration in many developing countries. If planning was to be effective, these problems had to be addressed and the soft state had to be replaced by strong, centralized governments, managed by well-trained and efficient administrators. The commitment to technocratic management in Myrdal's work is characteristic of other statist approaches, and while he may have overstated the problem, most statist interventionists would agree with his proposals for improving planning and administrative skills in developing countries.

Myrdal's writings also reveal a strong commitment to egalitarianism. This commitment is clearly inspired by the Swedish social democratic movement which placed great stress on the reduction of class inequalities. Myrdal (1968, 1970) argues that the problem of inequality is a major impediment to economic and social progress in the Third World and that the reduction of inequality is a precondition for development. Entrenched class and caste differences, inequalities in land distribution, the urban–rural divide, the oppression of women and unequal access to the social services all need to be addressed. These ideas were subsequently restated by many neo-institutionalist writers but they do not exert much influence in development circles today.

In addition, some neo-institutionalists do not stress the need for egalitarian strategies. As was shown in the last chapter, Paul Streeten and his colleagues (1981) have argued that the reduction of inequality is not an overriding requirement in development, and that the satisfaction of basic needs should be given priority instead. Although Streeten is a neo-institutionalist, and owes a clear intellectual debt to Myrdal, he differs from the neo-institutionalist mainstream by advocating a more pragmatic, empiricist approach and emphasizing the provision of services by the state rather than the promotion of egalitarianism (Preston, 1982). Nevertheless, the provision of basic needs requires planning, the implementation of programmes by trained administrators and, ultimately, the existence of a strong central government with the resources and determination to resolve pressing social problems.

The notion of *market socialism* marks the most recent development in the ongoing effort to forge an accommodation between capitalism and socialism. Although market socialism is not a new idea, it has gained currency as socialists struggle to identify ways of appealing to electorates that apparently no longer respond to calls for nationalization, workers' control and other socialist beliefs. Pranab Bardhan and

John Roemer (1993: introduction) point out that the principles underlying market socialism were first advocated by the Polish economist,
Oskar Lange, who sought to combine collective ownership with market
principles to determine prices and set production quotas. While
Lange's contribution was seminal, Janos Kornai (1993) notes that the
gradual liberalization of the Eastern European economies provided a
more practical basis for integrating social ownership with market principles. He suggests that various countries, but especially Yugoslavia
and Hungary, were able to forge a successful integration of the two
approaches. However, in their examination of market socialism's potential relevance to Britain, Julian Le Grand and Saul Estrin (1989) do not
see much prospect for nationalization and suggest instead that cooperatives and planning offer the best prospect for harmonizing free
market and socialist objectives.

The Theory of Corporatism
Another influence on the institutional perspective in social development is corporatism. Corporatism is a representational theory based on
studies of the way governments in many industrial societies have sought
to create lasting compacts between themselves, organized labour and
business in an attempt to reduce conflict, plan the economy and promote social welfare. Corporatist societies differ from socialist or
communist states in that their governments do not own or control the
economy. They also differ from capitalist societies in that their governments are far more interventionist and committed to directing
economic and social policy in coalition with both labour and industry
(Crouch, 1979; Pekkarinen et al., 1992; Schmitter and Lehmbruch,
1979).

As Peter Williamson (1989) reveals, the origins of corporatism can be
traced to nineteenth-century guild socialism, syndicalism and
Mussolini's attempts to unite workers and employers within a fascist
political system. However, it was really in the post-Second World War
era that corporatist forms have emerged, largely as a response to the
growth of organized labour and the growing power of highly organized groups of industrialists and business leaders. The rise of
contemporary corporatism is most frequently associated with the growing power of the labour movement and attempts to mitigate the
disruptions caused by labour unrest.

There is, however, considerable disagreement about which societies
can properly be designated as corporatist. While some commentators
believe that all Western industrial nations may be characterized as corporatist, many others use the term in a more restricted way to connote
only those societies which have successfully implemented corporatist
arrangements. Usually, Austria, Japan, the Scandinavian countries and

Switzerland are categorized as corporatist. The United States and Britain are seldom regarded as corporatist. However, these categories are not universally accepted. Walter Korpi (1983) has challenged the inclusion of the Scandinavian countries in the corporatist category, and Wolfgang Blaas (1992) claimed that Switzerland and Japan are in fact paternalist-liberal rather than corporatist societies.

Another problem is that corporatist forms are subject to change. Some writers believe that corporatism is no longer as widespread as it once was, and that increased economic integration and de-industrialization, which have resulted in the growth of the service sector, have lessened the need for corporatist arrangements (Pekkarinen et al., 1992). On the other hand, Robin Archer (1992) believes that Australia has recently become a corporatist society with highly structured state, labour and industry relationships. In addition, while many societies, including Britain, have sought to create corporate structures, they have not always succeeded.

In his classic definition, Philippe Schmitter (1974) suggests that corporatism is a social system in which interest groups are organized into a limited number of non-competitive and functionally differentiated categories through the active agency of the state. These groups are granted monopoly rights to represent their members and they agree to participate in the corporate structure and to be bound by agreements. Corporatism is, therefore, largely based on negotiations and the prospect of securing favourable advantage for constituency groups. However, it is also characterized by an underlying desire to reduce conflict and foster an equilibrium of interests. Corporatism is driven by the idea that negotiated agreements between government, labour and business will promote the interests of all and enhance the common good.

In a typical corporatist system, agreements are negotiated around issues such as prices, profits, economic policy, working conditions, incomes and social welfare. These agreements seek to create favourable outcomes for all participants. Successful corporatist arrangements, therefore, ensure that business and industry are advantaged by, for example, obtaining adequate rates of return on investments, by limiting labour disputes and by finding suitable opportunities for expansion. Similarly, the interests of labour are promoted through favourable wage settlements, improvements in working conditions and expanded social services. Government benefits because conflict is reduced, and the flow of revenues for public projects is ensured. While these outcomes are not always achieved, proponents of corporatism believe that it offers an effective compromise between the struggles of capital and labour and a useful basis for accommodating their diverse ideological approaches.

IMPLEMENTING AN INSTITUTIONAL PERSPECTIVE

The institutional perspective is inspired by the ideal of toleration and the desirability of fostering a compromise between divergent ideological positions. The institutional perspective is also informed by critiques of narrowly focused economic theories, and by analyses of the importance of social institutions in economic life undertaken by scholars such as Veblen, Keynes and Galbraith. Similarly, the pragmatism of Dewey and James and the welfarism of Beveridge and Titmuss have made a major contribution to the articulation of this approach. The idea that the state should actively take responsibility for managing social development has been influenced not only by the writings of statist thinkers such as Tawney, Titmuss and Myrdal, but by corporatism and Keynesian interventionism as well.

The following account of how the institutional perspective in social development can be implemented begins with a discussion of the organizational and professional personnel arrangements needed to support this approach. It also considers the role of government in coordinating strategies for achieving social development goals. It reviews the different socio-spatial settings in which social development strategies should be introduced and then considers the mechanisms by which social and economic development policies can be integrated.

The Organizational Basis for Social Development

Strategies for promoting social development do not occur spontaneously. Nor do they occur in a vacuum. These strategies are implemented by actual people within specific organizational contexts. As the discussion in the previous chapter revealed, proponents of different social development strategies place different emphasis on the sponsorship and thus the organizational basis for social development.

Proponents of the statist approach argue that social development programmes should be formulated and implemented by government agencies, usually at the central level. Individualists and communitarians challenge this position. Communitarians believe that social development can best be fostered at the local level through the efforts of local people themselves. The organizational basis for the communitarian approach, therefore, rests on local institutions such as village councils, local committees and community organizations. All involve a high degree of popular participation and attribute political authority to local people themselves rather than to parliamentary officials who are elected through conventional electoral means. Communitarians also recognize the contribution of non-governmental organizations in promoting social development. They believe that these organizations provide a more effective organizational basis for social development than government agencies which they often accuse of being inefficient, remote and even corrupt.

Advocates of individualist social development strategies agree with the communitarian critique of state intervention. They believe that state control of social development fosters complacency and dependency and is inimical to individual responsibility for welfare. However, proponents of the individualist approach do not have a clearly articulated view of the organizational framework needed to implement social development effort. Nevertheless, they acknowledge that the effective implementation of the enterprise strategy requires an organizational base, the deployment of personnel and a commitment on the part of political leaders. Most advocate the creation of quasi-governmental organizations which operate like community development agencies to stimulate and support entrepreneurial efforts. Others believe that these tasks should be contracted out to non-governmental organizations. In addition, most recommend the introduction of fiscal incentives, easy credit and other measures designed to promote the enterprise approach to social development.

Many proponents of government-sponsored social development recognize that the statist approach of the 1950s and 1960s was excessively centralized and did little to acknowledge community and other non-governmental social development efforts. It is also true that government planning agencies responsible for economic and social development were often remote, unduly technocratic and unresponsive to local needs and conditions. Many assumed that the responsibility for social development was the exclusive purview of government. Today, the limitations of this approach have been acknowledged and there is a far greater emphasis on community-based interventions as well as policies and programmes that promote economic liberalization and the creation of opportunities for ordinary people to utilize the economic market more effectively. These new attitudes have been fostered by global political and economic changes which are inimical to centralized, totalitarian statism and more conducive to pluralist systems. In this new climate, it much more likely that different organizational structures for promoting social development will coexist. Indeed, non-governmental and commercial organizations today play a much more active role in social development than before.

However, there is still a need for an overall organizational framework by which the social development activities of diverse groups can be facilitated, coordinated and harmonized. In the absence of a framework of this kind, it is likely that social development efforts will be fragmented, disorganized and inefficient. For this reason, the institutional approach to social development requires that an organizational system be established and that overall responsibility for managing this system be entrusted to a government agency which is responsive to the interests of the diverse groups that are involved in social development.

It is important that any national agency which is established to direct, facilitate and coordinate social development should recognize, respect and seek to harmonize the efforts of other organizations responsible for implementing different strategic approaches to social development. This agency should recognize the validity of these different approaches and seek to foster their implementation. As suggested earlier, its style and approach should be one of *managed pluralism*. In the past, national social development agencies made little effort to facilitate pluralism, assuming that the state should be the primary if not the sole promoter of social development.

The organizational settings used to implement social development in the past can form a basis for the implementation of the institutional perspective. As was shown previously in this book, under the guidance of the United Nations, the promotion of social development in developing countries in the 1960s and early 1970s was entrusted to central planning ministries which were urged to adopt social planning as a counterpart of economic development planning. Many developing countries enhanced their central planning agencies by creating social planning divisions responsible for defining social development goals and formulating social plans. The social planning divisions were also responsible for coordinating the activities of social sectoral agencies such as ministries of education, health, housing and social welfare (Conyers, 1982; Hardiman and Midgley, 1982, 1989; Midgley, 1984a). Despite the setbacks of the 1980s, when structural adjustment policies undermined the authority and effectiveness of these agencies, many are slowly being revitalized in many countries. They can once again serve as an organizational locus for facilitating, coordinating and supporting social development endeavours.

Of course, these central planning agencies were largely confined to the developing countries. With the exception of the communist countries and some European nations such as France, central economic planning in the industrial countries is poorly developed and attempts to integrate social policies with economic development planning efforts have been minimal. In some countries such as Britain, attempts to introduce centralized economic planning in the 1960s were unsuccessful. Instead, most industrial countries have used Keynesian techniques to influence economic activity rather than producing directive development plans. This factor has also contributed to the compartmentalization of social and economic policies.

However, this does not preclude a fresh renewed effort to create organizational settings at the national level where social and economic development efforts can be harmonized and where overall responsibility for social development can be promoted. Hopefully, the efforts of the United Nations to encourage a renewed commitment to social development will facilitate the emergence of appropriate organizational structures conducive to effective social development in both the industrial and the developing countries.

Steps must also be taken to ensure that organizational structures for the promotion of social development extend to the regional and local levels. As was noted earlier, the remoteness of central planning ministries in the past has contributed to a disillusionment with state-sponsored social development. Government social development agencies must extend their activities to the local level and, at the same time, ensure that non-governmental organizations as well as local bodies that foster the participation of ordinary people in social development are fully involved. To ensure the effective implementation of an institutional perspective, social development efforts must not be dictated by politicians, bureaucrats or planners but involve all constituents.

Personnel and Professional Roles for Social Development

In addition to creating specific organizational structures for the implementation of an institutional approach to social development, personnel who are knowledgeable about social development and who are able to implement its strategies will need to be deployed. However, there are differences of opinion about the types of personnel needed to staff social development agencies, and about the expertise they need to carry out their duties.

As was noted in chapter 3, some experts believe that social development tasks are best undertaken by professional social development specialists who are specifically trained for this purpose. Others see no need for such specialists. Advocates of the former approach include Margaret Hardiman and James Midgley (1980) who established the social planning courses at the London School of Economics in the early 1970s. They believe that a multidisciplinary social science training with a specific preparation in social policy analysis and planning techniques is needed to implement social development programmes. Their approach is, of course, compatible with the institutional perspective and, as was noted earlier in this chapter, it is also compatible with the technocratic, statist approach advocated by Titmuss and other neo-institutionalist writers.

A different point of view comes from those who believe that social development tasks can be readily assumed by economists. This position is advocated by Nancy Birdsall and the authors of the United Nations Development Programme's *Human Development Reports* (1990, 1993) who seldom make reference to social development authors who are not economists. A similar argument against the deployment of professionally trained social development personnel comes from those who believe that a general training in the social sciences or in one or another social science discipline provides an adequate preparation for social development. These disciplines include sociology, anthropology and social work. Also relevant is the interdisciplinary field of development studies and the growing interest in development anthropology (Mair, 1984). Although many social workers have argued that a professional qualification in social work provides adequate expertise to work in social development settings, Midgley (1978, 1981) has questioned this conclusion, pointing out that few schools of social work provide an adequate training in social development or social planning.

On the other hand, proponents of communitarian social development strategies generally see little need for highly trained professionals to work in formal organizations concerned with social development. They argue that the emphasis on training, particularly at the tertiary level, fosters a technocratic approach to social development which is remote from local people and insensitive to their needs. Instead, they favour the deployment of local community workers who operate at the grass-roots level and are often drawn from the local community themselves. Training for these workers should be offered at local centres. As was noted earlier, communitarians also favour social development interventions that are managed by non-governmental organizations, and they thus prefer the deployment of personnel suited to work in these settings.

Despite the antipathy to professionalism among the proponents of the communitarian approach, it is difficult to escape the conclusion that specialized personnel with at least some formal training in the field are needed if social development goals are to be achieved. However, as the institutional perspective suggests, different types of personnel are required to implement different social development strategies. Obviously, training courses should be related to the needs of these different personnel. The personnel required to implement community social development programmes are very different from those needed to work in government social development agencies at the central level. Similarly, these different roles require different levels of expertise and skill, and thus call for different types of training. Community-level workers need to have very different skills from those working with economists and other specialists in central planning agencies. Similarly, social development specialists who work with people in the informal sector or who seek to promote entrepreneurial activities need very different skills from those who serve in governmental organizations.

As a profession, social work is well placed to provide a comprehensive training in social development. Its expertise in working with individuals and communities and in administrative settings is highly conducive to the implementation of social development policies and programmes. However, as was noted earlier, the profession has not taken steps to ensure that social work education is adequately prepared to provide an appropriate training for those who wish to pursue a career in the field. Yet there are signs that this situation is being rectified as more schools of social work in both the industrial and the developing countries introduce specialized social development courses (Midgley et al., 1994).

Social development professionals should have clearly identified roles and responsibilities. These are varied and include research into social needs and problems, the definition of specific social development objectives, the formulation of social development policies and programmes, the monitoring of outcomes and the removal of impediments to social progress. All of these tasks need to be undertaken in conjunction with a wider process of economic development. This requires close cooperation with economists at the various levels at which development initiatives are formulated. These include the local, community, regional and national levels. Also relevant is the type of intervention. Social and economic aspects need to be integrated in national as well as sectoral and project planning.

The Location of Development Effort
As was shown in chapter 1, efforts to promote social development take place within defined socio-spatial contexts. Social development, like economic development, is focused on specific socio-spatial entities, localities, regions and communities. All provide a locus for social development's macro-focus. The institutional perspective in social development requires that social development strategies be implemented at all three levels and that efforts at these different levels be properly coordinated.

The nation state has become the unit for much development activity. Nation states are largely a product of international diplomacy and political effort during the last two centuries. It is only in relatively recent times that the idea that ethnic groups or nations should be located within defined political boundaries and be governed by political leaders of the same ethnic or national background gained currency. The collapse of European imperialism after the Second World War resulted in the creation of many new nation states, not all of which consist exclusively of one ethnic group. Nevertheless, despite ongoing conflicts, the international community recognizes the legitimacy of the nation state and focuses attention on national development effort.

This is reflected in the way the international development agencies have focused resources on nation states for development purposes. Development aid and technical assistance are directed largely at individual countries, and reports on international development trends are compiled with reference to particular nations. Academic research in the field of development is based on a similar approach. While there are, of course, many examples of attempts to focus studies of development on international regions such as Africa, Asia or Latin America, the nation state remains the basic unit for analysis in much development research.

While social development can be fostered at the national level, the institutional perspective requires that social development policies and programmes be formulated and implemented at the regional and local levels as well and that these efforts be harmonized within a wider framework of national social development policy. Although neglected in the literature, social development strategies can be applied just as effectively in the context of regional development as in national development. Typically, regional development focuses on underdeveloped areas and seeks to promote their economic and social transformation.

Finally, social development takes place at the local level. The locality may be a small town, a village and its surrounding rural areas or an inner city community. As was shown previously in this book, rural communities have long featured prominently in the literature of social development. Indeed, social development began with efforts to promote community development in rural areas. However, the community action approach has tended to focus on political mobilization and people's participation in social programmes, with the result that economic development projects have been neglected. More recently, local community-based economic development is again being stressed, particularly with reference to the way community development can promote economic growth and enhance the incomes and standards of living of local people (Midgley and Simbi, 1993; Blakely, 1994; Galaway and Hudson, 1994).

If social development goals are to be achieved, it is important not only that social development strategies be integrated with economic development but that these be linked to different socio-spatial contexts. The institutional approach seeks to ensure that social and economic development efforts take place and are effectively harmonized at the national, regional and local levels. This multipronged approach can facilitate improvements at all levels and foster welfare for everyone.

The emphasis on harmonizing efforts between socio-spatial settings is compatible with the universalism of the institutional perspective. As the definition offered in chapter 1 revealed, social development is inclusive because it attempts to cover the population as a whole rather than focusing only on particularly needy groups of individuals. While social development is indeed concerned with those who have been neglected or excluded from development, it seeks to raise standards of living for all within wider socio-spatial contexts.

Nevertheless, social development is primarily concerned with needy communities. These communities include poor inner-city areas, low-income rural communities, particularly in remote areas, and deprived regions. Social development interventions that focus on these localities within the context of a broader development approach are justified in terms of what some writers have called 'positive discrimination' or 'priority area' policies (Glennerster and Hatch, 1974; Holterman, 1978). Positive discrimination uses economic, fiscal and social policies to direct resources to particularly needy groups on a geographic basis. Usually, social indicators are used to identify geographic areas which contain a significant proportion of needy or neglected groups of people. In addition to ensuring that these areas are adequately provided with social services, social development planners urge increased investments in programmes that enhance economic activity and enhance opportunities for people to obtain employment or engage in productive self-employment.

A variation on priority area policies is the community renewal or community revitalization approach. This approach focuses both government and private resources on low-income communities where the need for economic and social development is particularly pressing. In the United States, community renewal has found expression in various programmes including the community development and model cities programmes. More recently, it has fostered the creation of Empowerment Zones and Enterprise Zones. Urban and rural communities that are designated as Empowerment or Enterprise Zones not only receive direct budgetary aid to foster economic development and social service programmes, but are provided with numerous fiscal incentives and other special considerations which encourage private business investment and economic development.

Integrating Economic and Social Development Effort
As has been emphasized repeatedly in this book, social development differs from other approaches for promoting social welfare because it links social policies and programmes to a wider process of economic development. To be effective, the institutional perspective must, therefore, ensure that social development strategies are harmonized with economic development efforts. All the strategies discussed in the previous chapter are directly or indirectly associated with economic development. However, they can only be meaningfully implemented within the wider context of efforts to promote economic development.

It is for this reason that social development requires an appropriate economic development framework for its implementation.

Despite the criticisms made of economic growth, development has generated the resources needed to enhance people's welfare. The significant social improvements which have been recorded in many parts of the world during this century have been dependent on economic growth. However, as was argued in the introduction, economic growth of itself does not guarantee that levels of welfare will automatically improve or that economic improvements will benefit all sections of the population. The problem facing most countries today is not a lack of economic development, but a problem of distorted development. Distorted development occurs when economic growth is not accompanied by concomitant improvements in welfare for all sections of the population. For this reason, social development seeks to harmonize economic and social policies in ways that enhance social welfare for all.

There are three ways in which the social development approach seeks to harmonize economic and social efforts. First, it seeks to create formal organizational and institutional arrangements by which economic and social policies can be better integrated. In many countries, organizations that are responsible for economic development have no ongoing contacts let alone a close working relationship with agencies that are responsible for social service policies and programmes. On the other hand, countries that have successfully adopted a social development approach have ensured that economic development and social service agencies work closely together.

As was noted previously, the creation of social planning divisions within central planning agencies in developing countries at the behest of the United Nations in the 1960s and 1970s is an example of organizational efforts to foster such linkages. Such settings need to be established or strengthened in the industrial countries as well. Central planning agencies employ economic as well as social development professionals who formulate policies and plans, and work closely with sectoral organizations to coordinate and integrate development effort. While the creation of these organizational structures has taken place at the national level, they also exist at the regional and local levels. At both the regional and the national levels, the successful integration of social and economic development also requires a purposeful commitment on the part of economic planners, political leaders and ordinary people themselves to pursue growth strategies that raise levels of living among all sections of the population.

Second, the social development approach seeks to foster the integration of economic and social policy by ensuring that economic development has a direct impact on the social well-being of all citizens. The proponents of social development argue that economic growth which only benefits a section of the population is meaningless. They are critical of societies which experience economic growth but fail to ensure that growth fosters significant improvements in social well-being for people as a whole. In the introduction, it was argued that many countries are characterized by the condition of distorted development in which economic growth fails to benefit large numbers or significant groups of people. The institutional perspective requires the creation of an economic development framework that fosters growth and raises levels of living among all sections of the population. This framework involves the adoption of economic policies that encourage investment in productive economic enterprises and the adoption of policies and programmes that generate income among all sections of the population, particularly through enhancing employment and self-employment opportunities.

To promote the social well-being of all citizens, economic development policies must generate growth and increase the incomes of the population. Investments in enterprises that produce high rates of return are of little social value if the income produced is repatriated abroad, or if it only reaches a small, wealthy section of the population. To promote social development, investments must create employment or self-employment opportunities on a significant scale since it is largely through productive employment and self-employment that the incomes of ordinary people are increased.

Most social development experts emphasize the need for economic development strategies that generate productive employment and self-employment, and thus increase the incomes of ordinary people. These strategies are particularly needed in underdeveloped regions. Despite the shortcomings of the modernization approach, its insistence on employment generation remains valid. Today, employment creation continues to be stressed by most economists and the international agencies. For example, to alleviate conditions of mass poverty, the World Bank (1990) favours interventions that create labour-intensive industries, promote agricultural techniques that absorb labour and maximize self-employment opportunities among the urban and rural poor.

In addition to employment creation, productivity increases generate higher incomes and levels of welfare. Economic policies that introduce inexpensive, appropriate technologies that enhance the productivity of workers in the agricultural, manufacturing and service sectors should also be encouraged. Income can also be increased through the introduction of accessible credit to producers and through measures that increase asset ownership. In many poor countries, a more equitable distribution of land ownership would contribute significantly to agricultural production and enhance income generation. While many of these strategies are directed at the developing countries, they also have relevance for underdeveloped regions in the industrial nations.

The issue of asset ownership raises the issue of redistribution which remains controversial. The term itself usually invokes sharp reactions and ideological opposition. However, if human and social capital formation is to be encouraged, resources generated by economic development will need to be directed to programmes of this kind. Similarly, social service expenditures require redistributive social policies. Basic human needs cannot be met without redirecting resources to appropriate programmes. This does not involve the imposition of punitive taxes on the population, or the confiscation of private property as scaremongers have claimed, but the judicious application of various fiscal and other techniques that direct resources towards needed social programmes (Chenery et al., 1974).

Third, social development encourages the formulation of social policies and programmes that contribute positively to economic development. Proponents of the institutional perspective urge that social interventions that contribute positively to economic development be given priority over those that have a purely remedial or maintenance function. While remedial programmes will obviously be needed in all societies, social development seeks to identify interventions that refocus remedial approaches so that they have a developmental function and foster economic growth.

Policies and programmes that mobilize human capital should be given priority. Investments in human and social capital are urgently needed if people are to have the educational levels and skills to utilize the opportunities created by economic development. Economists such as George Psacharopoulos (1973, 1981, 1992) have demonstrated that public investments in education generate high rates of return and the World Bank's (1990) report on poverty argued strongly for greater investments of this kind. Educational investments, it noted, can generate rates of return to governments of between 13 per cent and 26 per cent. Similarly, investments in health care can increase productivity and obviate the social as well as private costs associated with debilitating diseases. Similar arguments have been made for expenditures on nutritional programmes, housing, maternal and child welfare services, drinking water supplies, sanitation, various income subsidies and supports, and other programmes. While some economists believe that social service programmes of this kind are a consumption expenditure and thus a drain on economic development, others have argued that they in fact enhance and support economic development. Social service expenditures are now widely regarded as investments in human capital. Many economists now accept that investments in human capital are highly conducive to high economic performance and that countries which invest extensively in education, health care, child welfare and other forms of human capital formation have higher levels of economic development than those that do not.

In addition, governments should adopt policies that foster the mobilization of social capital. Unfortunately, this term is defined in different ways in the literature. First, it has been used to connote the creation of civic associations, the development of strong bonds of community reciprocity and the strengthening of social relationships (Putnam et al., 1993) so that people are better able to participate in development. This definition is highly compatible with the ideational approach to social development discussed earlier in this book. Second, the term has been used in a materialist sense to refer to the creation of social infrastructure such as housing, schools, health clinics, sanitary and water supply projects and the other physical facilities that add to the social capital stock which communities and nations need to realize social development goals. A third definition of social capital draws on Michael Sherraden's (1991) important work on asset development among low-income groups. Sherraden is critical of the way social policies, particularly in the industrial countries, emphasize the provision of income benefits to maintain minimum consumption levels among the poor. He argues instead that income support programmes should provide incentives and resources that encourage savings among the poor. This will, he believes, accumulate the social investments they need to meet their needs and those of their children.

In addition to policies and programmes that create human and social capital, those that foster people's welfare by contributing simultaneously to economic development should be emphasized. The strategies for social development discussed in the previous chapter are examples of interventions of this kind. For example, community development programmes that mobilize people for cooperative effort not only to enhance physical and social amenities but to engage in productive economic activities make a positive contribution to development. It is also possible to formulate remedial approaches or interventions that cater for those with special needs in ways that enhance their participation in development. Instead of relying exclusively on residential care and similar maintenance-oriented social service approaches, social development experts recommend the introduction of programmes that integrate people with special needs into the economy through vocational training, job placement, the creation of micro-enterprises, cooperatives and community-based projects which encourage economic self-sufficiency and full integration into society.

These three methods of integrating economic and social development are designed to foster the emergence of a developmental perspective which blurs rather than accentuates the differences between the economic and social domains. Although both have distinctive characteristics, the harmonization of the two offers the best prospect of promoting human welfare today. However, it is important to recognize that the integration of the economic and social policies and programmes takes place within the context of a wider *development process.* As the definition offered earlier noted, social development strategies are implemented within a comprehensive and dynamic process of economic development.

Harmonizing Social Development Strategies
The different strategies for achieving social development described in the previous chapter are based on normative theories about the best way of organizing society and of achieving social goals. It is probably because of their ideological character that these strategies invoke fierce loyalties. Advocates of one or another strategy frequently claim that their preferred strategy offers the only viable means of achieving social development goals. Usually, these claims are based on ideological sentiments rather than a dispassionate, scientific evaluation of different forms of intervention.

While there are clear differences between the different strategies, the tendency to polarize debates about the best way of achieving social development overlooks the possibility that different strategies can be combined. While preferences for particular strategies should not be abandoned, the tendency to claim moral superiority for one or another strategy needs to be tempered by the realization that they have all helped to promote social development goals. There is no doubt that communitarian interventions have enhanced the welfare of many communities. Similarly, governments have played a major role in promoting social development in many parts of the world. In addition, while few proponents of social development have been enthusiastic supporters of a market-based approach, informal sector enterprises have also provided a livelihood for millions of people around the world.

These realities are gradually being recognized in the literature on social development. In the current global political climate, the tendency to dogmatically embrace one approach to the exclusion of the others is receding. This climate is not only more conducive to pluralism, but cognizant of the harsh fiscal realities facing many governments today. Faced with budgetary restraint, many governments now actively promote the harmonization of different strategies instead of relying exclusively on state sponsorship.

It is with reference to community involvement that the literature has begun to advocate greater integration of *statist and communitarian* social development strategies. Of course, this idea is not a new one.

Indeed, it formed the basis of the community development approach. There are many examples of the successful creation of government and community partnerships in community development. Governments and local communities have joined efforts to construct community centres, clinics and schools and they have engaged in rural development projects, squatter upgrading schemes and a host of other activities which have made a major contribution to raising production and increasing incomes. In addition, as Theodore Panayotou (1993) reveals, there have been notable successes in implementing the sustainable development approach because of the successful linking of government with local effort.

However, these successes are seldom lauded in the academic and popular literature on community participation which prefers to focus on alleged incompatibility of state and community efforts. Many writers have claimed that a meaningful partnership between the two is impossible since the state inevitably seeks to co-opt local effort, suppress the true aspirations of the people and manipulate community endeavour for its own ends. While this criticism is often overstated (Midgley et al., 1986), there are problems in harmonizing state and community approaches. Bureaucratic indifference is a problem, corruption does exist, resources are limited and governments do have their own agendas. However, these problems can be addressed. A positive step in this direction is John Montgomery's (1988) attempt to formulate proposals for increasing the effectiveness of administrators in community projects and for enhancing relations between the two. Another example is Franklyn Lisk's (1985) detailed discussion of policies and procedures needed for harmonizing the basic needs and community participation approaches. Although people's involvement had been an integral element of basic needs service delivery since the inception of this approach, Lisk and the other contributors to his volume examine a variety of technical, policy and political aspects related to the integration of these two approaches.

Steps have also been taken to harmonize an *enterprise approach with the communitarian and statist perspectives*. There are many examples of governments successfully promoting and supporting informal sector enterprises, and of using the enterprise approach to address the problems of low-income groups. It was shown in the last chapter that countries such as the Philippines have fostered the creation and development of small enterprises as an integral element of their national development strategies. This policy has focused particularly on low-income groups, and has sought to use micro-enterprises to enhance the levels of living of poor people. These efforts have been actively supported by international agencies such as the United Nations Development Programme and the World Bank which have advocated a 'market friendly' development strategy (United Nations Development Programme, 1990; World Bank, 1990, 1991).

Other governments have not made the promotion of small enterprises a central component of their social development policies but have, nevertheless, sought to strengthen the enterprise sector by removing a variety of restrictions on informal economic activities and by introducing measures that promote these activities. These include the provision of credit by government agencies, the construction of markets and industrial parks for small businesses, and the introduction of training and technical assistance. Some governments have sought to integrate the informal and larger formal sector by encouraging larger businesses to subcontract with informal sector enterprises, and to increase the goods and services they purchase from these enterprises. As these examples reveal, there is considerable scope for governments to facilitate and support an enterprise approach to social development.

The promotion of an enterprise approach among low-income groups needs to focus not only on individuals and families but also on communities. Indeed, some writers such as Thomas Dichter (1989) have been critical of the emphasis in community development on activities that do not expand economic activities but focus instead on non-material aspects such as strengthening community relationships and identity, and enhancing the quality of community leadership. Dichter argues that community participation strategies should seek to create productive enterprises that increase incomes and enhance levels of living for the community as a whole. Other writers have echoed these ideas, emphasizing the need for local economic development (Midgley and Simbi, 1993; Blakely, 1994; Galaway and Hudson, 1994). This can be done by encouraging individual community members to establish enterprises in loose collaboration with others, or by creating cooperatives which can collectively undertake economically viable activities. Although few examples of the successful harmonization of the communitarian and enterprise approaches are available, the experiences of cooperatives have been well documented. Indeed, the literature on cooperatives reveals that groups of people working together have competed effectively on the market to increase their incomes and raise their standards of living (Worsley, 1971; Mendoza, 1980; Young et al., 1981; Csaki and Kislev, 1993).

As these examples reveal, it is possible to harmonize the different social development strategies within the framework of an institutional perspective that recognizes the validity of different approaches and seeks to promote their implementation in different socio-spatial settings. As was argued earlier, this requires that these different approaches be recognized as compatible rather than competitive. It also requires the creation of appropriate organizational arrangement.

Although various organizations should be encouraged to engage in social development, the state should play an activist role in fostering the systematic implementation of these approaches. Through a strategy of managed pluralism, committed governments can adopt an institutional perspective to promote social development and enhance the well-being of all citizens.

ACHIEVING SOCIAL DEVELOPMENT: SOME CASE ILLUSTRATIONS

It has already been argued that it is possible to implement an institutional perspective that integrates different social development strategies and harmonizes social and economic policies. As was shown in the last section, the literature reveals that statist approaches can be effectively linked with community-based and enterprise approaches. Similarly, communitarian and enterprise approaches can also be harmonized. The idea that the major strategies for achieving social development are mutually exclusive has not only been invalidated, but more examples of how these approaches can be integrated are being provided in the literature. These examples come from accounts of the achievements of particular countries, but examples of the successful application of the institutional social development approach at the local and regional levels can also be provided.

The first case illustration focuses on a local community in Thailand and describes its efforts to simultaneously promote economic and social development by utilizing different strategic approaches. The second reports on a regional development initiative which is in the process of being implemented in the Mississippi Delta in the United States. Third, case illustrations are given of the efforts of different countries to promote social development by adopting a 'middle-way' position based on the institutional ideas and strategy of managed pluralism described earlier in this chapter. These illustrations suggest that it is possible to implement an institutional approach to social development and to enhance the social welfare of the population as a whole.

Achieving Social Development at the Local Level
One example of how the three major strategic approaches described in the last chapter can be harmonized is provided by Shin'ichi Shigetomi (1994) of the Institute of Developing Economies in Japan. Shigetomi spent several years working in rural development in North-East Thailand, and he reports how the village of Sri Phon Thong was able, under the leadership of a particularly energetic headman, to enhance its economic and social development by successfully utilizing the resources

of the government, creating communitarian institutions and fostering local enterprises.

The village of Sri Phon Thong is located in a particularly poor part of the country and its members are dependent on agriculture for their livelihood. Many of the young have migrated to the cities and numerous poor farmers have sought to increase their incomes by working as labourers in neighbouring villages and towns. The headman attempted to organize the villagers to initiate new projects which would improve their lives. He came from a farming family, and had previously migrated to Bangkok where he operated a small food-vending business. He had also previously challenged the traditional village leadership and had been accused of communist sympathies. However, on his return to the village in 1980, he was elected headman and began to secure the backing of village members for his proposals. Eventually, more than two thirds of the village's households enthusiastically supported his initiatives.

These initiatives involved all three strategies discussed in the last chapter. First, the villages sought to strengthen local cooperative activities and this in turn fostered greater community integration. It also helped them to construct needed facilities and to cooperate on economic projects that increased their incomes. By acting cooperatively they were better able to negotiate for improved government services. Indeed, a good deal of time was spent visiting government officials to secure improved services and amenities. In addition, the village obtained support from a local non-governmental organization which was promoting a variety of development projects in the area. This organization assisted the village with a number of its initiatives.

Local economic initiatives included the creation of a rice bank, a savings and credit society, a cooperative retail store, a rice mill, a village fish farm, a communal forest and a fertilizer production facility. In addition, steps were taken to assist local farmers to increase their incomes through improved agricultural techniques and similar activities. These activities were designed not only to increase agricultural yields but to help farmers market their products externally. By adopting an 'export-oriented' approach, the village sought to increase the flow of external resources into the community.

Not all the village members participated in all projects and, in some cases, the projects were managed and owned by particular groups. For example, the credit cooperative was managed largely by women who collected subscriptions and made low-interest loans to farmers and others who sought aid. The credit society proved to be a success. Within a few years, its membership had trebled and, in 1990, it joined the Credit Union League of Thailand.

Many cooperative activities were specifically designed to increase the income of their members. With the help of the government's Department of Agriculture, the village cleaned a polluted swamp and established a cooperative fish farming enterprise. Fish were sold to neighbouring villages and towns, and profits were shared among the members. The rice mill increased the income of farmers because it ended their dependence on a privately owned mill some distance away, as well as their reliance on the middlemen who transported the rice for milling. The rice bank was established to provide security against shortages and to assist members to purchase additional rice when needed at low cost. The bank was built with government aid and it reduced dependence on the large farmers in the neigbourhood who sold rice at high cost during periods of shortage.

Some of the projects established by the villagers had direct benefits for the environment. At the invitation of a non-governmental organization working in the area, the people of Sri Phon Thong joined with neighbouring villages to demarcate an area of the natural forest for preservation and communal ownership. By 1990, eight villages had joined the project and agreed not to cut wood and disturb the natural habitat. With technical assistance from the non-governmental organization as well as the government, they learned forestry management and derived economic benefit from the forest's resources. Another environmentally sound project was the local rice husk fertilizer production project. This project used rice husks mixed with animal manure instead of synthetic chemical fertilizers. This innovation proved to be successful, increasing production yields and at the same time protecting the environment.

As Shigetomi's account reveals, it is possible to integrate different strategic approaches to social development at the local level and to foster the promotion of social development within the context of economic development effort. The villagers also utilized the resources of the state in a positive way. The combination of the communitarian and individualist perspectives is particularly interesting. Although the village created cooperatives and engaged in communal activities, these activities did not abolish individual enterprise but sought rather to supplement and strengthen the capacities of farmers to increase their incomes. Nor did all village members join every cooperative. Households were free to participate in as many or few projects as they wished. As it became clear that some cooperative activities were bringing tangible benefits to their members, more people joined. However, even for those who did not join or who participated in only one or a few projects, the community created a milieu in which all households benefited and in which solidaristic sentiments were enhanced. Above all, their material welfare improved significantly.

Although Shigetomi's example deals with a rural community, it is possible to foster the integration of different social development approaches in urban communities, and at the regional and national levels as well. As has been argued already, it is possible for different social development strategies to be harmonized, and to be integrated with economic development efforts to cover deprived regions and the nation state as a whole.

Social Development at the Regional Level
As was shown in chapter 3, regional planning is now a recognized field of physical or spatial planning. Although regional planning has long sought to combine physical, economic and social strategies for the improvement of deprived regions, emphasis has traditionally been placed on the development of infrastructure and the creation of industries. Usually, central government revenues have been used to build networks of roads, irrigation projects and other forms of physical infrastructure. Economic development has been encouraged through offering incentives to businesses, and particularly large corporations, to establish manufacturing plants or other facilities in the region. While social planning has been a recognized component of regional planning, it has not been given the same emphasis as infrastructural and economic development. It has traditionally been assumed that social conditions will improve as infrastructural and economic development creates employment and raises incomes.

Despite the achievements of well-publicized regional development projects in both the industrial and the developing countries, regional planning lost momentum during the 1980s. Economic difficulties as well as the ascendancy of Radical Right-wing ideology impeded the expansion of regional development projects in many parts of the world. Governments were unable or unwilling to mobilize the resources required to invest in large-scale infrastructural and economic development projects and, in any case, the idea that government should assume responsibility for managing the development of whole regions was less acceptable than before. Indeed, right-wing critics often attacked the work of regional development planners, claiming that they not only interfered with the smooth operation of the market but were responsible for numerous planning blunders and had done more harm than good. In this climate, regional planning has lost much of the appeal it enjoyed in the 1950s and 1960s, and fewer governments are today committed to regional development planning than before. Consequently, fewer large-scale regional development projects have been initiated in recent years.

One exception is the Mississippi Delta project which was mentioned in the introduction. This project focuses on an area of the United States which is characterized by a severe form of distorted development.

Although the region is a major agricultural producer, a locus for petro-chemical industries and tourism, its poorest counties have the highest incidence of poverty in the country, and its infant mortality rates exceed those of several so-called developing countries.

Faced with these problems, the governors of the Delta's three major states (Arkansas, Louisiana and Mississippi) requested the federal government of the United States to fund the preparation of a major development plan for the region. This request was approved and, in 1988, a Commission responsible for preparing the plan was established under the chairmanship of Bill Clinton, the former governor of Arkansas. The Commission's headquarters was located in Memphis, Tennessee, and it began to undertake studies of the region's social and economic problems and to formulate policies for dealing with them. The result of the Commission's efforts was the publication in 1990 of a comprehensive plan for the economic and social development of the region. The plan was entitled *The Delta Initiatives* (Lower Mississippi Delta Development Commission, 1990).

While some may view this document as just another regional development plan, this would be inaccurate. The plan differs significantly from most regional development plans in that it does not place the same emphasis on infrastructural development as is common in regional planning, nor does it rely on the traditional approach of attracting external investors to create large-scale manufacturing facilities within the region. In addition, it is less top-down in its approach than most regional development plans. It not only stresses the need for local participation but gives priority to policies that support indigenous economic enterprises, particularly in agriculture, processing and local, small-scale industries. Emphasis is also placed on small-scale industries that utilize new electronic technologies. The Commission's cognizance of developments in electronics is accompanied by a recommendation that appropriate infrastructure be created to support industries of this kind. Community development is also given priority as are environmental issues. Above all, the plan differs from most regional development plans by its heavy emphasis on social development. Indeed, instead of viewing the Commission's report as yet another regional development plan, it should be seen as an attempt to implement an updated version of the unified socio-economic development approach which was advocated by the United Nations in the 1970s.

The report places prime emphasis on social development. One quarter of its recommendations are directed at human capital development, and many of the plan's other sections dealing with economic development and the environment also address social development issues directly. The plan contends that increased investments in education and health are essential prerequisites for economic development. It argues that, in the absence of rapid social improvements, economic development efforts are likely to be of little value. The plan also emphasizes the need for improvements in housing conditions which, it notes, are very unsatisfactory. A variety of social programmes are examined, and the plan recommends that ways be found of harmonizing these programmes with development objectives.

The Delta plan also goes beyond the traditional social services to examine intergroup relationships, discrimination and social exclusion. It notes that two centuries of institutionalized racism in the region has created conditions of deep disadvantage and deprivation which can only be addressed through comprehensive race relations and affirmative action policies that enhance opportunities for minorities. In addition to these methods, it urges that economic development ensure the inclusion of minorities through small-business training for minority entrepreneurs, as well as loans and technical assistance to minority businesses.

The plan's economic development proposals are closely linked with the region's social realities and social development needs. Rather than relying exclusively on job creation through external investments, the plan seeks to enhance the productive capacity of the region's people themselves. Emphasis is placed on agricultural improvements, local business development and other indigenous resources such as tourism that build economic strengths from within. In this regard, the plan realistically faces the limited prospects of creating employment in the large-scale corporate sector and seeks instead to stimulate local productive activities that will generate employment and self-employment through endogenous means. This strategy not only is cognizant of local social realities but requires that resources be allocated for human capital and social development. The plan's emphasis on local development is obviously predicated on the ability of local people to utilize economic opportunities and this, in turn, requires human capital investments to ensure that people have the necessary qualifications and skills.

Although efforts are currently under way to implement the Delta plan, it has not been fully funded and no comprehensive organizational structure has been created to manage its implementation. The federal deficit and political factors have impeded its implementation. However, steps are being taken to introduce legislation in the United States Congress which hopefully will begin the process of implementation. In addition, several federal agencies have taken administrative action to introduce programmes in the region that are compatible with the Commission's recommendations. Local political leaders, numerous community and voluntary groups and several universities are also involved in the process of implementation. Hopefully, the Commission's proposals for the economic and social development of the region will not only be implemented, but offer a framework for the development of other regions where the need to address the problem of distorted development is equally pressing.

Social Development at the National Level
The social development approach has been implemented by several governments with some success. The experiences of some of these countries will be considered. Although there are, of course, many more examples of countries that have not attempted to address social needs, those that have adopted a 'middle-way' position compatible with the institutional perspective reveal that it is possible to combine economic and social objectives in development with positive results.

Examples include high-income industrial countries such as Austria, Denmark, Japan and Sweden, newly industrializing countries such as Costa Rica, Malaysia and the 'four little tigers' of East Asia, as well as developing countries such as Botswana and Sri Lanka. Few of these countries regard themselves as socialist, but all have governments which have intervened extensively in their economies and in social affairs. Although none are utopias, all have made significant progress in promoting balanced social and economic development in recent decades.

Despite their historic commitment to democratic socialism, Sweden and the other Scandinavian welfare states have all retained the market as a basis for economic activity. However, their governments have also intervened extensively in the economy and invested heavily in social programmes. For example, in the mid-1980s, Sweden and Denmark devoted about a third of all government expenditures to the social services and levels of taxation in both countries were among the highest in the Western world (OECD, 1988). Like the other Scandinavian welfare states, the social services in Sweden and Denmark are generous, comprehensive and universal and are intended to mitigate class divisions. Both countries have very high standards of living. Life expectancy in Sweden is now 78 years, while in Denmark it is 76 years. Despite recent economic difficulties, both countries have very high per capita incomes (in excess of US $20,000 per annum) and both recorded annual economic growth rates in excess of 2.2 per cent during the recessionary 1980s (World Bank, 1993a).

The Scandinavian countries, and Sweden in particular, have sought to harmonize economic and social policies to promote the welfare of their populations. In Sweden, as Gøsta Esping-Andersen (1992) points out, social policy performs a 'productivist' function. As he notes, the country's social policies have sought to foster employment and economic growth rather than responding reactively to social need.

Compared to most other European welfare states, the Swedish government spends far more on employment generation through education, job training, employment placement and similar services than on unemployment benefits. Its health, educational, child care and family service expenditures are regarded as productive investments rather than consumption expenditures. By using social policy deliberately to foster a healthy, educated and efficient labour force, Sweden thus invests in human capital, fosters economic growth and generates employment. This, in turn, produces the revenues needed for further social investments (Hort, 1993). Because of the close links between social policy and economic development, Sweden may more appropriately be classed as an example of the adoption of the social development rather than social administration approach. Indeed, while the term 'social development' is hardly known in the other industrial countries, it is frequently used in the Scandinavian literature.

While it is true that the Swedish electorate has revealed its dissatisfaction with the Social Democratic Party in recent elections, the party's electoral setbacks hardly mark the end of the country's commitment to social development (Hort, 1993). While it is likely that the Social Democrats will introduce greater market elements into social policy, this does not mean that the Swedish welfare state is being 'dismantled' as some in the American media have claimed (*New York Times*, 15 December 1993: B6). Even if significant changes are introduced, it is likely that the Swedish welfare state will be closer to the German 'social market' than the current, fragmented and increasingly privatized British or American welfare state. Indeed, the defeat of the centre-right coalition government in 1994 and the re-election of the Social Democrats suggests that Swedes are not eager to embrace the Anglo-American model.

Austria typifies the corporatist type of society described earlier in this chapter. Indeed, its *social partnership* model, which emerged after 1957 when the Joint Commission on Wages and Prices was established, represents what Ramesh Mishra describes as a 'strongly institutionalized form of social consensus' (1990: 52). As in other corporatist societies, the social partnership maintains a compact between employers, workers and the state, and ensures that prices, wages and social benefits are controlled rather than dictated by market forces. Austria is undoubtedly a capitalist society, but its corporatism promotes a collective effort to direct the economy and to ensure that economic development benefits society as a whole. Austria, like most other European countries, has suffered from economic recession and, during the 1980s, it relied on deficit financing to control the rate of unemployment and maintain its social programmes. However, because of these policies, the country maintained a low unemployment rate during the 1980s and avoided many of the problems that characterized other industrial countries at the time. Despite economic difficulties, Austrians enjoy one of the highest standards of living in the world. The country's life expectancy is 76 years, its infant mortality rate of 8 per 1,000 is one of the lowest, it has one of the best physician–population ratios in the world, and its population is highly educated (World Bank, 1993a).

Japan's economic and social development achievements are well known and widely recognized. With substantial foreign aid from the United States, the country emerged from the devastation of the Second World War to become an industrial and economic giant. Japan is a capitalist country but none of its postwar governments have believed that an unrestrained free market is the best way of promoting development. Instead, the government has directed its economic growth through a combination of corporatist and technocratic means. The government has relied extensively on highly trained economic planners to manage the economy not through bureaucratic Soviet-style five-year plans but through incentives, negotiation, Keynesian principles and other techniques. As a recent World Bank study (1993b) revealed, industrialization was given high priority, innovation was encouraged, infant industries were protected and exporters were assisted. By the end of the 1980s, Japan's GNP per capita was the third highest of the industrial nations (after Switzerland and Finland) and well above that of the United States. Another feature of Japanese development is the important role played by local communities and small producers. Although Japan spends less on social programmes than most other welfare states, the country has achieved a high level of social development. Its life expectancy is 79 years and educational standards are envied. Crime rates are low and the society is marked by a high degree of solidarity (World Bank, 1993a).

Among the high-income or 'newly industrializing' developing countries, the 'four little tigers' of East Asia (Hong Kong, Korea, Singapore and Taiwan) are recognized to have experienced exceptional rates of growth during the last three decades. None had been identified as having much potential for development in the 1950s. Indeed, leading development economists such as Paul Rosenstein-Rodan (1961) regarded Korea and Singapore as countries with very limited prospects. By the mid-1970s, however, most economists were using superlatives to describe the economic performances of these countries. Some economists such as Milton Friedman (1980) argued that their achievements were a testimony to the power of the free market. By allowing the market to operate free of government control, real economic and social progress had been achieved. However, few economists today accept that the economic and social attainments of the newly industrializing East Asian countries are due to unrestrained capitalism. Indeed, most believe that their success is due not to *laissez-faire* but to the adoption of Japanese-style *dirigisme* by which governments successfully directed economic development through export-driven industrialization (Luedde-Neurath, 1984; Wade, 1984; World Bank, 1993b). As in Japan, small producers have played a major role in fostering this approach and linkages between local economic effort and larger corporations have been carefully forged. In addition, as Midgley (1986) revealed, the social services have played an important role in their development. Housing policies in Hong Kong and Singapore ensured that workers had adequate shelter while health care and income maintenance were linked to overall development strategies. The integration of economic and social policies in these countries is being increasingly replicated. Malaysia, Indonesia and Sri Lanka are just some of the other countries that are seeking to harmonize market and statist approaches in an effort to promote the development of their societies.

Costa Rica is frequently described as the Third World's most advanced welfare state. Since the country's successful 1948 revolution against dictatorship which resulted in the disbanding of its military forces, successive governments have sought to promote economic development in ways that foster social progress for the population as a whole. During the 1960s and 1970s, the economy sustained growth rates of about 3 per cent per year. Although these rates were moderate, they were combined with social policies that maximized investments in human capital and enhanced levels of welfare. In addition to investing heavily in education, Costa Rica attracted international attention for its primary health care policies which sought to ensure adequate sanitation and clean drinking water for all citizens. Mass immunization was also introduced and created networks of clinics which provided ready access to primary health care, particularly for women and children. At a time when many other developing countries were allocating substantial resources to hospital construction, the number of hospitals in Costa Rica actually declined. Unlike many other countries where investments in hospital construction detracted from primary health care, especially in rural areas, Costa Rica ensured that access to primary health care for ordinary people increased. Between 1970 and 1980, the number of outpatient facilities providing primary health care rose from about 350 to 1,150 (United Nations Development Programme, 1990).

Costa Rica's health policies are indicative of its overall approach to social development. By harmonizing economic and social goals, and by formulating social policies that are both appropriate to local needs and universal in scope, the country has succeeded in raising the levels of living of the population, even though economic growth has been moderate. Despite recent economic difficulties associated with indebtedness and global recession, Costa Rica has some of the most favourable social indicators in Latin America today.

Another country that is frequently cited as having achieved significant social gains despite limited economic achievements is Sri Lanka. Even before independence from British rule, the government had introduced free primary and secondary education, free primary health care and a universal food subsidy programme. These programmes were consolidated and expanded after independence. Like Costa Rica, Sri Lanka attracted international attention for its public health campaigns and particularly its efforts to eradicate malaria. Social and economic policies were closely integrated and the country's social policies ensured that the levels of living of low-income groups increased. Social programmes were universal and social expenditures high. Nevertheless, the country achieved moderate economic growth rates and, compared to many other developing countries, recorded remarkable gains in levels of literacy and educational attainment. Life expectancy is high and infant mortality rates are low. Also, Sri Lanka has long been characterized by low income inequality. However, the exploitation of ethnic tensions by political leaders fostered increased hostility between the major ethnic groups and eventually resulted in widespread communal conflict. The suffering that this has caused reveals that social policies that enhance material welfare without addressing ethnic divisions and seeking to enhance solidarity fail in the long term to create conditions conducive to the well-being of all.

Botswana is one of few African countries to experience sustained economic and social development. While many African countries have recorded negative rates of growth in recent years, Botswana maintained average annual rates in excess of 8 per cent between 1960 and 1990 and is now no longer classed as a low-income nation (World Bank, 1993a). While much of this wealth comes from minerals, the government has promoted economic diversification and invested in programmes that enhance both economic and social development. Social expenditures rose steadily during the 1970s and are now about 10 per cent of GDP, which is higher than many other African developing countries. Investments in education and health have increased and supplementary feeding for children has been expanded. During the mid-1980s, the country suffered severe drought but a rapid response by the government, which relied on community-based interventions, prevented widespread death and suffering. As an arid country, Botswana faces continued climatic adversity but as the United Nations Development Programme (1990) reported, the adoption of policies designed to respond to natural disasters at moderate cost have ensured that the most vulnerable sections of the population are protected. In addition, the implementation of appropriate social policies has resulted in significant gains in educational standards, literacy, infant mortality and life expectancy, particularly when compared to other African countries.

THE CHALLENGE AHEAD

As this chapter has attempted to show, social development is not an abstract ideal but a realistic approach for promoting people's welfare. It differs from the other major approaches to social welfare such as philanthropy, social work and social administration by its attempt to link social policies and programmes with economic development efforts. Although different strategies for promoting social development have been formulated, the approach adopted in this book advocates the harmonization of these approaches by mobilizing different social institutions to enhance social welfare. It has been argued that the resources of the market, community and state can all be tapped to foster the attainment of social development goals. As the final section of this chapter has shown, it is possible to utilize these institutions to promote social development, particularly within the framework of an activist style of intervention which has been called *managed pluralism* in this book. Social development is best promoted when governments play a positive role in facilitating, coordinating and directing the efforts of diverse groups of individuals, groups and communities and effectively utilizing the market, community and state to promote social development.

The chapter has demonstrated that it is possible to realize significant improvements in social welfare by mobilizing the market, community and state within the context of a wider process of economic development. In the case illustrations given above, the role of the state in fostering social development has been paramount but this has not resulted in the abolition of the market. Instead, market mechanisms have been effectively utilized to promote growth and economic development. Nor has the state abrogated individual rights or local community efforts as has been the case in the communist world. Indeed, in many of the countries mentioned, local effort has complemented market and state involvement, and frequently community-based programmes have formed a major part of social development endeavours.

However, it must be stressed that the case illustrations do not suggest that social development offers some quick and easy path to utopia. The countries mentioned have made real gains but they also face numerous challenges, and many have problems which detract from their social development attainments. Also, it is important to recognize that these case illustrations represent only a small minority of the world's nations and communities. There are many more examples of countries where social development efforts have not been implemented or where they have been ineffectively or haphazardly adopted. In most countries today, the absence of any meaningful social development effort perpetuates the conditions of distorted development discussed in the introduction. The challenge is whether the social development approach will in fact be adopted to ameliorate situations of social deprivation and neglect. There is little point in complacently lauding the achievements of a handful of societies or communities. Instead, concerted efforts are needed to ensure that social development has wider appeal. Hopefully, renewed international interest in social development, as exemplified by the recent United Nations World Summit on Social Development, will facilitate its global adoption.

References

Adorno, Theodore and Horkheimer, Max (1944) *Dialectic of Enlightenment*. London: Allen Lane.

Alinsky, Saul (1946) *Reveille for Radicals*. Chicago, IL: University of Chicago Press.

Alinsky, Saul (1971) *Rules for Radicals*. New York: Random House.

Andersen, Dennis and Khambata, Farida (1981) *Small Enterprises and Development Policy in the Philippines: A Case Study*. Washington, DC: World Bank.

Apthorpe, Raymond (1970) 'Development Studies and Social Planning', in Raymond Apthorpe (ed), *People, Planning and Development Studies*. London: Frank Cass. pp. 1–28.

Archer, Robin (1992) 'The Unexpected Emergence of Australian Corporatism', in Jukka Pekkarinen, Matti Pohjola and Bob Rowthorn (eds), *Social Corporatism: A Superior Economic System?* Oxford: Clarendon Press. pp. 377–418.

Arndt, H. W. (1978) *The Rise and Fall of Economic Growth: A Study in Contemporary Thought*. Chicago, IL: University of Chicago Press.

Bairoch, Paul (1973) *Urban Unemployment in Developing Countries*. Geneva: International Labour Office.

Bardhan, Pranab K. and Roemer, John E. (eds) (1993) *Market Socialism: The Current Debate*. New York: Oxford University Press.

Baster, Nancy (1972) *Measuring Development*. London: Frank Cass.

Bauer, Peter T. (1976) *Dissent on Development*. London: Weidenfeld & Nicolson.

Becker, Gary (1964) *Human Capital: A Theoretical and Empirical Analysis with Special Reference to Education*. New York: Columbia University Press.

Bell, Daniel (1960) *The End of Ideology: On the Exhaustion of Political Ideas in the 50s*. Glencoe, IL: Free Press. pp. 369–75.

Bennis, Warren G., Benne, Kenneth D. and Chin, Robert (1961) 'Introduction', in Warren G. Bennis, Kenneth D. Benne and and Robert Chin (eds), *The Planning of Change*. New York: Holt, Rinehart and Winston. pp. 1–17.

Bhattacharyya, S. N. (1970) *Community Development: An Analysis of the Programme in India*. Calcutta: Academic Publishers.

Billups, James (1994) 'The Social Development Model as an Organizing Framework for Social Work Practice', in Roland G. Meinert, John T. Pardeck and William P. Sullivan (eds), *Issues in Social Work: A Critical Analysis*. Westport, CT: Auburn House. pp. 21–38.

Birch, David L. (1987) *Job Creation in America*. New York: Free Press.

Birdsall, Nancy (1993) *Social Development is Economic Development*. Washington, DC: World Bank.

Birkbeck, Chris (1979) 'Garbage, Industry and the Vultures of Cali, Colombia', in Ray Bromley and Chris Gerry (eds), *Casual Work and Poverty in Third World Cities*. Chichester: John Wiley & Sons. pp. 161–84.

Blaas, Wolfgang (1992) 'The Swiss Model: Corporatism or Liberal Capitalism?', in Jukka Pekkarinen, Matti Pohjola and Bob Rowthorn (eds), *Social Corporatism: A Superior Economic System?* Oxford: Clarendon Press. pp. 363–76.

178   Social development

Blakely, Edward J. (1994) *Planning Local Economic Development: Theory and Practice.* Thousand Oaks, CA: Sage.
Bluestone, Barry and Harrison, Bennett (1982) *The DeIndustrialization of America.* New York: Basic Books.
Boeke, Julius H. (1953) *Economics and Economic Policy of Dual Societies.* Haarlem: Willink.
Boserup, Ester (1970) *Women's Role in Economic Development.* London: Allen & Unwin.
Boulding, Kenneth E. (1967) 'The Boundaries of Social Policy', *Social Work* 12 (1): 3–11.
Brandt, Willy (1980) *North–South: A Programme for Survival.* London: Pan Books.
Brokensha, David and Hodge, Peter (1969) *Community Development: An Interpretation.* San Francisco, CA: Chandler.
Bromley, Ray and Gerry, Chris (eds) (1979) *Casual Work and Poverty in Third World Cities.* Chichester: John Wiley & Sons.
Brown, Lester (1974) *In the Human Interest.* Oxford: Pergamon Press.
Burkey, Stan (1993) *People First: A Guide to Self-Reliant, Participatory Rural Development.* London: Zed Books.
Case, John (1992) *From the Ground Up: The Resurgence of American Entrepreneurship.* New York: Simon & Schuster.
Cernea, Michael (1985) *Putting People First: Sociological Variables in Rural Development.* New York: Oxford University Press.
Chambliss, Rollin (1954) *Social Thought from Hammurabi to Comte.* New York: Holt, Rinehart and Winston.
Chandler, Susan (1982) 'Towards a Social Development Analysis', in Daniel S. Sanders (ed), *The Developmental Perspective in Social Work.* Manoa, HI: University of Hawaii Press. pp. 77–88.
Chenery, Hollis, Ahluwalia, Montek, Bell, Clive, Duloy, John H. and Jolly, Richard (1974) *Redistribution with Growth.* Oxford: Oxford University Press.
Chodak, Szymon (1973) *Societal Development: Five Approaches with Conclusions from Comparative Analysis.* New York: Oxford University Press.
Chomsky, Noam (1994) *World Orders Old and New.* New York: Columbia University Press.
Coleman, James S. (1972) 'The Resurrection of Political Economy', in Norman T. Uphoff and Warren F. Ilchman (eds), *The Political Economy of Development.* Berkeley, CA: University of California Press. pp. 30–9.
Conyers, Diana (1982) *An Introduction to Social Planning in the Third World.* Chichester: John Wiley & Sons.
Cornia, Giovanni, Jolly, Richard and Stewart, Frances (1987) *Adjustment with Human Face.* Oxford: Clarendon Press.
Cosio, Ignacio Algara (1981) 'Community Development in Mexico', in Ronald Dore and Zoë Mars (eds), *Community Development.* London: Croom Helm. pp. 337–432.
Crouch, Colin (ed) (1979) *State and Economy in Contemporary Capitalism.* London: Croom Helm.
Csaki, Csaba and Kislev, Yoav (1993) *Agricultural Cooperatives in Transition.* Boulder, CO: Westview Press.
Dabbagh, Affaf (1993) 'Ideology and Non-Western Culture: An Islamic Perspective', *Social Development Issues* 15 (1): 17–18.
de Schweinitz, Karl (1943) *England's Road to Social Security.* Philadelphia, PA: University of Pennsylvania Press.
de Soto, Hernando (1989) *The Other Path: The Invisible Revolution in the Third World.* New York: Harper & Row.

Dichter, Thomas W. (1989) 'The Enterprise Concept: A Comment on Innovations in Participatory Approaches to Development', in William P. Lineberry (ed), *Assessing Participatory Development: Rhetoric versus Reality.* Boulder, CO: Westview Press. pp. 131–7.

Dore, Ronald and Mars, Zoë (eds) (1981) *Community Development.* London: Croom Helm.

Drucker, Peter (1985) *Innovation and Enterprise: Practice and Principles.* New York: Harper & Row.

Eatwell, John (1982) *Whatever Happened to Britain?* London: Duckworth.

Elliott, Doreen (1993) 'Social Work and Social Development: Towards an Integrative Model for Social Work Practice', *International Social Work* 36 (1): 21–37.

Else, John F. and Raheim, Salome (1992) 'AFDC Clients as Entrepreneurs: Self-Employment Offers an Important Option', *Public Welfare* 50 (4): 36–41.

Erlich, Paul (1969) *The Population Bomb.* London: Pan Books.

Esping-Andersen, Gøsta (1992) 'The Making of a Social Democratic Welfare State', in Klaus Misgeld, Karl Molin and Klas Amark (eds), *Creating Social Democracy: A Century of the Social Democratic Labor Party in Sweden.* University Park, PA: State University of Pennsylvania Press. pp. 35–66.

Estes, Richard (1985) *The Social Progress of Nations.* New York: Praeger.

Estes, Richard (1993) 'Towards Sustainable Development: From Theory to Praxis', *Social Development Issues* 15 (3): 1–29.

Etzioni, A. (1993) *The Spirit of Community: Rights, Responsibilities and the Communitarian Agenda.* New York: Crown Publishers.

Farvar, M. Taghi and Glaeser, Bernard (1979) *The Politics of Ecodevelopment.* Berlin: International Institute for Environment and Society.

Frank, André Gunder (1967) *Capitalism and Underdevelopment in Latin America.* New York: Monthly Review Press.

Frank, André Gunder (1969) *Latin America: Underdevelopment or Revolution?* New York: Monthly Review Press.

Freire, Paulo (1972) *Pedagogy of the Oppressed.* Harmondsworth: Penguin Books.

Friedman, Milton (1962) *Capitalism and Freedom.* Chicago, IL: University of Chicago Press.

Friedman, Milton (with Friedman, Rose) (1980) *Free to Choose.* London: Secker & Warburg.

Fukuyama, Francis (1992) *The End of History and the Last Man.* New York: Basic Books.

Galaway, Burt and Hudson, Joe (eds) (1994) *Community Economic Development: Perspectives on Research and Policy.* Toronto: Thompson Publishing.

Galbraith, John Kenneth (1958) *The Affluent Society.* Boston, MA: Houghton Mifflin.

Ghai, D. P., Khan, A. R., Lee, E. L. H. and Alfthan, T. (eds) (1977) *The Basic Needs Approach to Development.* Geneva: International Labour Office.

Gil, David (1985) 'Dialectics of Individual Development and Global Social Welfare', in Brij Mohan (ed), *New Horizons in Social Welfare Policy.* Cambridge, MA: Schenkman. pp. 15–46.

Glaeser, Bernard (ed) (1984) *Ecodevelopment: Concepts, Projects, Strategies.* Oxford: Pergamon Press.

Glennerster, Howard and Hatch, Stephen (1974) *Positive Discrimination and Inequality.* London: Fabian Society.

Glennerster, Howard and Midgley, James (eds) (1991) *The Radical Right and the Welfare State: An International Assessment.* Hemel Hempstead: Harvester Wheatsheaf.

Goode, William J. (1963) *World Revolution and Family Patterns.* New York: Free Press.

Gow, David D. and VanSant, Jerry (1983) 'Beyond the Rhetoric of Community Development Participation: How can it be Done?' *World Development* 11 (5): 427–46.

Gran, Guy (1983) *Development by People.* New York: Praeger.

Griffin, Keith (1976) *Land Concentration and Rural Poverty.* London: Macmillan.

Griffin, Keith (1978) *International Inequality and National Poverty.* London: Macmillan.

Griffin, Keith and James, J. (1981) *The Transition to Egalitarian Development.* London: Macmillan.

Habermas, Jürgen (1976) *Legitimation Crisis.* London: Heinemann.

Hagan, Everett (1962) *On the Theory of Social Change.* Homewood, IL: Dorsey Press.

Hall, Anthony and Midgley, James (1988) *Development Policies: Sociological Perspectives.* Manchester: Manchester University Press.

Harbison, Frederick H. (1967) *Educational Planning and Human Resource Development.* Paris: UNESCO.

Harbison, Frederick H. (1973) *Human Resources as the Wealth of Nations.* London: Oxford University Press.

Hardiman, Margaret and Midgley, James (1980) 'Training Social Planners for Social Development', *International Social Work* 23 (3): 1–14.

Hardiman, Margaret and Midgley, James (1982) *The Social Dimensions of Development: Social Policy and Planning in the Third World.* Chichester: John Wiley & Sons.

Hardiman, Margaret and Midgley, James (1989) *The Social Dimensions of Development: Social Policy and Planning in the Third World.* (Revised edition) Aldershot: Gower.

Hart, Keith (1973) 'Informal Income Opportunities and Urban Employment in Ghana', *Journal of Modern African Studies* 11 (1): 61–89.

Hayek, Friedrich von (1944) *The Road to Serfdom.* London: Routledge & Kegan Paul.

Hayek, Friedrich von (1949) *Individualism and Economic Order.* London: Routledge & Kegan Paul.

Higgins, Benjamin (1956) 'The Dualistic Theory of Underdeveloped Areas', *Economic Development and Cultural Change* 4 (1): 22–115.

Hirsch, Fred (1977) *The Social Limits to Growth.* London: Routledge & Kegan Paul.

Hobhouse, Leonard T. (1911) *Liberalism.* New York: Holt.

Hobhouse, Leonard T. (1924) *Social Development: Its Nature and Conditions.* London: Allen & Unwin.

Hodge, Peter (1973) 'Social Policy: An Historical Perspective as Seen in Colonial Policy', *Journal of Oriental Studies* 9 (4): 207–19.

Hokenstad, Merle C., Khinduka, Shanti K. and Midgley, James (eds) (1992) *Profiles in International Social Work.* Washington, DC: NASW Press.

Hollnsteiner, Marie R. (1977) 'People Power: Community Participation in the Planning of Human Settlements', *Assignment Children* 40 (1): 11-47.

Hollnsteiner, Marie R. (1982) 'The Participatory Imperative in Primary Health Care', *Assignment Children* 59/60 (1): 43–64.

Holterman, Sally (1978) 'The Welfare Economics of Priority Area Policies', *Journal of Social Policy* 7 (1): 23–40.

Hopps, June Gary and Pinderhughes, Elaine B. (1992) 'Social Work in the United States: History, Context and Issues', in Merle C. Hokenstad, Shanti K. Khinduka and James Midgley (eds), *Profiles in International Social Work.* Washington, DC: NASW Press. pp. 163–80.

Hort, Sven E. Olsson (1993) 'Welfare Policy in Sweden', in Thomas P. Boje and Sven E. Olsson Hort (eds), *Scandinavia in a New Europe.* Oslo: Scandinavian University Press. pp. 71–86.

Hozelitz, Bert F. (1960) *Sociological Factors in Economic Development*. New York: Free Press.

Inkeles, Alex and Smith, David H. (1974) *Becoming Modern*. London: Heinemann.

Inter-American Development Bank (1988) *Ten Years of Small Projects*. Washington, DC.

International Labour Office (1972) *Employment, Incomes and Equality: A Strategy for Increasing Productive Employment in Kenya*. Geneva.

International Labour Office (1976) *Employment, Growth and Basic Needs: A One World Problem*. Geneva.

International Labour Office (1979) *Follow-up of the World Employment Conference: Basic Needs*. Geneva.

International Labour Office (1984) *Rural Small Scale Industries and Employment in Africa and Asia*. Geneva.

International Labour Office (1985) *Informal Sector in Africa*. Geneva.

Israel, Arturo (1987) *Institutional Development: Incentives to Performance*. Baltimore, MD: Johns Hopkins University Press.

Jones, John and Pandey, Rama (eds) (1981) *Social Development: Conceptual, Methodological and Policy Issues*. New York: St Martin's Press.

Kahn, Herman (1979) *World Economic Development 1979 and Beyond*. Boulder, CO: Westview Press.

Kahn, Herman and Wiener, Anthony J. (1967) *The Year 2000*. London: Macmillan.

Karger, Howard J. (1992) 'Welfare, the Global Political Economy and the State: The American Experience', *Social Development Issues* 14 (1): 83–95.

Keller, Douglas (1990) 'The Postmodern Turn: Positions, Problems and Prospects', in George Ritzer (ed), *Frontiers of Social Theory: The New Synthesis*. New York: Columbia University Press. pp. 255–86.

Kitching, Gavin (1982) *Development and Underdevelopment in Historical Perspective*. London: Methuen.

Koenigsberger, Otto (1976) 'Urban Pioneers of the New West', *The Guardian* 31 May: 17.

Kornai, Janos (1993) 'Market Socialism Revisited', in Pranab K. Bardhan and John E. Roemer (eds), *Market Socialism: The Current Debate*. New York: Oxford University Press. pp. 42–68.

Korpi, Walter (1983) *The Democratic Class Struggle*. London: Routledge.

Korten, David C. (1983). 'Social Development: Putting People First', in David C. Korten and Felipe B. Alonso (eds), *Bureaucracy and the Poor: Closing the Gap*. West Hartford, CT: Kumarian Press. pp. 201–21.

Korten, David C. and Klaus, Rudi (1984) *People Centered Development: Contributions towards Theory and Planning Frameworks*. West Hartford, CT: Kumarian Press.

Lasch, Christopher (1991) *The True and Only Heaven: Progress and its Critics*. New York: Norton.

Lash, Scott and Urry, John (1987) *The End of Organized Capitalism*. Cambridge: Polity Press.

Le Grand, Julian and Estrin, Saul (eds) (1989) *Market Socialism*. Oxford: Clarendon Press.

Lee, Judith A. B. (ed) (1988) *Group Work with the Poor and Oppressed*. New York: Haworth Press.

Lerner, Daniel (1958) *The Passing of Traditional Society*. New York: Free Press.

Lewis, Oscar (1966) 'The Culture of Poverty', *Scientific American* 214 (1): 19–25.

Lewis, W. Arthur (1954) 'Economic Development with Unlimited Supplies of Labour', *The Manchester School* 22 (2): 139–99.

Lewis, W. Arthur (1955) *The Theory of Economic Growth*. London: Allen & Unwin.

Lindblom, Charles E. (1959) 'The Science of Muddling Through', *Public Administration* 19 (2): 79–99.

Lipton, Michael (1977) *Why Poor People Stay Poor: A Study of Urban Bias in World Development*. London: Temple Smith.

Lisk, Franklyn (ed) (1985) *Popular Participation in Planning for Basic Needs*. New York: St Martin's Press.

Livingston, Arthur (1969) *Social Policy in Developing Countries*. London: Routledge & Kegan Paul.

Lloyd, Gary A. (1982) 'Social Development as a Political Philosophy', in Daniel S. Sanders (ed), *The Developmental Perspective in Social Work*. Manoa, HI: University of Hawaii Press. pp. 43–50.

Lower Mississippi Delta Development Commission (1990) *The Delta Initiatives: Realizing the Dream, Fulfilling the Potential*. Memphis, TN.

Luedde-Neurath, Richard (1984) 'State Intervention and Foreign Direct Investment in South Korea', *IDS Bulletin* 15 (2): 18–25.

Lusk, Mark (1992) 'Social Development and the State in Latin America: A New Approach', *Social Development Issues* 14 (1): 10–21.

Maas, Henry (1984) *People and Contexts: Social Development from Birth to Old Age*. Englewood Cliffs, NJ: Prentice Hall.

MacPherson, Stewart (1982) *Social Policy in the Third World*. Brighton: Wheatsheaf.

MacPherson, Stewart and Midgley, James (1987) *Comparative Social Policy and the Third World*. Brighton: Wheatsheaf.

Mair, Lucy (1944) *Welfare in the British Colonies*. London: Royal Institute of International Affairs.

Mair, Lucy (1984) *Anthropology and Development*. London: Macmillan.

Manning, D. J. (1976) *Liberalism*. London: Dent and Sons.

Manuel, Frank E. and Manuel, Fritzie P. (1979) *Utopian Thought in the Western World*. Oxford: Basil Blackwell.

Marcuse, Herbert (1964) *One Dimensional Man*. London: Routledge & Kegan Paul.

Marsden, David and Oakley, Peter (1982) 'Radical Community Development in the Third World', in Gary Craig, Nick Derricourt and Martin Loney (eds), *Community Work and the State*. London: Routledge & Kegan Paul. pp. 153–63.

Matthews, R. C. O. (1986) 'The Economics of Institutions and Sources of Growth', *Economic Journal* 96 (4): 903–18.

Mazumdar, Dipak (1976) 'The Urban Informal Sector', *World Development* 4 (8): 665–79.

McClelland, David (1964) 'A Psychological Approach to Economic Development', *Economic Development and Cultural Change* 12 (2): 320–4.

McRobie, George (1981) *Small is Possible*. London: Jonathan Cape.

Mead, Margaret (1962) *Male and Female: A Study of the Sexes in a Changing World*. Hardmondsworth: Penguin Books.

Meadows, Donella H., Meadows, Dennis L., Randers, Jorgen and Behrens, William W. (1972) *The Limits to Growth*. New York: Universe Books.

Meinert, Roland G. (1991) 'A Brief History of the IUCISD: From Informal Interest Group to International Organization', *Social Development Issues* 13 (3): 1–13.

Meinert, Roland G. and Kohn, Ezra (1987) 'Towards Operationalization of Social Development Concepts', *Social Development Issues* 10 (3): 4–18.

Meinert, Roland G., Kohn, Ezra and Strickler, Gayle (1984) 'International Survey of Social Development Concepts', *Social Development Issues* 8 (1/2): 70–88.

Mendoza, Eugenio V. (1980) *Agricultural Cooperatives in Developing Countries*. London: International Cooperative Alliance.

Midgley, James (1978) 'Development Roles for Social Work in the Third World: The Prospect of Social Planning', *Journal of Social Policy* 7 (2): 173–88.

Midgley, James (1981) *Professional Imperialism: Social Work in the Third World*. London: Heinemann.

Midgley, James (1984a) 'Fields of Practice and Professional Roles for Social Planners: An Overview', in James Midgley and David Piachaud (eds), *The Fields and Methods of Social Planning*. London: Heinemann Educational Books. pp. 11–33.

Midgley, James (1984b) *Social Security, Inequality and the Third World*. New York: John Wiley & Sons.

Midgley, James (1984c) 'Social Work Services in the Third World: Towards the Integration of Remedial and Developmental Orientations', *Social Development Issues* 8 (2): 89–104.

Midgley, James (1984d) 'Social Welfare Implications of Development Paradigms', *Social Service Review* 58 (2): 181–98.

Midgley, James (1986) 'Industrialization and Welfare: The Case of the Four Little Tigers', *Social Policy and Administration* 20 (3): 225–38.

Midgley, James (1989) 'Social Work in the Third World: Crisis and Response', in Pam Carter, Tony Jeffs and Mark Smith (eds), *Social Work and Social Welfare Yearbook I*. London: Open University Press. pp. 33–45.

Midgley, James (1990) 'International Social Work: Learning from the Third World', *Social Work* 35 (3): 295–301.

Midgley, James (1991) 'The Radical Right, Politics and Society', in Howard Glennerster and James Midgley (eds) *The Radical Right and the Welfare State: An International Assessment*. Hemel Hempstead: Harvester Wheatsheaf. pp. 3–23.

Midgley, James (1993) 'Ideological Roots of Social Development Strategies', *Social Development Issues* 15 (1): 1–13.

Midgley, James (1994) 'The Challenge of Social Development: Their Third World and Ours', *Social Development Issues* 16 (2): 1–12.

Midgley, James and Hamilton, Donald (1978) 'Local Initiative and the Role of Government in Community Development', *International Social Work* 21 (1): 2–11.

Midgley, James and Piachaud, David (eds) (1984) *The Fields and Methods of Social Planning*. London: Heinemann Educational.

Midgley, James and Sanzenbach, Paul (1989) 'Social Work, Religion and the Global Challenge of Fundamentalism', *International Social Work* 32 (1): 273–87.

Midgley, James and Simbi, Peter (1993) 'Promoting a Development Focus in the Community Organization Curriculum: Relevance of the African Experience', *Journal of Social Work Education* 29 (3): 269–78.

Midgley, James, Cox, David, Elliott, Doreen and Kaseke, Edwell (1994) 'Social Work Education and Social Development: State of the Art', in Karl-Ernst Hesser (ed), *Social Work Education: State of the Art* (Proceedings of the 27th Congress of the International Association of Schools of Social Work). Amsterdam: Hogeschool van Amsterdam. pp. 177–82.

Midgley, James, Hall, Anthony, Hardiman, Margaret and Narine, Dhanpaul (1986) *Community Participation, Social Development and the State*. New York: Methuen.

Mishan, Edward J. (1967) *The Costs of Economic Growth*. Harmondsworth: Penguin Books.

Mishra, Ramesh (1984) *The Welfare State in Crisis*. Brighton: Wheatsheaf.

Mishra, Ramesh (1990) *The Welfare State in Capitalist Society: Policies of Retrenchment*

184   *Social development*

and Maintenance in Europe, North America and Australia. London: Harvester Wheatsheaf.

Montgomery, John D. (1988) *Bureaucrats and People: Grassroots Participation in Third World Development.* Baltimore, MD: Johns Hopkins University Press.

Morris, D. M. (1979) *Measuring the Conditions of the World's Poor.* Oxford: Pergamon Press.

Moser, Caroline O. N. (1989) *Gender Planning and Development: Theory, Practice and Training.* London: Routledge.

Mosse, Julia Cleves (1993) *Half the World, Half a Chance: An Introduction to Gender and Development.* Oxford: Oxfam.

Mould, Peter S. (1966) 'Rural Improvement through Communal Labour in the Bombali District of Sierra Leone', *Journal of Administration Overseas* 5 (1): 29–47.

Murdoch, George P. (1937) 'Comparative Data on the Division of Labour by Sex', *Social Forces* 15 (4): 551–3.

Mushi, Samuel (1981) 'Community Development in Tanzania', in Ronald Dore and Zoë Mars (eds), *Community Development.* London: Croom Helm. pp. 139–244.

Myrdal, Gunnar (1968) *Asian Drama: An Inquiry into the Poverty of Nations.* Harmondsworth: Penguin Books.

Myrdal, Gunnar (1970) *The Challenge of World Poverty.* Harmondsworth: Penguin Books.

Newell, Kenneth (ed) (1975) *Health by the People.* Geneva: World Health Organisation.

Niemeyer, Gerhart (1993) 'This Terrible Century', *The Intercollegiate Review* 29 (1): 3–10.

Nisbet, Robert (1980) *History of the Idea of Progress.* New York: Basic Books.

North, Charles C. (1932) *Social Problems and Social Planning: The Guidance of Social Change.* New York: McGraw Hill.

North, Douglas (1991) 'Institutions', *Journal of Economic Perspectives* 5 (1): 97–112.

Nurkse, Ragnar (1953) *Problems of Capital Formation in Underdeveloped Countries.* London: Oxford University Press.

Oakley, Ann (1972) *Sex, Gender and Society.* London: Temple Smith.

Oakley, Peter (1991) *Projects with People.* Geneva: International Labour Office.

O'Connor, James (1973) *The Fiscal Crisis of the State.* New York: St Martin's Press.

Omer, Salima (1979) 'Social Development', *International Social Work* 22 (3): 11–26.

Organization for Economic Cooperation and Development (OECD) (1988) *Aging Populations: Social Policy Implications.* Paris.

Paiva, F. J. X. (1977) 'A Conception of Social Development', *Social Service Review* 51 (2): 327–36.

Paiva, F. J. X. (1982) 'The Dynamics of Social Development and Social Work', in Daniel S. Sanders (ed), *The Developmental Perspective in Social Work.* Manoa, HI: University of Hawaii Press. pp. 1–11.

Panayotou, Theodore (1993) *Green Markets: The Economics of Sustainable Development.* San Francisco, CA: ICS Press.

Pekkarinen, Jukka, Pohjola, Matti and Rowthorn, Bob (eds) (1992) *Social Corporatism: A Superior Economic System?* Oxford: Clarendon Press.

Philippines (1971) *Report of the First Asian Conference of Ministers Responsible for Social Welfare.* Manila: Department of Social Welfare.

Piachaud, David (1989) 'Social Policy and the Economy: Introduction', in Martin Bulmer, Jane Lewis and David Piachaud (eds), *The Goals of Social Policy.* London: Unwin Hyman. pp. 261–6.

Plant, Robert (1983) *A Short Guide to the ILO World Employment Programme.* Geneva: International Labour Office.

Popper, Karl (1945) *The Open Society and its Enemies*. London: Routledge & Kegan Paul.
Popper, Karl (1957) *The Poverty of Historicism*. London: Routledge & Kegan Paul.
Portes, Alejandro, Castells, Manuel and Benton, Lauren A. (eds) (1989) *The Informal Economy: Studies in Advanced and Less Developed Countries*. Baltimore, MD: Johns Hopkins University Press.
Preston, P. W. (1982) *Theories of Development*. London: Routledge & Kegan Paul.
Prigoff, Arline (1992) 'Women, Social Development and the State in Latin America: An Empowerment Approach', *Social Development Issues* 14 (1): 56–71.
Psacharopoulos, George (1973) *Returns to Education: An International Comparison*. Amsterdam: Elsevier.
Psacharopoulos, George (1981) 'Returns to Education: An Updated International Comparison', *Comparative Education* 17 (3): 321–41.
Psacharopoulos, George (1992) *Returns to Investment in Education: A Global Update*. Washington, DC: World Bank.
Putnam, Robert D. with Leonardi, Roberto and Nanetti, Raffaella Y. (1993) *Making Democracy Work: Civic Traditions in Modern Italy*. Princeton, NJ: Princeton University Press.
Rao, Vijaya (1983) *World Guide to Social Work Education*. Vienna: International Association of Schools of Social Work.
Redclift, Michael (1987) *Sustainable Development: Exploring the Contradictions*. London: Routledge.
Reich, Robert B. (1991) *The Work of Nations*. New York: Alfred Knopf.
Reidy, Angela (1981) 'Welfarists in the Market', *International Social Work* 24 (2): 36–46.
Rodney, Walter (1972) *How Europe Underdeveloped Africa*. Dar-es-Salaam: Tanzania Publishing House.
Rogers, Barbara (1980) *The Domestication of Women: Discrimination in Developing Societies*. London: Tavistock.
Rosenstein-Rodan, Paul (1943) 'Problems of Industrialization of South and Eastern Europe', *Economic Journal* 53 (2): 205–11.
Rosenstein-Rodan, Paul (1961) 'International Aid for Underdeveloped Countries', *Review of Economics and Statistics* 43 (2): 107–38.
Rostow, Walt W. (1960) *The Stages of Economic Growth: A Non-Communist Manifesto*. Cambridge: Cambridge University Press.
Rostow, Walt W. (1963) *The Economics of Take-Off into Sustained Growth*. London: Macmillan.
Ruiz-Perez, Sonia (1979). 'Begging as an Occupation in San Christoballas Casas, Mexico', in Ray Bromley and Chris Gerry (eds), *Casual Work and Poverty in Third World Cities*. Chichester: John Wiley & Sons. pp. 229–50.
Sachs, Ignacy (1980) *Stratégies de l'Ecodéveloppement*. Paris: Les Editions Ouvrières.
Sanders, Daniel S. (ed) (1982) *The Developmental Perspective in Social Work*. Manoa, HI: University of Hawaii Press.
Sassen-Koob, Saskia (1989) 'New York City's Informal Economy', in Alejandro Portes, Manuel Castells and Lauren A. Benton (eds), *The Informal Economy: Studies in Advanced and Less Developed Countries*. Baltimore, MD: Johns Hopkins University Press. pp. 60–77.
Schmitter, Philippe (1974) 'Still the Century of Corporatism?', in Frederick B. Pike and Thomas Stritch (eds), *The New Corporatism: Social and Political Structures in the Iberian World*. Notre Dame, IN: University of Notre Dame Press. pp. 85–131.
Schmitter, Philippe and Lehmbruch, George (eds) (1979) *Trends Towards Corporatist Interest Intermediation*. London: Sage.

Schumacher, Ernst Frederich (1974) *Small is Beautiful*. London: Sphere Books.

Seers, Dudley (1972) 'The Meaning of Development', in Norman T. Uphoff and Warren F. Ilchman (eds), *The Political Economy of Development*. Berkeley, CA: University of California Press. pp. 123–9.

Sergio, Alessandrini and Dellagio, Bruno (eds) (1987) *The Unofficial Economy*. Aldershot: Gower.

Sherraden, Michael (1991) *Assets and the Poor: A New American Welfare Policy*. Armonk, NY: M. E. Sharpe.

Shigetomi, Shin'ichi (1994) 'The Experience of Sri Phon Thong in Thailand'. Paper presented at the United Nations Centre for Regional Development Expert Group Meeting on Self-Organizing Capability of Local Communities, Nagoya, Japan, January.

Shiva, Vandana (1989) *Staying Alive: Women, Ecology and Development*. London: Zed Books.

Smart, Barry (1992) *Modern Conditions, Postmodern Controversies*. London: Routledge.

Spengler, Oswald (1926) *The Decline of the West*. New York: Alfred Knopf.

Spergel, Irving (1978) 'Social Development and Social Work', in Simon Slavin (ed), *Social Administration*. New York: Haworth Press. pp. 24–35.

Spergel, Irving (1982) 'The Role of the Social Developer', in Daniel S. Sanders (ed), *The Developmental Perspective in Social Work*. Manoa, HI: University of Hawaii Press. pp. 12–30.

Stepick, Alex (1989) 'Miami's Two Informal Sectors', in Alejandro Portes, Manuel Castells and Lauren A. Benton (eds), *The Informal Economy: Studies in Advanced and Less Developed Countries*. Baltimore, MD: Johns Hopkins University Press. pp. 111–31.

Stern, E. Mark (ed) (1990) *Psychotherapy and the Poverty Patient*. New York: Haworth Press.

Stewart, Frances (1985) *Basic Needs in Developing Countries*. Baltimore, MD: Johns Hopkins University Press.

Streeten, Paul and Burki, Shahid Javed (1978) 'Basic Needs: Some Issues', *World Development* 6 (3): 411–21.

Streeten, Paul with Burki, Shahid Javed, Ul Haq, Mahbub, Hicks, Norman and Stewart, Frances (1981) *First Things First: Meeting Basic Needs in Developing Countries*. New York: Oxford University Press.

Tawney, R. H. (1921) *The Acquisitive Society*. London: G. Bell & Sons.

Thomas, J. J. (1992) *Informal Sector Activity*. Ann Arbor, MI: University of Michigan Press.

Titmuss, Richard M. (1960) *The Irresponsible Society*. London: Fabian Society.

Titmuss, Richard M. (1963) 'The Social Divisions of Welfare', in Richard M. Titmuss, *Essays on the Welfare State*. London: Allen & Unwin. pp. 34–55.

Titmuss, Richard M. (1968) 'Social Policy and Economic Progress', in Richard M. Titmuss, *Commitment to Welfare*. London: Allen & Unwin. pp. 153–65.

Titmuss, Richard M. (1971) *The Gift Relationship*. London: Allen & Unwin.

Titmuss, Richard M. (1974) *Social Policy: An Introduction*. London: Allen & Unwin.

Titmuss, Richard M., Abel-Smith, Brian and Lynes, Tony (1961) *Social Policy and Population Growth in Mauritius*. London: Methuen.

Toffler, Alvin (1971) *Future Shock*. London: Pan Books.

Toffler, Alvin (1983) *The Third Wave*. London: Pan Books.

Turner, Bryan S. (ed) (1990) *Theories of Modernity and Postmodernity*. London: Sage.

United Kingdom (1954) *Social Development in the British Colonial Territories*. London: Colonial Office, HMSO.

United Kingdom (1960) *The UK Colonial Development and Welfare Acts*. London: Central Office of Information, HMSO.

United Nations (1969) *Proceedings of the International Conference of Ministers Responsible for Social Welfare*. New York: United Nations.

United Nations (1971a) 'Social Policy and Planning in National Development', *International Social Development Review* no. 3: 4–15.

United Nations (1971b) *Popular Participation in Development*. New York.

United Nations (1975) *Popular Participation in Decision Making for Development*. New York.

United Nations Children's Fund (UNICEF) (1982) 'Popular Participation in Basic Services: Lessons Learned through UNICEF's Experience', *Assignment Children* 59/60 (1): 121–32.

United Nations Development Programme (1990) *Human Development Report 1990*. New York.

United Nations Development Programme (1993) *Human Development Report 1993*. New York.

van den Hombergh, Heleen (1993) *Gender, Environment and Development: A Guide to the Literature*. Utrecht: International Books.

Veblen, Thorstein (1899) *The Theory of the Leisure Class: An Economic Study of Institutions*. New York: Macmillan.

Wade, Robert (1984) 'Dirigisme Taiwan Style', *IDS Bulletin* 15 (2): 65–70.

Ward, Barbara and Dubos, René (1972) *Only One Earth*. London: Deutsch.

Warren, Bill (1980) *Imperialism: Pioneer of Capitalism*. London: Verso.

Waterston, Albert (1965) *Development Planning: Lessons from Experience*. Baltimore, MD: Johns Hopkins University Press.

Weeks, John (1975) 'Policies for Expanding Employment in the Informal Urban Sector of Developing Countries', *International Labour Review* 111 (1): 1–13.

Wilensky, Harold and Lebeaux, Charles (1965) *Industrial Society and Social Welfare*. New York: Free Press.

Williamson, Peter J. (1989) *Corporatism in Perspective: An Introductory Guide to Corporatist Theory*. London: Sage.

Wilson, William Julius (1987) *The Truly Disadvantaged: The Inner City, the Underclass and Public Policy*. Chicago, IL: University of Chicago Press.

Wolfe, Marshall (1980) 'An Assessment', in United Nations Research Institute for Social Development, *The Quest for a Unified Approach to Development*. Geneva. pp. 63–142.

Wolfe-Phillips, Leslie (1979) 'Why Third World?', *Third World Quarterly* 1 (1): 105–14.

Woo, Jennie Hay (1991) 'Education and Economic Growth in Taiwan: A Case of Successful Planning', *World Development* 19 (8): 1029–44.

World Bank (1975) *The Assault on World Poverty*. Baltimore, MD: Johns Hopkins University Press.

World Bank (1978) *Employment and Development of Small Enterprises*. Washington, DC.

World Bank (1982) *World Development Report, 1982*. Washington, DC.

World Bank (1990) *World Development Report, 1990: Poverty*. Washington, DC.

World Bank (1991) *World Development Report, 1991: The Challenge of Development*. Washington, DC.

World Bank (1992) *World Development Report, 1992: Development and the Environment*. Washington, DC.

World Bank (1993a) *World Development Report, 1993: Investing in Health*. Washington, DC.

World Bank (1993b) *The East Asian Miracle: Economic Growth and Public Policy*. New York: Oxford University Press.

World Commission on Environment and Development (Brundtland Commission) (1987) *Our Common Future: From One Earth to One World*. Geneva.

World Health Organization (1981) *Global Strategy for Health for All by the Year 2000*. Geneva.

World Health Organization (1982) *Activities of the World Health Organization in Promoting Community Involvement for Health Development*. Geneva.

Worsley, Peter (ed) (1971) *Two Blades of Grass: Rural Cooperatives in Agricultural Modernization*. Manchester: Manchester University Press.

Worsley, Peter (1984) *The Three Worlds: Culture and Development*. London: Weidenfeld & Nicolson.

Young, Crawford, Sherman, Neal P. and Rose, Tim H. (1981) *Cooperatives and Development*. Madison, WI: University of Wisconsin Press.

Index

CPSIA information can be obtained at www.ICGtesting.com
Printed in the USA
LVOW12s0239221013

358005LV00001B/58/P

9 780803 977730